FINLAND
Helsinki
tinn ESTONIA
ga LATVIA
ilnuis LITHUANIA
Minsk
BELARUS
Kiev
UKRAINE
MOLDOVA
Budapest Chisinau
GARY
BIA ROMANIA
elgrade Bucharest
Sofia BULGARIA
Pristina
 ANIA Skopje
EECE

RUSSIAN FEDERATION

Moscow

Astana

KAZAKHSTAN

MONGOLIA
Ulan Bator

CHINA
Beijing

NORTH
KOREA
Pyongyang

SOUTH
KOREA
Seoul
Sejong City

JAPAN
Tokyo

GEORGIA Tbilisi
AZERBAIJAN
ARMENIA Baku
Ankara Yerevan
TURKEY
Nicosia SYRIA
CYPRUS Beirut
LEBANON Damascus
ISRAEL Amman
Jerusalem
JORDAN
Cairo
EGYPT

UZBEKISTAN
Tashkent
KYRGYZSTAN
Bishkek

TURKMENISTAN
TAJIKISTAN
Asgabat Dushanbe

Tehran

IRAQ IRAN
Baghdad
KUWAIT
Kuwait
BAHRAIN
Manama QATAR
Riyadh Doha
SAUDI Abu Dhabi
ARABIA UAE Muscat
OMAN
YEMEN

AFGHANISTAN
Kabul
Islamabad
PAKISTAN
New Delhi

NEPAL
Thimphu
Kathmandu BHUTAN
BANGLADESH
Dhaka
BURMA
[MYANMAR]
Nay Pyi Taw

Taipei
TAIWAN

SUDAN
Khartoum

ERITREA Sana
Asmara
DJIBOUTI
Djibouti
Addis Ababa

SOUTH
SUDAN
ngui Juba

ETHIOPIA

Socotra
[Yemen]

INDIA

Laccadive Islands
[India]

SRI LANKA
Colombo
Sri Jayewardenapura
Kotte

Andaman
Islands
[India]

LAOS
Hanoi
VIETNAM
Vientiane
THAILAND
Bangkok
CAMBODIA
Phnom Penh

MALDIVES
Male

Nicobar
Islands
[India]

PHILIPPINES
Manila

Northern
Mariana
Islands
[US]

Wake Island [US]

MARSHALL ISLANDS

Guam
[US]

BRUNEI
Bandar Seri Begawan

PALAU
Ngerulmud

MICRONESIA Palikir

Majuro

Baker &
Howland Islands
[US]

UGANDA
Kampala
Kigali
RWANDA
Bujumbura Nairobi
BURUNDI
Dodoma

KENYA

Mogadishu

SOMALIA

British Indian
Ocean Territory
[UK]

Christmas Island
[Australia]

KUALA LUMPUR
MALAYSIA
Putrajaya
SINGAPORE
Singapore

INDONESIA

Jakarta

PAPUA NEW GUINEA
Port Moresby

SOLOMON
ISLANDS
Honiara

NAURU
Bairiki

KIRIBATI

TUVALU
Fongafale

Tokelau
[NZ]
Apia

EM. REP.
CONGO

TANZANIA

SEYCHELLES
Victoria

COMOROS
Moroni

Mayotte
[France]

ZAMBIA MALAWI
Lusaka Lilongwe
ZIMBABWE
OTSWANA
aborone Pretoria
Mbabane Maputo
SWAZILAND
emfontein Maseru
OUTH LESOTHO
AFRICA

MOZAMBIQUE

MADAGASCAR
Antananarivo

MAURITIUS
Port Louis

Réunion
[France]

Amsterdam Island
[France]

St.-Paul Island
[France]

EAST
TIMOR
Dili

Ashmore & Cartier Islands
[Australia]

Cocos (Keeling) Island
[Australia]

WESTERN
AUSTRALIA

NORTHERN
TERRITORY

QUEENSLAND

AUSTRALIA
SOUTH
AUSTRALIA

NEW SOUTH
WALES

VICTORIA

TASMANIA

Coral Sea
Islands
[Australia]

New
Caledonia
[France]

VANUATU
Port-Vila

Suva
FIJI

Wallis
& Futuna
[France]

SAMOA

TONGA
Nuku'alofa

Canberra
AUSTRALIAN
CAPITAL
TERRITORY

Norfolk Island
[Australia]

Kermadec Islands
[New Zealand]

NEW ZEALAND
Wellington

Chatham Islands
[New Zealand]

Bounty Islands
[New Zealand]

Prince Edward
Islands
[South Africa]

Crozet Islands
[France]

Kerguelen
[France]

Auckland Islands
[New Zealand]

Macquarie Island
[Australia]

Country abbreviations

BEL.	Belgium
BOS. & HERZ.	Bosnia and Herzegovina
CZECH REP.	Czech Republic
KOS.	Kosovo
LIECH.	Liechtenstein
LUX.	Luxembourg
MAC.	Macedonia
MON.	Montenegro
NETH.	Netherlands
NZ	New Zealand
RUSS. FED.	Russian Federation
SM	San Marino
SLVN.	Slovenia
SWITZ.	Switzerland
UAE	United Arab Emirates
UK	United Kingdom
US	United States of America
VAT. CITY	Vatican City

ANTARCTICA

DK WHERE ON EARTH?
ATLAS

DK London
Senior editor Chris Hawkes
Senior art editor Rachael Grady
Editors Tom Booth, Anna Fischel, Anna Limerick
US editor Jenny Siklos
Designers David Ball, Chrissy Barnard, Mik Gates, Spencer Holbrook, Kit Lane
Illustrators Adam Benton, Stuart Jackon-Carter, Jon@kja-artists
Cartography Simon Mumford, Encompass Graphics

Jacket editor Claire Gell
Jacket designer Mark Cavanagh
Jacket design development manager Sophia MTT
Picture research Jayati Sood

Producer, pre-production Nadine King, Rob Dunn
Senior producer Gary Batchelor

Managing editor Francesca Baines
Managing art editor Philip Letsu
Publisher Andrew Macintyre
Publishing director Jonathan Metcalf
Associate publishing director Liz Wheeler
Art director Karen Self

First American Edition, 2017
Published in the United States by DK Publishing
1450 Broadway, New York, New York 10018

Copyright © 2017 Dorling Kindersley Limited
DK, a Division of Penguin Random House LLC
20 21 10 9 8 7 6 5
015–282938–April/17

A catalog record for this book is available from the Library of Congress.

ISBN 978-1-4654-5864-3

DK books are available at special discounts when purchased in bulk for sales promotions, premiums, fund-raising, or educational use. For details, contact: DK Publishing Special Markets, 1450 Broadway, New York, New York 10018
SpecialSales@dk.com

Printed and bound in Dubai

A WORLD OF IDEAS:
SEE ALL THERE IS TO KNOW

www.dk.com

CONTENTS

Early Earth

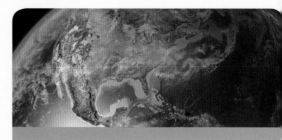

North America

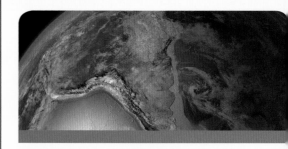

South America

Africa

Europe

Asia

Australia and Oceania

Polar regions

The oceans

Reference

Kangaroo

The South Pole

EARLY EARTH

Under attack
Rock and debris from space crashed into Earth's surface during its early formation, turning it molten and triggering volcanic activity.

Early Earth

Earth's formation started shortly after the birth of the Sun, 4.6 billion years ago. A star exploding in nearby space caused a vast amount of interstellar dust to collapse in on itself. This formed our Sun, and over time the rest of the surrounding debris clumped together into planets. As these grew larger, their steadily increasing gravity pulled them into spheres. One of these was our planet, Earth, a rocky ball with a molten metal core, and a thin shell, called a crust, at its surface.

The layered interior structure of Earth emerged early in its evolution. Heat from Earth's molten core forced the crust, which is made up of large slabs of rock called tectonic plates, to move constantly. As these plates shunted around and crashed into each other, they caused earthquakes and fiery volcanoes, formed mountain ranges and entire continents, and helped create the conditions in which life could emerge.

This illustration shows the sequence of Earth's formation—from small fragments of rock and dust sticking together, to a planet with its own atmosphere.

Atmosphere
The air was heavy with carbon dioxide. Atmospheric pressure was higher than it is today, which allowed water to stay liquid at a far higher temperature than its modern boiling point.

Clouds
Clouds of water droplets could be seen in the sky, much as today.

First oceans
Liquid water, in which the first life formed, would have become permanent oceans at some time between 4.4 and 4.2 billion years ago.

THE FIRST LIFE FORMS ON EARTH, THE ANCESTORS OF MODERN

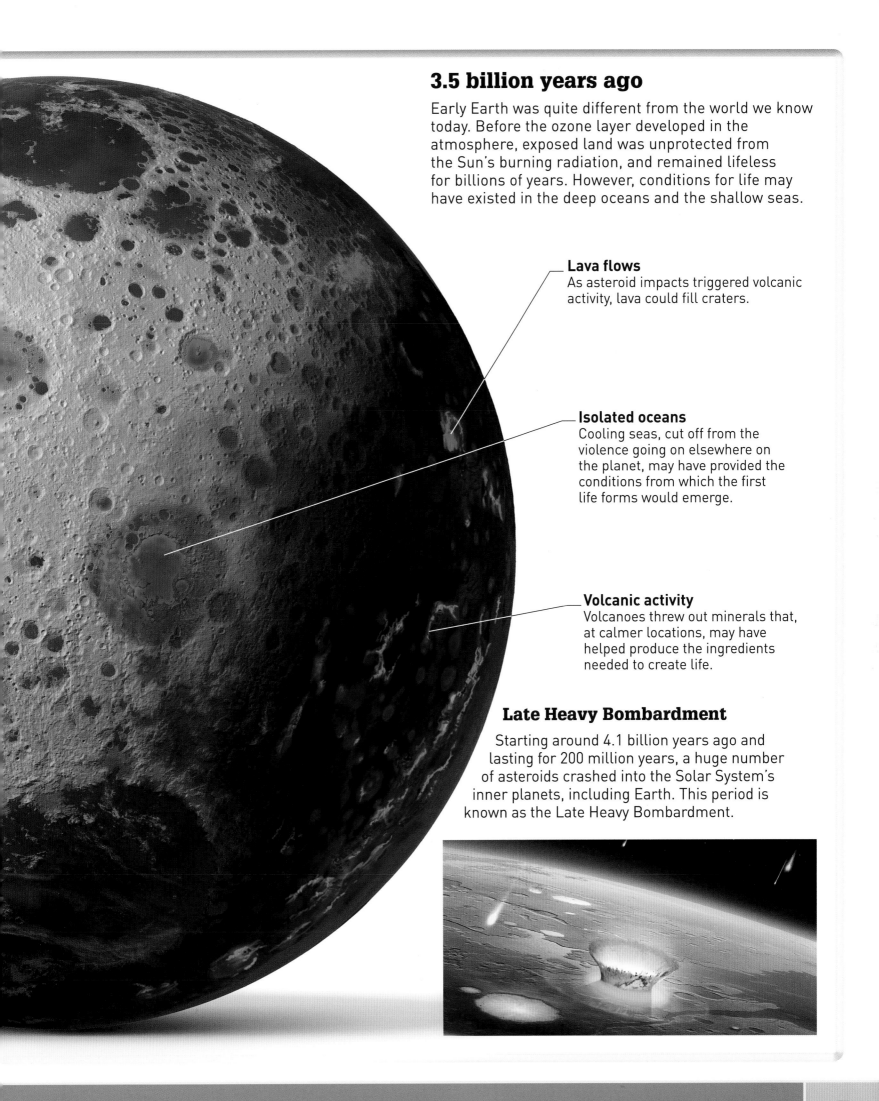

3.5 billion years ago

Early Earth was quite different from the world we know today. Before the ozone layer developed in the atmosphere, exposed land was unprotected from the Sun's burning radiation, and remained lifeless for billions of years. However, conditions for life may have existed in the deep oceans and the shallow seas.

Lava flows
As asteroid impacts triggered volcanic activity, lava could fill craters.

Isolated oceans
Cooling seas, cut off from the violence going on elsewhere on the planet, may have provided the conditions from which the first life forms would emerge.

Volcanic activity
Volcanoes threw out minerals that, at calmer locations, may have helped produce the ingredients needed to create life.

Late Heavy Bombardment

Starting around 4.1 billion years ago and lasting for 200 million years, a huge number of asteroids crashed into the Solar System's inner planets, including Earth. This period is known as the Late Heavy Bombardment.

BACTERIA, ARE THOUGHT TO HAVE EMERGED 3.5 BILLION YEARS AGO.

7

500 million years ago

By this stage of Earth's history two major continents had formed. The largest, Gondwana, was mainly tropical. Laurentia (now North America) had also drifted from the polar regions to the tropics and sat on the Equator. Temperatures were mild across the globe, but cooling.

In the water

Many life forms developed in the warm, shallow seas, including marine invertebrates such as *Hallucigenia*, a worm with limbs.

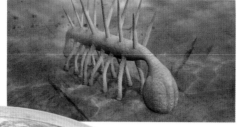

Hallucigenia

420 million years ago

Continents continued to shift. Avalonia (now split across present-day southern Britain and Canada) moved north to collide with Laurentia. Siberia headed north and Gondwana south, taking most of present-day Australia and Antarctica into the southern hemisphere. Sea levels started to rise.

LAURENTIA

LAURENTI

The giant continent of Gondwana sat on the tropics

Reverse view

Reverse view

Lifeless land

Carbon dioxide levels in the atmosphere were 15 times higher than today, and no animals could survive on land.

Early algae

There was no land vegetation, but many types of algae (plant-like oganisms that live in the sea) had appeared and diversified.

Animals

Millipedes, such as the one below, were the first known oxygen-breathing animals on land.

THE FIRST INSECTS ARE THOUGHT TO HAVE

In the water

The first coral reefs and fish appeared. *Guiyu oneiros* remains dating back to 419 million years ago have been found in Yunnan Province, China.

Guiyu oneiros

380 million years ago

Laurentia and Baltica collided, closing up the Iapetus Ocean and forming the continent of Eurasia. The collision created the Appalachian-Caledonide Mountain Range, which extended from Scandinavia to the Appalachian Mountains in North America. Gondwana rotated clockwise, approaching Eurasia.

In the water

The "Age of Fish" saw a variety of lobe-finned fish and jawed predators. Placoderms (armored fish) included the mighty *Dunkleosteus*.

Dunkleosteus

SIBERIA

EURASIA

GONDWANA

Reverse view

Plants

The tiny, but upright, *Cooksonia* was one of the first plants to colonize land. It was short, had branching stems, and lived in damp habitats.

Cooksonia

Fish with legs

The first tetrapods (four-legged animals) developed. The earliest were like fish with legs, such as *Ichthyostega*.

Ichthyostega

Archaeopteris

Plants

The landmasses turned green as woody, spore-bearing plants such as *Archaeopteris*, a treelike plant with ferny leaves, created major forests and swamps.

300 million years ago

By 300 million years ago, Eurasia had merged with Gondwana to form the supercontinent Pangea, which extended from high in the northern hemisphere to the South Pole, where ice caps spread. Siberia collided with eastern Europe, creating the Ural Mountains.

In the water

Fish and aquatic tetrapods, such as *Microbrachis* ("tiny limbs"), shared the seas with corals, crinoids (sea lilies), and brachiopods (mollusks).

Microbrachis

250 million years ago

All the continents were absorbed into the giant supercontinent Pangea. Global sea levels fell, while, in Siberia, massive volcanic eruptions poured out ash and gases, poisoning both the atmosphere and the oceans. Such events led to a global mass extinction.

SIBERIA

PANGEA

Reverse view

PANGEA

Reverse view

Animals

The shelled egg evolved, so tetrapods, such as *Ophiacodon*, could lay eggs on land without them drying out.

Plants

Lush swamps dominated by tree ferns laid the foundations for rich deposits of coal, and provided a habitat for arthropods, such as winged insects.

Animals

About 70 percent of land species became extinct, including *Dimetrodo*

Ophiacodon

Dimetrodon

AROUND 250 MILLION YEARS AGO, A MASS EXTINCTION WIPED

Helicoprion

In the water
Falling sea levels exposed reefs. An estimated 95 percent of marine species died out in the mass extinction—*Helicoprion* was one of the few survivors.

220 million years ago

Pangea was at its largest—it extended from pole to pole— and sea levels had lowered. The supercontinent moved north, rotating counterclockwise. New life forms, including dinosaurs, started to evolve on the land.

In the water
Marine reptiles included turtles, frogs, crocodiles, and dolphinlike ichthyosaurs, such as *Mixosaurus*. Corals and mollusks also evolved new forms.

Mixosaurus

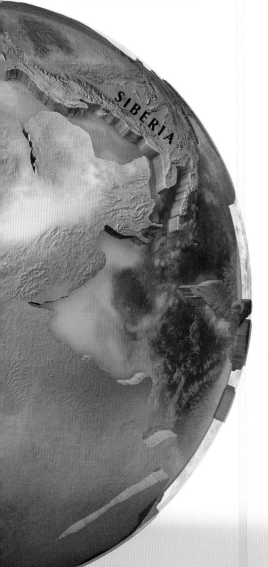
SIBERIA

PANGEA

Reverse view

Plants
Half of all plant species died out. *Glossopteris*, widespread for 50 million years, declined, as did conifers, horsetails, and ferns.

Glossopteris

Animals
The first flies evolved, and early archosaurs (ruling reptiles), such as *Euparkeria*, paved the way for dinosaurs.

Euparkeria

Dicroidium

Plants
Vegetation adapted to the dry climate. Flora included conifers and the seed fern *Dicroidium*, which was distributed throughout Pangea.

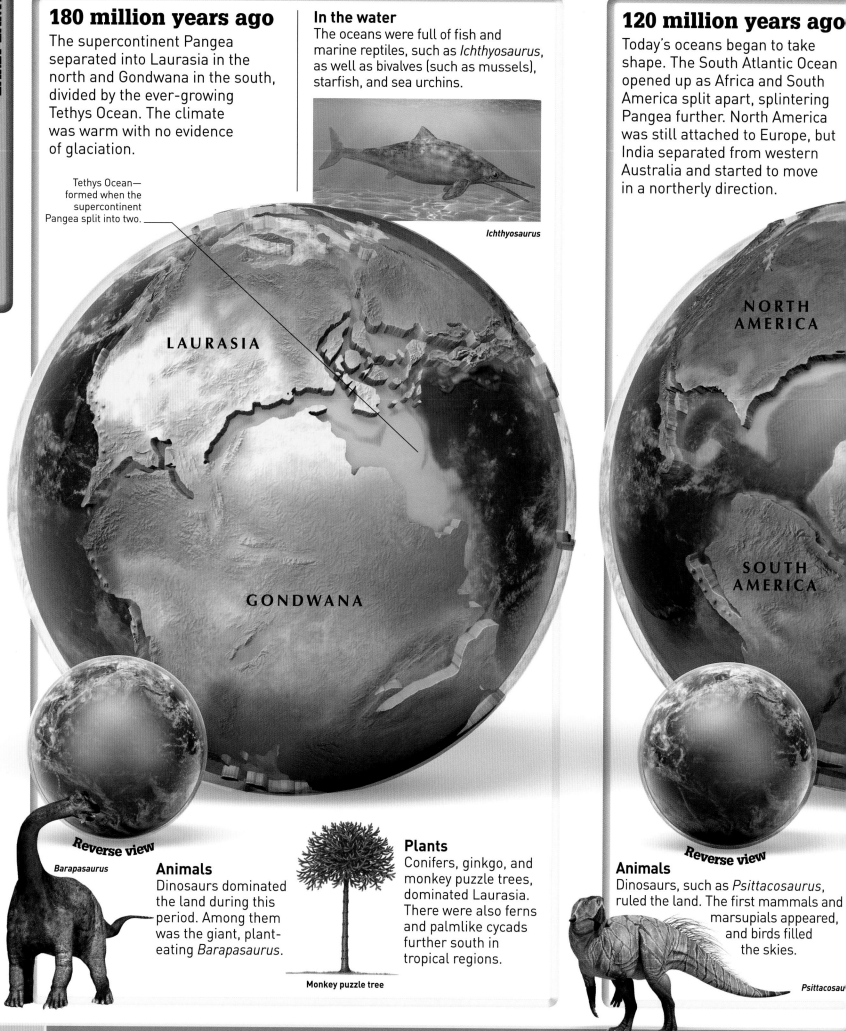

180 million years ago

The supercontinent Pangea separated into Laurasia in the north and Gondwana in the south, divided by the ever-growing Tethys Ocean. The climate was warm with no evidence of glaciation.

Tethys Ocean—formed when the supercontinent Pangea split into two.

In the water

The oceans were full of fish and marine reptiles, such as *Ichthyosaurus*, as well as bivalves (such as mussels), starfish, and sea urchins.

Ichthyosaurus

LAURASIA

GONDWANA

Reverse view

Barapasaurus

Animals

Dinosaurs dominated the land during this period. Among them was the giant, plant-eating *Barapasaurus*.

Plants

Conifers, ginkgo, and monkey puzzle trees, dominated Laurasia. There were also ferns and palmlike cycads further south in tropical regions.

Monkey puzzle tree

120 million years ago

Today's oceans began to take shape. The South Atlantic Ocean opened up as Africa and South America split apart, splintering Pangea further. North America was still attached to Europe, but India separated from western Australia and started to move in a northerly direction.

NORTH AMERICA

SOUTH AMERICA

Reverse view

Animals

Dinosaurs, such as *Psittacosaurus*, ruled the land. The first mammals and marsupials appeared, and birds filled the skies.

Psittacosau

MODERN-DAY MAMMAL GROUPS BEGAN TO

In the water

Archelon (giant sea turtles) and other sea reptiles flourished. New species of strangely coiled creatures called ammonoids thrived, as did sea snails and anemones.

Archelon

AFRICA

India had split from Africa.

80 million years ago

High sea levels flooded much of North America and created a seaway that extended from the Gulf of Mexico to the newly forming Atlantic Ocean. By 65 million years ago, India had collided with Asia, causing volcanic eruptions. An asteroid had hit Mexico, causing a mass extinction.

In the water

New types of shellfish continued to evolve and peculiar sea reptiles, such as the long-necked *Albertonectes*, came into being.

Albertonectes

NORTH AMERICA

EURASIA

SOUTH AMERICA

AFRICA

INDIA

Reverse view

Plants

The first angiosperms (flowering plants), such as magnolia, colonized the land, evolving alongside pollinating insects, including bees.

Triceratops

Animals

New dinosaurs evolved, including *Triceratops*. Snakes, ants, and termites also emerged.

Plants

More flowering plants started to appear on land. Conifers and palmlike cycads spread, thanks to the success of their seed-bearing cones.

40 million years ago

North and South America were separate, and Antarctica split away from Australia. These isolated landmasses saw animals and plants develop independently. Mountain ranges, such as the Rocky Mountains and the Himalayas, formed along plate margins, and the closing of the Tethys Ocean forced up the Alps.

In the water
Single-celled plankton were at their most diverse and coral reefs grew. At the other end of the size scale, *Basilosaurus* was an early whale.

Basilosaurus

50,000–18,000 years ago

Part of a cycle of ice ages, ocean levels fell and rose as glaciers advanced and retreated. India nudged further into Asia, Australia into Indonesia, and Africa and the Middle East into Europe and Asia. France and England were joined until rising sea levels created the English Channel.

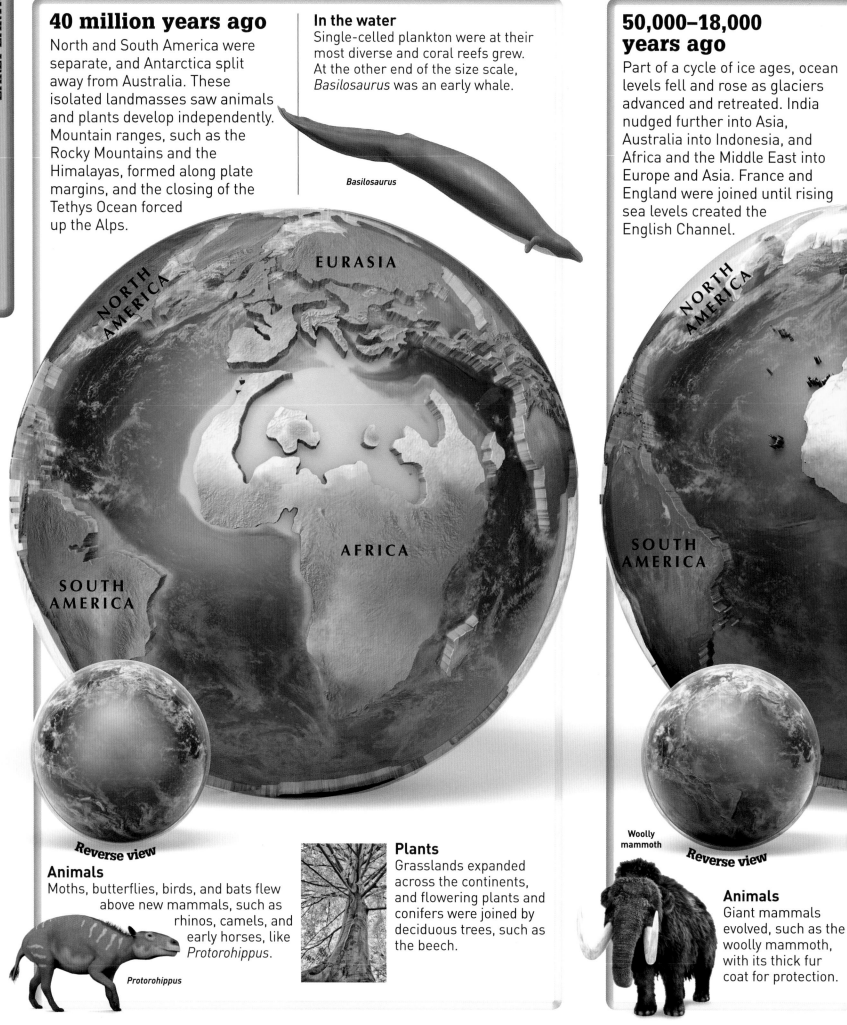

EURASIA

NORTH AMERICA

SOUTH AMERICA

AFRICA

NORTH AMERICA

SOUTH AMERICA

Reverse view

Animals
Moths, butterflies, birds, and bats flew above new mammals, such as rhinos, camels, and early horses, like *Protorohippus*.

Protorohippus

Plants
Grasslands expanded across the continents, and flowering plants and conifers were joined by deciduous trees, such as the beech.

Woolly mammoth

Reverse view

Animals
Giant mammals evolved, such as the woolly mammoth, with its thick fur coat for protection.

THE OLDEST PAINTED CAVE ART—A RED DOT—WAS MADE IN

Bottlenose dolphin

the water
quatic mammals such as olphins shared the seas with ankton species that adapted successive changes in the ater temperature.

Present day
The last ice age ended and giant mammals became extinct around 12,000 years ago. By that time, humans had started to make their mark on the world. Human activity has triggered global warming and has affected natural cycles of glaciation. The consequences of this could have a major impact on life on Earth.

In the water
Coral reefs provide a habitat for up to a quarter of all marine species. Marine life is still diverse, with an estimated 2 million species living in the oceans.

Fish at coral reef

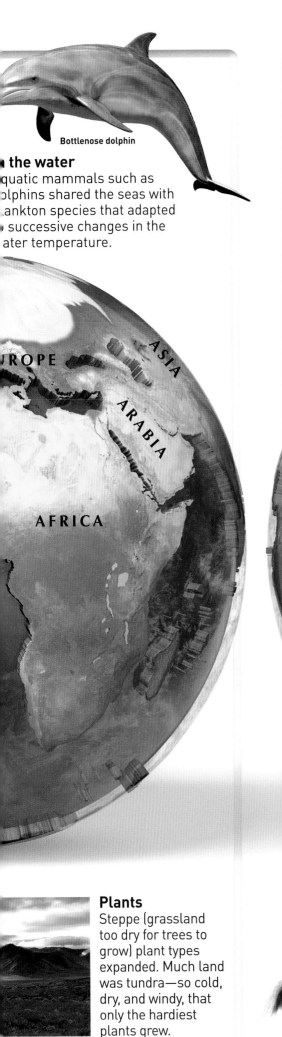

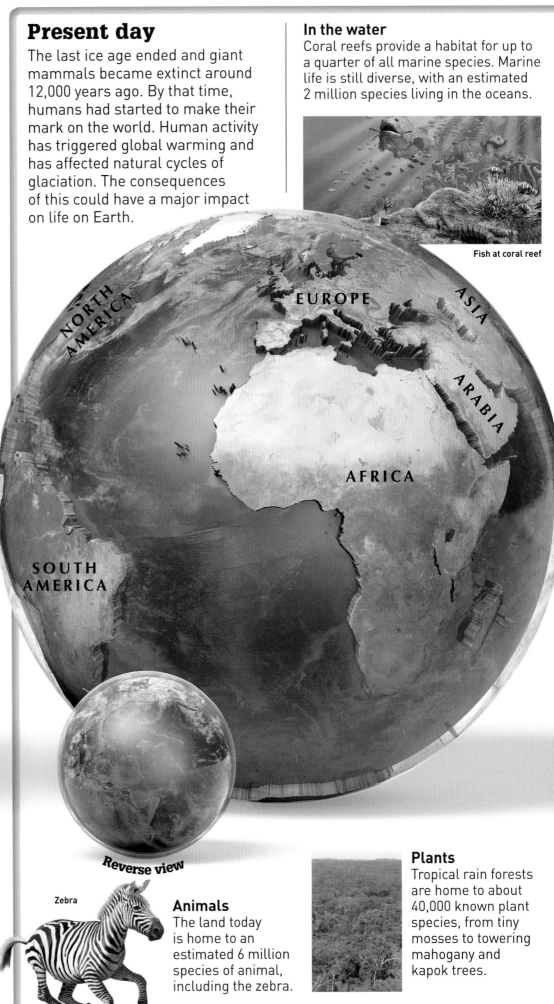

EUROPE

ASIA

ARABIA

AFRICA

NORTH
AMERICA

EUROPE

ASIA

ARABIA

AFRICA

SOUTH
AMERICA

Reverse view

Plants
Steppe (grassland too dry for trees to grow) plant types expanded. Much land was tundra—so cold, dry, and windy, that only the hardiest plants grew.

Zebra

Animals
The land today is home to an estimated 6 million species of animal, including the zebra.

Plants
Tropical rain forests are home to about 40,000 known plant species, from tiny mosses to towering mahogany and kapok trees.

NORTH AMERICA

North America from space
North America is a huge continent that dominates the northern half of Earth's western hemisphere. From space, the Great Lakes and the Rocky Mountains are clearly visible.

North American Free Trade Agreement

Established in 1994, the North American Free Trade Association, also known as NAFTA, is an agreement signed by the United States, Canada, and Mexico. Its aim is to increase the flow of trade between the three countries.

Greenland
(to Denmark)

ARCTIC OCEAN

Ellesmere Island

Baffin Bay

Baffin Island

Alaska
The United States bought Alaska from Russia for $7.2 million in 1867.

Beaufort Sea

ASIA

ALASKA

● Anchorage

Bering Sea

NUNAVUT

Hudson Bay

NORTHWEST TERRITORIES

YUKON

MANITOBA

ONTARI

C A N A D A

ALBERTA   SASKATCHEWAN

Edmonton ●   Saskatoon ●   Winnipeg ●   MINNES

● Regina   NORTH DAKOTA

● Calgary   ● Bismarck

● Juneau

Gulf of Alaska

BRITISH COLUMBIA

SOUTH DAKOTA

Queen Charlotte Islands

Vancouver ●

MONTANA   NEBRA

● Helena

Honolulu
HAWAII

Hawaiian Islands

PACIFIC OCEAN

Seattle ●
WASHINGTON

WYOMING

U N I T E D   S T

Hawaii
The volcanic Pacific islands became the United States' 50th state in 1959.

Vancouver Island

Portland ●
OREGON

IDAHO
● Boise

United States of America
The United States is a country made up of 50 states.

Salt Lake City ●

Denver ●   KAN

COLORADO

O F   A M E R

NEVADA   UTAH

Albuquerque ●
NEW MEXI

Las Vegas ●

El Pa

San Francisco ●

ARIZONA
Phoenix ●

CALIFORNIA

Los Angeles ●

San Diego ●

Chihua

Tijuana ●

PACIFIC OCEAN

FAST FACTS

Total land area:
9,358,340 sq miles
(24,238,000 sq km)

Total population:
576 million

Number of countries: 23

Largest country:
Canada—
3,855,103 sq miles
(9,984,670 sq km)

Smallest country:
St. Kitts and Nevis—
101 sq miles (261 sq km)

Largest country population:
United States of America—
321 million

Countries and borders

The continent of North America is dominated by Canada, the second largest country in the world, and the United States of America, the richest. The seven countries of Central America have struggled with the problems of poverty and war in the past, but have experienced peace and economic recovery in recent years.

Greenland
Although part of Denmark, Greenland has been self-governing since 1979. It is the world's largest island.

Canada
North America's largest country, Canada gained its independence from the United Kingdom in 1931 and has 10 provinces.

US-Mexico border
This border is the most frequently crossed international border in the world.

Dividing line
Panama's border with Colombia marks the divide between North and South America.

KEY
- Capital city
- Major city

ATLANTIC OCEAN

Caribbean Sea

Gulf of Mexico

SOUTH AMERICA

① **Denali**

At 20,321 ft (6,194 m), Denali, located in south-central Alaska, is the highest peak in North America. Denali means "tall" or "high" in Kokuyon, the language used by the people who live in the area that surrounds the mountain.

④ *Greenland*

Baffin Bay

Davis Str

Baffin Island

Parry Islands

Foxe Basin

Beaufort Sea

Victoria Island

ASIA

Mackenzie Bay

Hudson Bay

Bering Strait

Brooks Range

Denali 20,321 ft / 6,194 m

Great Bear Lake

C a n a d i a n S

Mackenzie

Great Slave Lake

① *Alaska Range*

Mackenzie Mountains

Lake Athabasca

Reindeer Lake

Bering Sea

Aleutian Range

Lake Winnipeg

Coast Mountains

C e n t r a l

Lake Manitoba

Aleutian Islands

Gulf of Alaska

R o c k y

W e s t e r n

G r e a t   L o

Mount Rainier 14,410 ft / 4,392 m

Hawaiian Islands

PACIFIC OCEAN

M o u n t a i n s

G r e a t   P l a i n

Cascade Range

Great Salt Lake

Western Cordillera

A system of parallel mountain ranges that extends along the continent's western coast.

Hawaii

Great Basin

Colorado Plateau

Death Valley -282 ft / -86 m

Grand Canyon

C o r d i l l e

Sierra Nevada

Colorado

San Joaquin Valley

Mojave Desert

Sonoran Desert

Coast Ranges

Lower California

Gulf of Califor

Landscape

North America lies between the Atlantic Ocean to the east and the Pacific Ocean to the west, and stretches from the Arctic in the north to just short of the equator in the south. The continent is also home to Greenland, the world's largest island.

PACIFIC OCEAN

BEFORE THE ISTHMUS OF PANAMA FORMED 20 MILLION YEARS

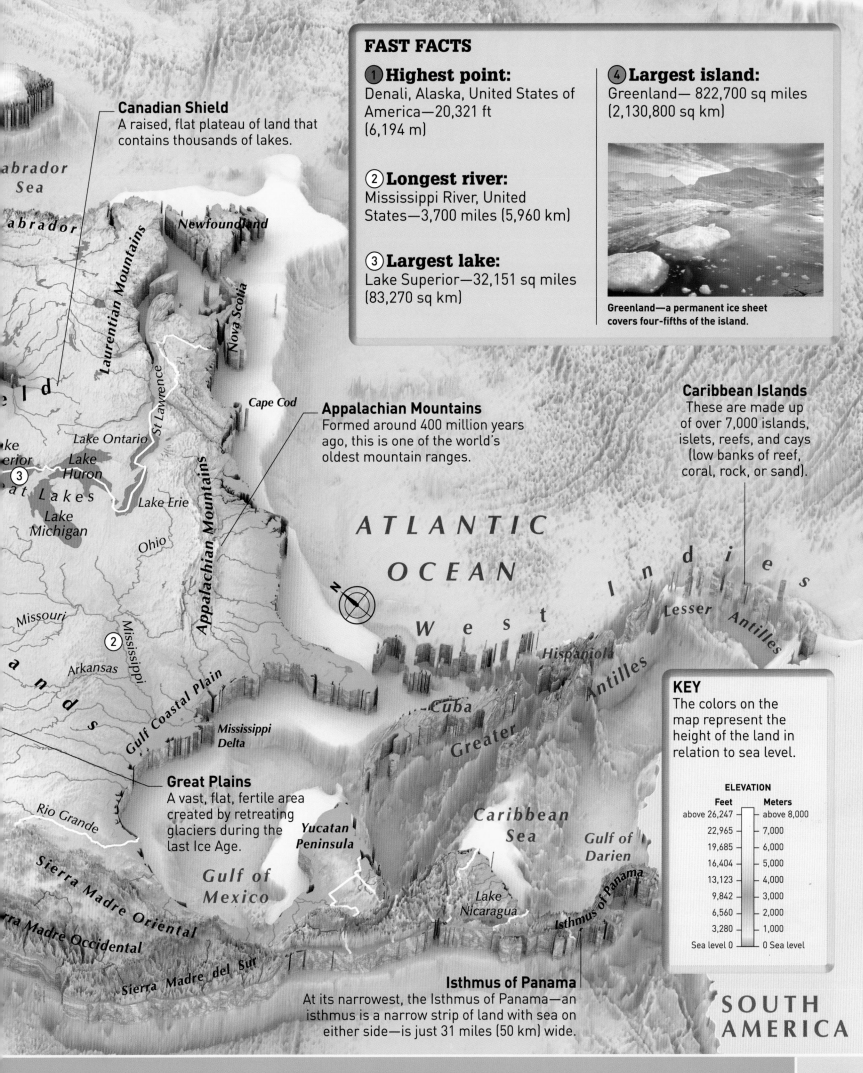

Canadian Shield
A raised, flat plateau of land that contains thousands of lakes.

Labrador Sea

Labrador

Newfoundland

Laurentian Mountains

Nova Scotia

St Lawrence

Cape Cod

Lake Ontario

Lake Erie

Lake Huron

Lake Michigan

Ohio

erior

ke

eld

l d

at Lakes

③

Appalachian Mountains
Formed around 400 million years ago, this is one of the world's oldest mountain ranges.

Appalachian Mountains

Missouri

Mississippi

Arkansas

ands

②

Gulf Coastal Plain

Great Plains
A vast, flat, fertile area created by retreating glaciers during the last Ice Age.

Mississippi Delta

Rio Grande

Sierra Madre Oriental

rra Madre Occidental

Sierra Madre del Sur

Yucatan Peninsula

Gulf of Mexico

FAST FACTS

① **Highest point:**
Denali, Alaska, United States of America—20,321 ft (6,194 m)

② **Longest river:**
Mississippi River, United States—3,700 miles (5,960 km)

③ **Largest lake:**
Lake Superior—32,151 sq miles (83,270 sq km)

④ **Largest island:**
Greenland— 822,700 sq miles (2,130,800 sq km)

Greenland—a permanent ice sheet covers four-fifths of the island.

Caribbean Islands
These are made up of over 7,000 islands, islets, reefs, and cays (low banks of reef, coral, rock, or sand).

ATLANTIC OCEAN

West Indies

Lesser Antilles

Hispaniola

Antilles

Cuba

Greater

Caribbean Sea

Gulf of Darien

Lake Nicaragua

Isthmus of Panama

Isthmus of Panama
At its narrowest, the Isthmus of Panama—an isthmus is a narrow strip of land with sea on either side—is just 31 miles (50 km) wide.

KEY
The colors on the map represent the height of the land in relation to sea level.

ELEVATION

Feet		Meters
above 26,247		above 8,000
22,965		7,000
19,685		6,000
16,404		5,000
13,123		4,000
9,842		3,000
6,560		2,000
3,280		1,000
Sea level 0		0 Sea level

SOUTH AMERICA

Fascinating facts

Largest lake: **Lake Superior, United States/ Canada**—32,151 sq miles (83,270 sq km)

Deepest lake

Great Slave Lake, Canada— **2,014 ft (614 m) deep**

Longest tunnels

 Railroad tunnel
Mount Macdonald Tunnel, British Columbia, Canada —9.1 miles (14.7 km)

Subway tunnel
Angrignon–Honoré-Beaugrand (Line 1 Green), Montreal Metro, Canada— 13.7 miles (22.1 km)

Road tunnel
Ted Williams Extension, Boston United States— 2.6 miles (4.2 km)

Number of time zones 10

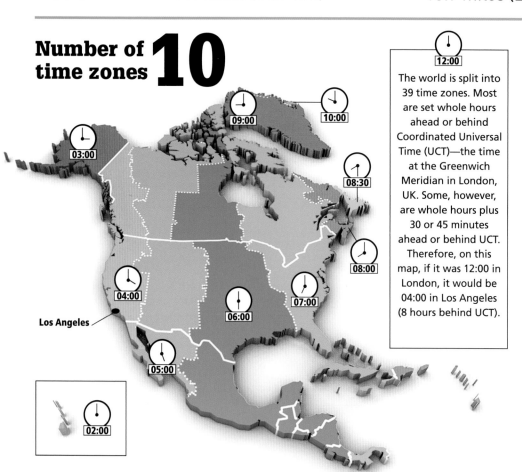

Los Angeles

The world is split into 39 time zones. Most are set whole hours ahead or behind Coordinated Universal Time (UCT)—the time at the Greenwich Meridian in London, UK. Some, however, are whole hours plus 30 or 45 minutes ahead or behind UCT. Therefore, on this map, if it was 12:00 in London, it would be 04:00 in Los Angeles (8 hours behind UCT).

Most active volcano

Kilauea, Hawaii

Official languages **7**

Amerindian languages ▪ **Creole** ▪ Danish (Greenland) ▪ **Dutch** ▪ English ▪ **French** ▪ Spanish

 **Busiest airport**

Hartsfield-Jackson Atlanta International Airport, Atlanta— **101,489,887 passengers per year**

Fastest train

North America's fastest train is the **Acela Express**, in the US, which can reach speeds of up to **150 mph (240 km/h)**

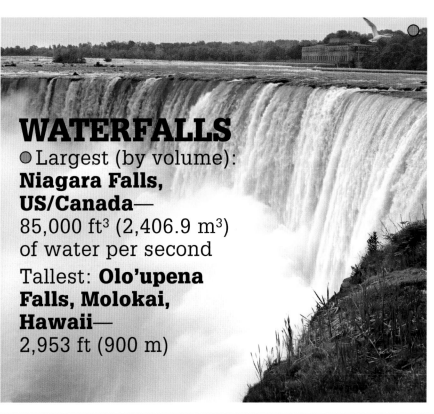

WATERFALLS

⦿ Largest (by volume):
Niagara Falls, US/Canada—85,000 ft³ (2,406.9 m³) of water per second

Tallest: **Olo'upena Falls, Molokai, Hawaii**—2,953 ft (900 m)

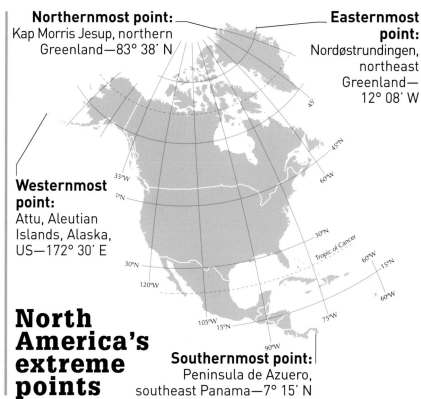

North America's extreme points

Northernmost point: Kap Morris Jesup, northern Greenland—83° 38′ N

Easternmost point: Nordøstrundingen, northeast Greenland—12° 08′ W

Westernmost point: Attu, Aleutian Islands, Alaska, US—172° 30′ E

Southernmost point: Peninsula de Azuero, southeast Panama—7° 15′ N

Longest coastline

Canada—**125,567 miles (202,080 km)**

Longest bridge

Lake Pontchartrain Causeway, Louisiana — **23.89 miles (38.442 km)**

Tallest bridge

Royal Gorge Bridge, Colorado — **955 ft (291 m)**

BIGGEST GLACIER
Bering Glacier, Alaska

Most visited cities (Visitors per year)

New York, US
12.27 million

Los Angeles, US
5.2 million

Miami, US
4.52 million

Toronto, Canada
4.18 million

Vancouver, Canada
3.76 million

Tallest buildings

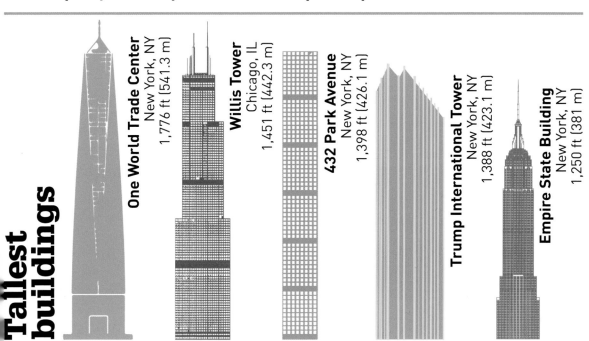

One World Trade Center New York, NY 1,776 ft (541.3 m)

Willis Tower Chicago, IL 1,451 ft (442.3 m)

432 Park Avenue New York, NY 1,398 ft (426.1 m)

Trump International Tower New York, NY 1,388 ft (423.1 m)

Empire State Building New York, NY 1,250 ft (381 m)

① Mexico City

Mexico's capital is located in the Valley of Mexico and sits at an altitude of 7,350 ft (2,240 m). Continuously inhabited since 1325, it is the oldest city in North America and also the most populous, with 8.85 million inhabitants.

Greenland

The world's largest island has the lowest population density in the world – 0.03 people per sq km (0.08 people per sq mile).

Anchorage

Alaska's most populated city, with 298,695 residents, Anchorage is the 65th largest city in the United States.

Edmonton

The capital of Alberta, Edmonton is the most northern city in North America with a metropolitan population of more than 1 million people.

Honolulu

The westernmost and southernmost city in the United States, Honolulu has a population of 352,769.

Hawaiian Islands

PACIFIC
OCEAN

Vancouver

The most densely populated city in Canada, with 13,590 inhabitants per sq mile (5,249 per sq km).

Population

Much of North America's landmass is sparsely populated, particularly in the frozen north. Population densities are highest along the United States' east and west coasts, around the Great Lakes, in the highlands of Mexico, and in the Caribbean islands, where the amount of available land is limited.

Los Angeles

The second largest city in the United States, it has a population of 3.97 million.

NINE OF NORTH AMERICA'S 10 MOST DENSELY POPULATED

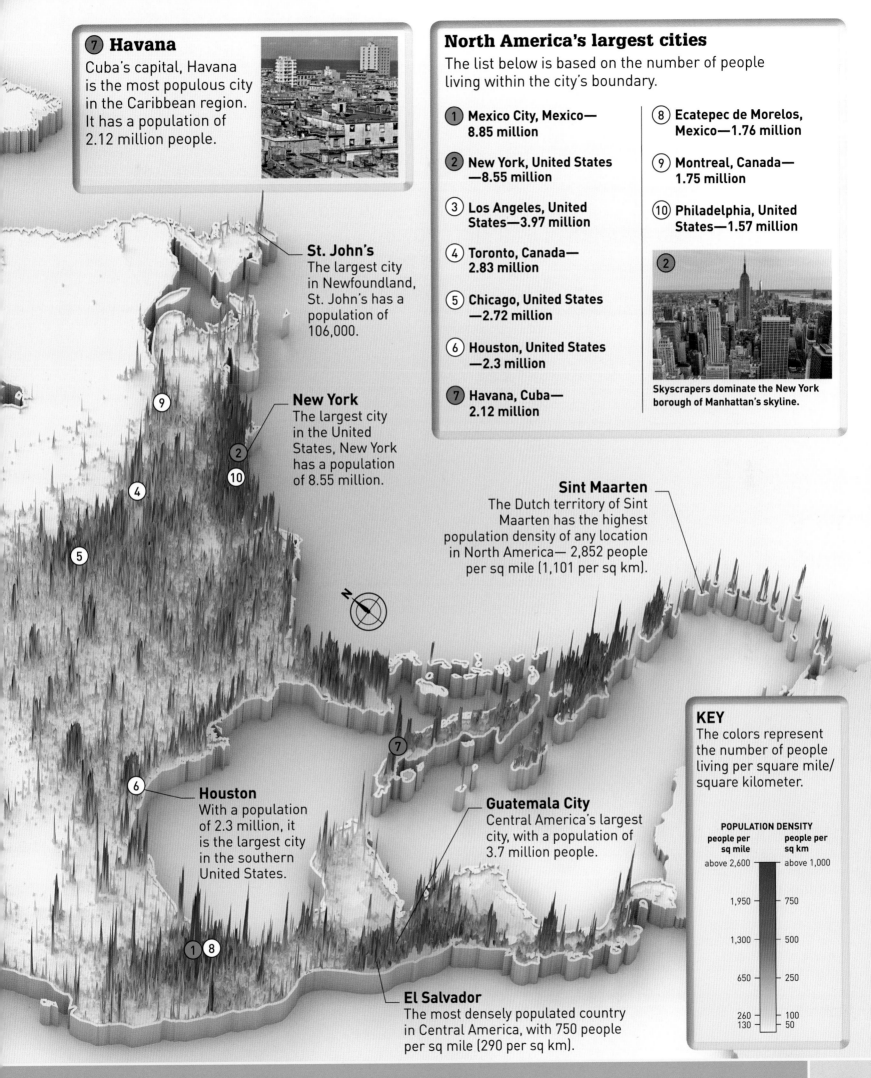

⑦ Havana

Cuba's capital, Havana is the most populous city in the Caribbean region. It has a population of 2.12 million people.

North America's largest cities

The list below is based on the number of people living within the city's boundary.

① **Mexico City, Mexico—8.85 million**

② **New York, United States —8.55 million**

③ **Los Angeles, United States—3.97 million**

④ **Toronto, Canada—2.83 million**

⑤ **Chicago, United States —2.72 million**

⑥ **Houston, United States —2.3 million**

⑦ **Havana, Cuba—2.12 million**

⑧ **Ecatepec de Morelos, Mexico—1.76 million**

⑨ **Montreal, Canada—1.75 million**

⑩ **Philadelphia, United States—1.57 million**

Skyscrapers dominate the New York borough of Manhattan's skyline.

St. John's

The largest city in Newfoundland, St. John's has a population of 106,000.

New York

The largest city in the United States, New York has a population of 8.55 million.

Sint Maarten

The Dutch territory of Sint Maarten has the highest population density of any location in North America— 2,852 people per sq mile (1,101 per sq km).

Houston

With a population of 2.3 million, it is the largest city in the southern United States.

Guatemala City

Central America's largest city, with a population of 3.7 million people.

KEY

The colors represent the number of people living per square mile/ square kilometer.

POPULATION DENSITY

people per sq mile	people per sq km
above 2,600	above 1,000
1,950	750
1,300	500
650	250
260	100
130	50

El Salvador

The most densely populated country in Central America, with 750 people per sq mile (290 per sq km).

The Grand Canyon

Formed over millions of years by the flow of the Colorado River, the Grand Canyon is a steep-sided canyon in the state of Arizona. It is 277 miles (446 km) long, 18 miles (29 km) wide at its widest point, and reaches a depth of 6,093 ft (1,857 m).

Granite Gorge
The most-visited section of the Grand Canyon, it is the starting point for the majority of rafting trips through the canyon along the Colorado River.

Grand Canyon Village

Grand Canyon

Gran

Colorado River

Granite Gorge

Grand Canyon Lodge

Bright Angel Canyon

Walhalla Plateau

Cape Royal

Desert View

Colorado River

Painte

South Rim
Approximately 90 percent of tourists catch their first dramatic glimpse of the Grand Canyon from here.

Painted Desert
Starting at the eastern edge of the Grand Canyon, the Painted Desert is 7,500 sq miles (19,425 sq km). It is named for its multi-colored layers of rock, which range from gray to purple, and from orange to pink.

THE FIRST EUROPEAN TO SEE THE GRAND CANYON WAS GARCIA

Tuckup Canyon
A 100-mile (160-km) long
trail route on the North Rim
of the Grand Canyon.

Tuckup Canyon

Grand Canyon Village
Occupied since the
1800s, Grand Canyon Village
was originally built around
the terminus for the Grand
Canyon Railroad, which
brought tourists to the area.

North Rim
Temperatures
on the North Rim
are usually lower
than those at
the South Rim
because it is 1,000 ft
(300 m) higher.

Colorado River

Kanab Plateau

Kaibab Plateau
Reaching an elevation of 9,200 ft
(2,817 m), this heavily forested
plateau contrasts sharply with
the arid lowlands to its south.

Great Thumb Mesa

Powell Plateau

rge

*Kaibab
Plateau*

Cockscomb

Cockscomb
A trail area running to the north of
the Grand Canyon, its highest point
is Cockscomb Rock at 5,009 ft (1,527 m).

**Kaibab
National Forest**
A 1.6 million-acre
(670,000-hectare)
forest that borders
both the north
and south of the
Grand Canyon.

Marble Canyon

Desert

Colorado River
From its source in the Rocky
Mountains, the Colorado River flows
for 1,450 miles (2,330 km) and
passes through Mexico before
emptying into the Gulf of California.

Marble Canyon
This marks the beginning of the
Grand Canyon. Despite its name,
the canyon contains no marble
—it gets its name from the color
of its limestone walls, which
resemble the color of marble.

○ **Chichen Itza**

The largest and most famous Mayan site, Chichen Itza, Mexico, was a major urban center between 750 and 1200 CE. The highlight of the site is the El Castillo pyramid, whose four sides are made up of 365 steps (one for each day of the solar year).

Illulisat Icefjord
Located 220 miles (350 km) north of the Arctic Circle, the area's many icebergs have made Illulisat a popular tourist destination.

Illulisat Icefjord,
Greenland

Mount Shishaldin,
Alaska,
United States

Mount Shishaldin
The highest mountain peak on the Aleutian Islands (9,373 ft/2,857 m), Mount Shishaldin is the most symmetrical cone-shaped volcano on Earth.

Ninstints,
British Columbia,
Canada

The Bow,
Calgary,
Canada

Mount Rushmore,
South Dakota,
United States

Old Faithful,
Wyoming, United States

Space Needle,
Seattle, United States

Mauna Loa,
Hawaii, United States

Hawaiian Islands

PACIFIC OCEAN

Redwood National Park,
California, United States

Golden Gate Bridge
When it opened in 1937, it had the longest main span (4,200 ft/1,280 m) of any suspension bridge in the world.

Golden Gate Bridge,
San Francisco,
United States

Hoover Dam,
Nevada-Arizona,
United States

Chaco Canyon
New Mexico,
United States

HOLLYWOOD

Hollywood Sign,
Los Angeles,
United States

The **United States** is the world's **second-** most-visited country.

KEY
○ **Landmark location**

Famous landmarks

L'Anse aux Meadows
A Viking settlement that dates to 1000 CE —nearly 500 years before Columbus discovered the New World.

...uk ...thedral, *...eenland*

L'Anse aux Meadows, *...wfoundland, Canada*

CN Tower, *Toronto, Canada*

Chateau Frontenac, *Québec City, Canada*

Lunenburg Church, *Nova Scotia, Canada*

Statue of Liberty, *New York, United States*

The White House, *Washington D.C., United States*

Niagara Falls, *United States–Canada*

From towering volcanoes, giant redwood forests, and thunderous waterfalls, to spectacular skyscrapers, the ruins of ancient civilizations, and the architectural legacies of the region's colonial past, North America's most famous landmarks are a stunning mix of natural wonders and manmade masterpieces.

● Niagara Falls

Niagara Falls is the collective name for three waterfalls that straddle the Canada-United States border. The largest, the Horseshoe Falls, has an average drop of 188 ft (57 m).

The White House
Built between 1792 and 1800, it is the official residence of the US president.

Kennedy Space Center, *Florida, United States*

Poverty Point, *Louisiana, United States*

The Alamo, *Texas, United States*

Gran Teatro, *Cuba*

National Palace, *Dominican Republic*

Bridgetown Clocktower, *Barbados*

Panama Canal
This 48-mile (77-km), manmade waterway connects the Atlantic and Pacific Oceans.

Chichen Itza, *Mexico*

Metropolitan Cathedral, *Mexico*

Panama Canal, *Panama*

Hospicio Cabañas, *Mexico*

Copán, *Honduras*

Teatro Nacional, *Costa Rica*

⊙ Tornado Alley

Tornado Alley is a nickname given to an area in the southern United States that experiences a high number of tornadoes. A tornado is a column of air that spins at high speed while maintaining contact with both the ground and the storm clouds above.

Coldest inhabited place
Prospect Creek Camp, in Alaska, is the coldest inhabited place in North America. On January 23, 1971, the thermometer there tumbled to -80°F (-62.2°C).

Lowest
The lowest temperature ever recorded in North America is -81.4°F (-63°C) at Snag, Yukon, in Canada, on February 3, 1947.

Wettest
Henderson Lake, British Columbia, Canada, received an average of 276 in (7 m) of rain and snow when measurements were taken between 1923 to 1935 and 1998 to 2000.

Highest
The highest temperature ever recorded in North America is 134°F (56.7°C) in Death Valley, California on July 10, 1913.

EISMITTE 0 10

RESOLUTE 0 9

IQALUIT 0 6

COPPERMINE 0 9

CHURCHILL 3 9

ANCHORAGE 3 8

FORT VERMILION 1 10

WINNIPEG 5 10

CALGARY 5 12

SIOUX CITY 5 12

VANCOUVER 3 10

BOISE 4 14

DENVER 7 11

HONOLULU 7 10
Hawaiian Islands
PACIFIC OCEAN

LAS VEGAS 8 13

SAN FRANCISCO 5 10

LOS ANGELES 7 11

GUAYMAS 7 9

Climate

The climate in North America ranges from freezing Arctic conditions in the far north to desert in the southwest, and tropical conditions in Florida, Central America, and the Caribbean. Central and southern regions are prone to severe storms, including hurricanes and tornadoes.

Driest
Batagues in Baja California, Mexico, is the driest place in North America. It receives just 1.2 in (30.5 mm) of rain per year.

IN 1998-99, A WORLD RECORD 95 FT (29 M) OF SNOW FELL ON THE

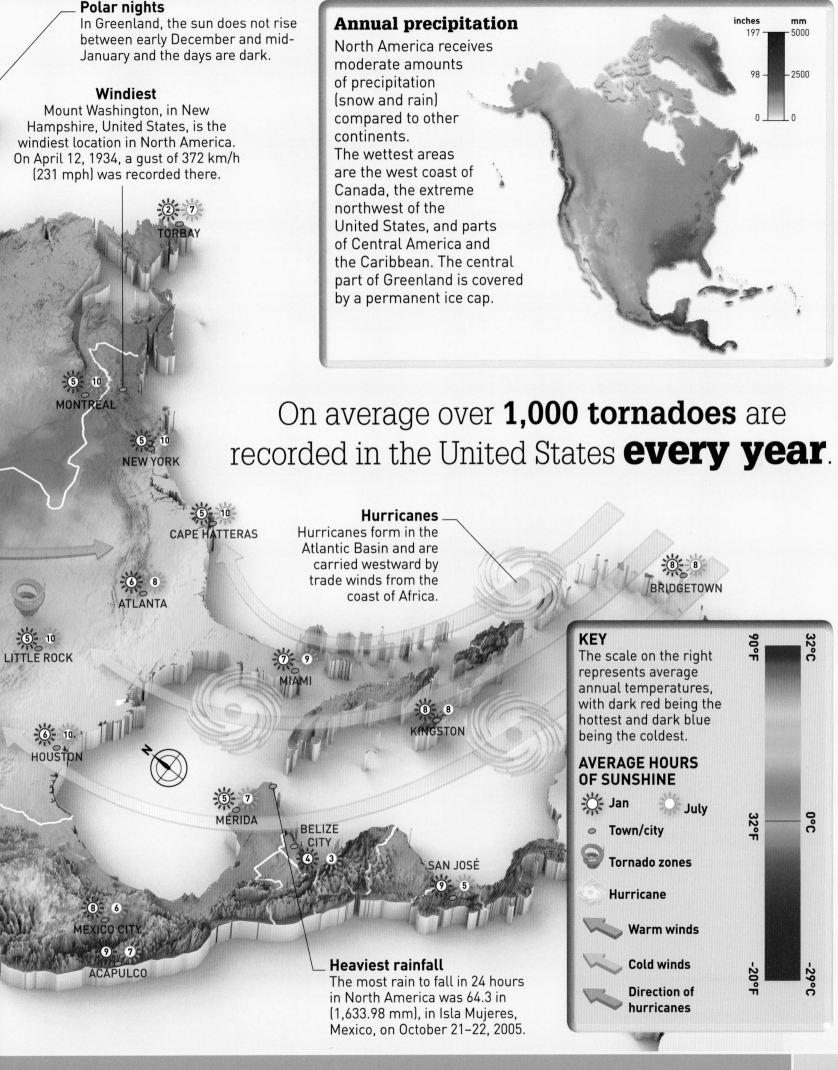

Polar nights
In Greenland, the sun does not rise between early December and mid-January and the days are dark.

Windiest
Mount Washington, in New Hampshire, United States, is the windiest location in North America. On April 12, 1934, a gust of 372 km/h (231 mph) was recorded there.

Annual precipitation
North America receives moderate amounts of precipitation (snow and rain) compared to other continents. The wettest areas are the west coast of Canada, the extreme northwest of the United States, and parts of Central America and the Caribbean. The central part of Greenland is covered by a permanent ice cap.

inches | mm
197 — 5000
98 — 2500
0 — 0

On average over **1,000 tornadoes** are recorded in the United States **every year**.

Hurricanes
Hurricanes form in the Atlantic Basin and are carried westward by trade winds from the coast of Africa.

KEY
The scale on the right represents average annual temperatures, with dark red being the hottest and dark blue being the coldest.

90°F — 32°C
32°F — 0°C
-20°F — -29°C

AVERAGE HOURS OF SUNSHINE
☀ Jan   ○ July
⬭ Town/city
⬭ Tornado zones
🌀 Hurricane
⬅ Warm winds
⬅ Cold winds
⬅ Direction of hurricanes

Heaviest rainfall
The most rain to fall in 24 hours in North America was 64.3 in (1,633.98 mm), in Isla Mujeres, Mexico, on October 21–22, 2005.

TORBAY (2) (7)
MONTREAL (5) 10
NEW YORK (5) 10
CAPE HATTERAS (5) 10
ATLANTA (6) 8
LITTLE ROCK (5) 10
MIAMI (7) 9
HOUSTON (6) 10
KINGSTON (8) 8
BRIDGETOWN (8) 8
MÉRIDA (5) 7
BELIZE CITY (4) 3
SAN JOSÉ (9) 5
MEXICO CITY (8) 6
ACAPULCO (9) 7

BIOMES

North America has a number of different biomes—large geographical areas of distinctive plant and animal groups—from deciduous forests in the south to tundra in the far north.

- Ice
- Tundra
- Boreal forest/Taiga
- Temperate coniferous forest
- Temperate broadleaf forest
- Temperate grassland
- Mediterranean
- Tropical coniferous forest
- Tropical broadleaf forest
- Tropical dry broadleaf forest
- Tropical, sub-tropical grassland
- Desert
- Flooded grassland
- Mangrove

Walrus
This mammal uses its tusks to haul its enormous 3,000 lb (1,500 kg) body out of the water.

Harbor seal
This common se slows its heartb when swimmir underwater.

Musk ox
Gets its name from the strong odor males emit during the rutting season.

Ringed seal
This seal can hold its breath underwater for 45 minutes.

Snowy owl
An unusual owl because it hunts by day.

American black bear
Short, non-retractable claw make it an excell tree-climber.

American bison
North America's largest land mammal, it can weigh up to 1 ton (907 kg).

Antelope
The fastest land animal in North America, the antelope can reach speeds of 55 mph (88.5 km/h).

Arctic ground squirrel
This squirrel doubles its weight during summer to prepare for a seven-month hibernation.

Elk
Male elk clas antlers in batt for mating righ

Steller sea lion
The largest sea lion species. Male bulls can be 2,205 lb (1,000 kg).

Dall sheep
This sheep has thick, curled horns that stop growing in the winter.

Gray wolf
Wolf pairs can track prey for up to 50 miles (80 km).

Coyote
A nocturnal canine that will eat whatever it finds.

Striped skunk
This mammal's foul-smelling oil can be smelled up to 1 mile (1.6 km) away.

Hawaiian Islands

PACIFIC OCEAN

Hawaiian monk seal
The only species of seal native to Hawaii. It is highly endangered.

Great white shark
A streamlined swimmer with powerful jaws that contain seven rows of knifelike teeth.

Golden eagle
North America's largest bird of prey can reach speeds of 200 mph (320 km/h) in a vertical dive.

Bighorn sheep
The horns of a male can weigh more than its whole skeleton.

Wildlife

A diverse array of animals roams North America's lands and waters. The contrasting biomes—from freezing tundra in the north to tropical rain forest in the south—provide a remarkable range of habitats for countless species to survive and thrive.

Gray seal
Two fur layers and blubber help this seal keep warm in freezing water.

Starnosed mole
Nose tentacles help this mole identify food.

Raccoon
Dextrous front paws help this mammal snatch fish from rivers and pick snacks from the trash.

River otter
Webbed feet and sleek body make this playful mammal an excellent swimmer.

● Oldest and largest
Situated above a dormant (inactive) volcano, and boasting more than half of the world's great geysers, Yellowstone, in Wyoming, became the world's first national park in 1872. This has helped preserve the landscape from human exploitation, and protect its animal herds from poachers.

Beaver
Powerful jaws help this rodent fell trees and build dams in deep water.

Lemon shark
A stocky shark that lives in groups in tropical coastal waters.

Rattlesnake
Highly venomous, this snake grows new "rattle" segments when it sheds its skin.

American alligator
This extremely territorial and powerful predator can be 13 ft (4 m) long.

Caribbean reef shark
This shark lives on reefs, and can dive to 1,250 ft (380 m).

Prairie dog
A rodent that lives in underground towns on grasslands.

Magnificent frigatebird
An agile flier with long wings and a forked tail.

Olive Ridley sea turtle
A solitary, open-ocean dweller; females return to land to lay eggs.

American crocodile
The largest crocodile species, it lives in brackish (slightly salty) water.

ARACHNIDS (SPIDERS AND SCORPIONS), 914 BIRDS, AND 662 REPTILES.

Canada

Despite its vast size (only the Russian Federation is larger), almost 90 percent of Canada is uninhabitable. The cold temperatures in the country's frozen north are too extreme for humans to live there.

Hawaii

With 953,000 people, O'ahu is the most populous of Hawaii's main islands.

PACIFIC OCEAN

Hawaiian Islands

California

The Los Angeles-Long Beach-Anaheim area is the most densely populated region in the United States.

By night

This image of North America at night provides a fascinating insight into where people live. The major urban areas are found in the eastern half of the United States, California, and central Mexico, but much of the northern half of the continent is uninhabited.

OF THE 50 STATES THAT MAKE UP THE UNITED STATES,

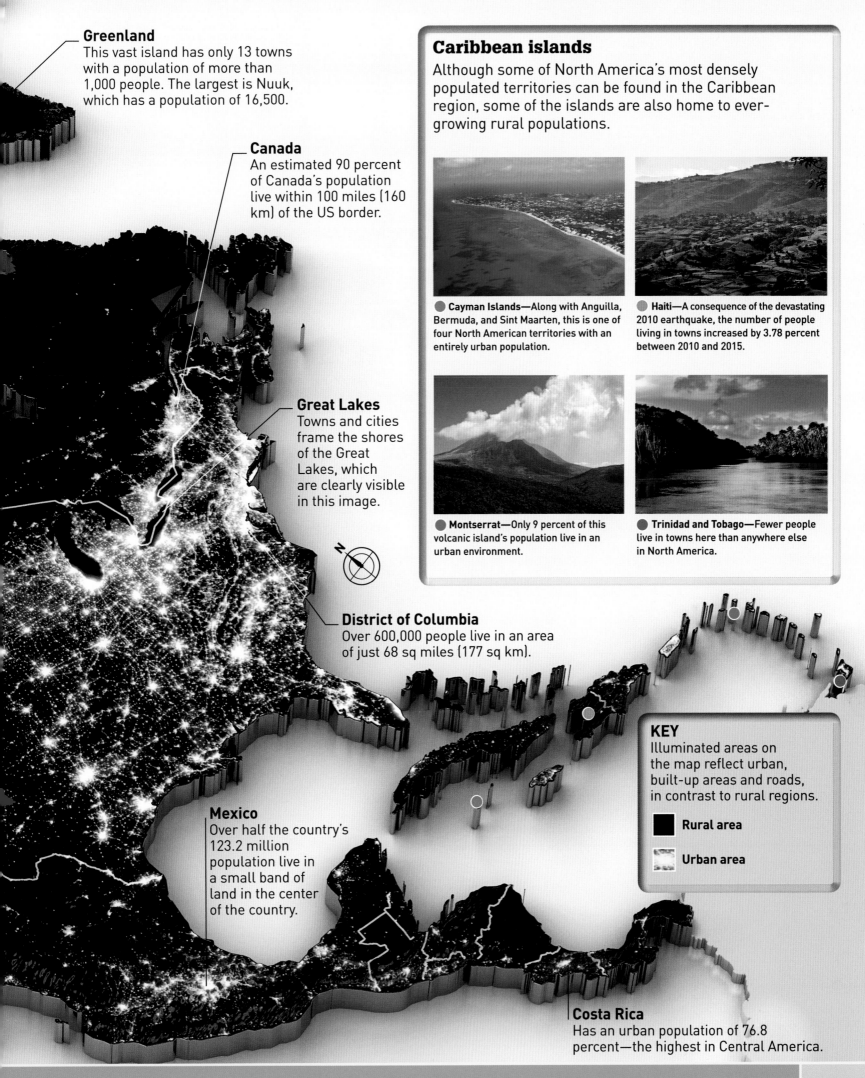

Greenland
This vast island has only 13 towns with a population of more than 1,000 people. The largest is Nuuk, which has a population of 16,500.

Canada
An estimated 90 percent of Canada's population live within 100 miles (160 km) of the US border.

Great Lakes
Towns and cities frame the shores of the Great Lakes, which are clearly visible in this image.

District of Columbia
Over 600,000 people live in an area of just 68 sq miles (177 sq km).

Mexico
Over half the country's 123.2 million population live in a small band of land in the center of the country.

Costa Rica
Has an urban population of 76.8 percent—the highest in Central America.

Caribbean islands
Although some of North America's most densely populated territories can be found in the Caribbean region, some of the islands are also home to ever-growing rural populations.

● **Cayman Islands**—Along with Anguilla, Bermuda, and Sint Maarten, this is one of four North American territories with an entirely urban population.

● **Haiti**—A consequence of the devastating 2010 earthquake, the number of people living in towns increased by 3.78 percent between 2010 and 2015.

● **Montserrat**—Only 9 percent of this volcanic island's population live in an urban environment.

● **Trinidad and Tobago**—Fewer people live in towns here than anywhere else in North America.

KEY
Illuminated areas on the map reflect urban, built-up areas and roads, in contrast to rural regions.

■ Rural area

▨ Urban area

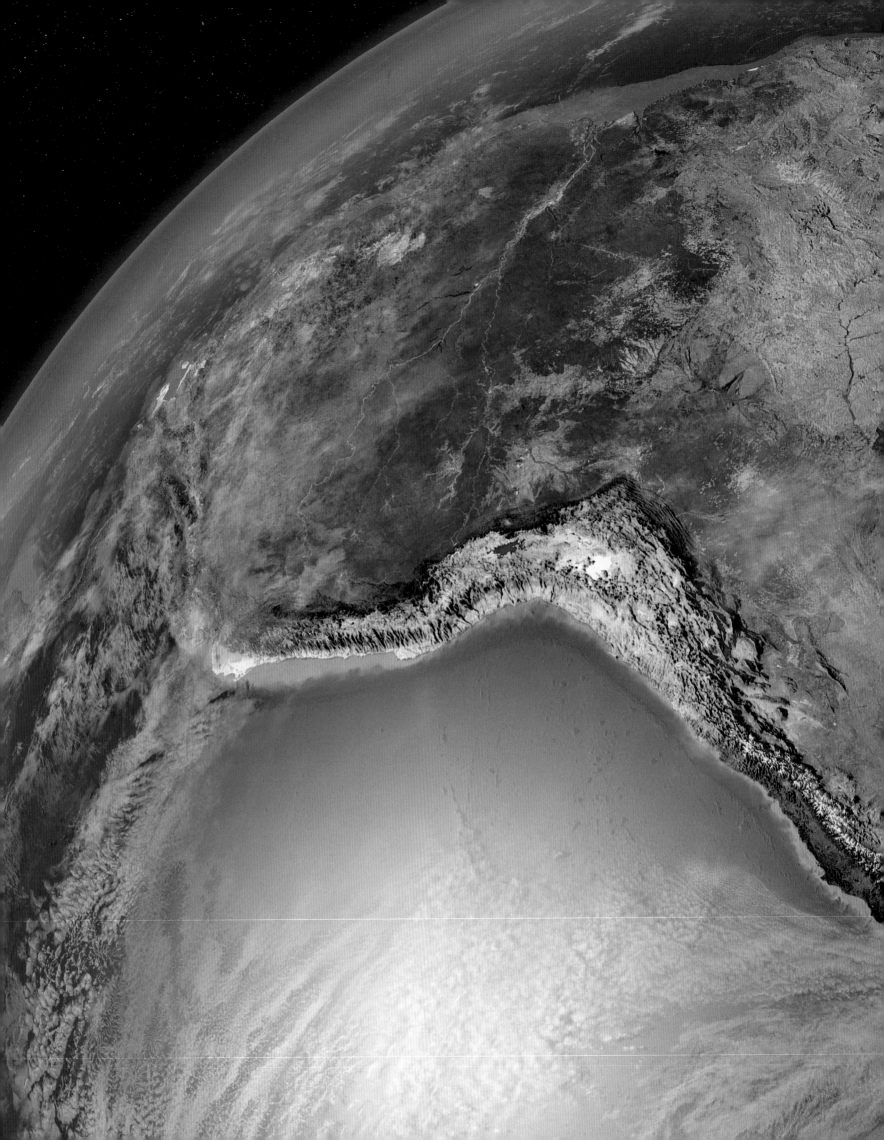

SOUTH AMERICA

Mountains and forests
The Andes mountain range and
the mighty Amazon rain forest
dominate South America, which
runs from the Caribbean Sea
in the north to the Tierra del Fuego
in the south.

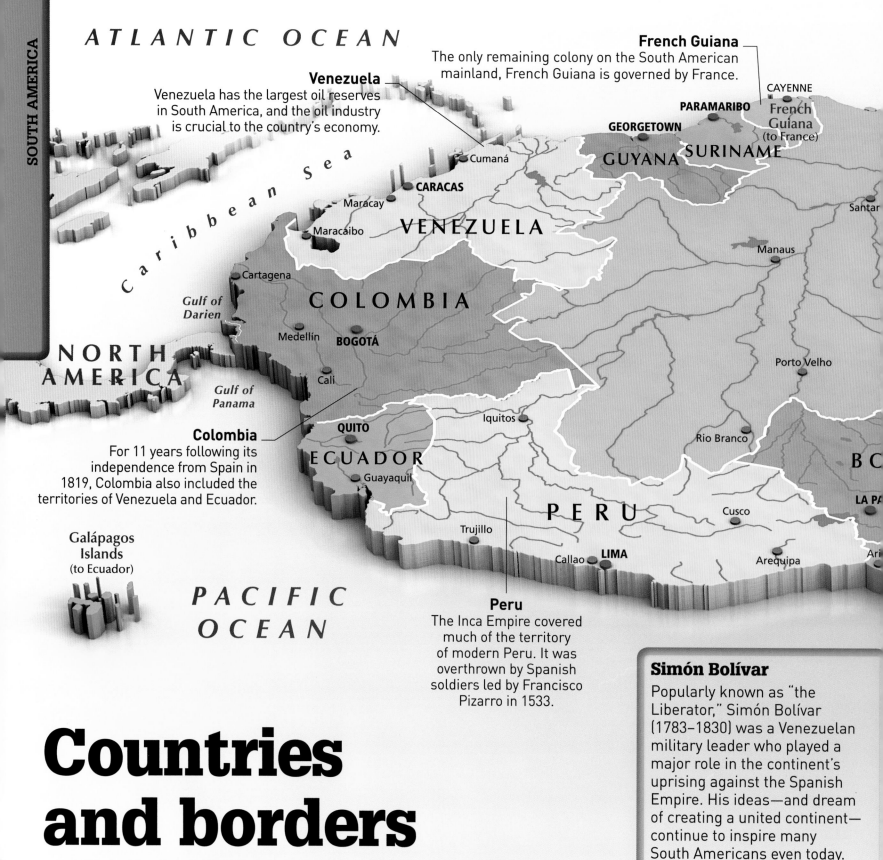

ATLANTIC OCEAN

French Guiana
The only remaining colony on the South American mainland, French Guiana is governed by France.

CAYENNE

PARAMARIBO

French Guiana
(to France)

GEORGETOWN

Venezuela
Venezuela has the largest oil reserves in South America, and the oil industry is crucial to the country's economy.

Cumaná

GUYANA SURINAME

Santar

CARACAS

Maracay

VENEZUELA

Maracaibo

Manaus

Caribbean Sea

Cartagena

COLOMBIA

Gulf of Darien

Medellín

BOGOTÁ

Porto Velho

NORTH AMERICA

Cali

Gulf of Panama

Iquitos

Rio Branco

Colombia
For 11 years following its independence from Spain in 1819, Colombia also included the territories of Venezuela and Ecuador.

QUITO

ECUADOR

Guayaquil

B C

PERU

Cusco

LA PA

Galápagos Islands
(to Ecuador)

Trujillo

PACIFIC OCEAN

Callao LIMA

Arequipa

Ari

Peru
The Inca Empire covered much of the territory of modern Peru. It was overthrown by Spanish soldiers led by Francisco Pizarro in 1533.

Simón Bolívar
Popularly known as "the Liberator," Simón Bolívar (1783–1830) was a Venezuelan military leader who played a major role in the continent's uprising against the Spanish Empire. His ideas—and dream of creating a united continent—continue to inspire many South Americans even today.

Countries and borders

For centuries, most of South America was under Spanish or Portuguese rule. Although the majority of countries became independent in the early 19th century, the languages and cultures of their past rulers have shaped the lives of people living there today.

Brazil
The Treaty of Tordesillas, signed in 1494, divided South America between Spain and Portugal. The Portuguese were given the lands to the east that would one day become Brazil.

Fortaleza
Natal
Recife
Belém
São Luís
Salvador

B R A Z I L

Palmas de Tocantins

Vitória
BRASÍLIA
Goiânia
Belo Horizonte
Cuiabá
Rio de Janeiro
Campinas
São Paulo
Campo Grande
Curitiba

Santa Cruz
A
bamba
UCRE

PARAGUAY
Ciudad del Este
ASUNCIÓN
Porto Alegre

Resistencia

URUGUAY

Salta

A
R
Santa Fe
MONTEVIDEO
Rosario
La Plata
Antofagasta
Córdoba
BUENOS AIRES

C
G

Bolivia
Named after Simón Bolívar, Bolivia became an independent republic in 1825.

E
Mendoza
N
Bahía Blanca

SANTIAGO
T
Valparaíso
I

Chile
Bernardo O'Higgins and José de San Martín were the revolutionaries who led Chile to independence in 1818. Today, they are two of the country's greatest national heroes.

L
N

Puerto
Montt

A

Punta Arenas

FAST FACTS
Total land area:
6,890,000 sq miles
(17,840,000 sq km)

Total population:
410 million

Number of countries: 12

Largest country:
Brazil—3,287,957 sq miles
(8,515,770 sq km)

Smallest country:
Suriname—63,251 sq miles
(163,820 sq km)

Largest country population:
Brazil—204.3 million

The Brazilian city of Rio de Janeiro is home to the world's biggest carnival.

ATLANTIC

OCEAN

Falkland Islands
The islands are a self-governing British colony. In 1982, Argentina invaded, leading to a brief, but bloody, war.

STANLEY

Falkland Islands
(to UK)

KEY
● Capital city
● Major city

The Orinoco
This river flows in a vast arc through Venezuela, passing through the flat Llanos, where it creates vast floodplains during the rainy season.

Guiana Highlands
The tablelike mountains of the Guiana Highlands are surrounded by cliffs that rise up to 1,300 ft (400 m).

ATLANTI

Tumuc-Humac Mountains

Pakaraima Mountains

Guiana Highlands

②

Amazon

Tapajós

Orinoco

Caribbean Sea

Punta Gallinas

Lake Maracaibo

Llanos

Represa Balbina

Branco

Rio Negro

Amazon

Gulf of Darien

Cordillera Oriental

Magdalena

Cauca

Cordillera Central

Japurá

Amazon

Madeira

Amazon Basin

Gulf of Panama

Cordillera Occidental

Putumayo

Purus

Chimborazo
20,702 ft /
6,310 m

Cordillera Real

Amazon

Juruá

The Colombian Andes
The Andes separate into three ranges in Colombia. Two of the country's great rivers, the Río Magdalena and the Río Cauca, have their sources here.

Nevado Huascarán
22,205 ft /
6,768 m

Marañón

Ucayali

Lake Titicaca

③

Altip

Gulf of Guayaquil

Andes

Punta Negra

Galápagos Islands
This isolated group of volcanic islands is home to a number of unique animal species.

Galápagos Islands

The Andes
Spanning 4,350 miles (7,000 km) along the western side of South America, the Andes is the longest mountain range on Earth.

The Altiplano
The second highest plain in the world, the Altiplano, in Bolivia, has an average altitude of 12,303 ft (3,750 m).

PACIFIC OCEAN

Landscape

South America boasts an extraordinary range of landscapes, from the tropical forests on the northern coast to the icy fjords of Tierra del Fuego. The Andes mountains extend along the west coast, while the Amazon Basin dominates the heart of the continent. To the south lie the grasslands of the Pampas.

③ Lake Titicaca
South America's largest lake, Lake Titicaca is the highest navigable body of water in the world, with an elevation of 12,500 ft (3,800 m). It is home to the Uros people, who live on floating islands made from reeds. One island even houses a meeting hall and a school.

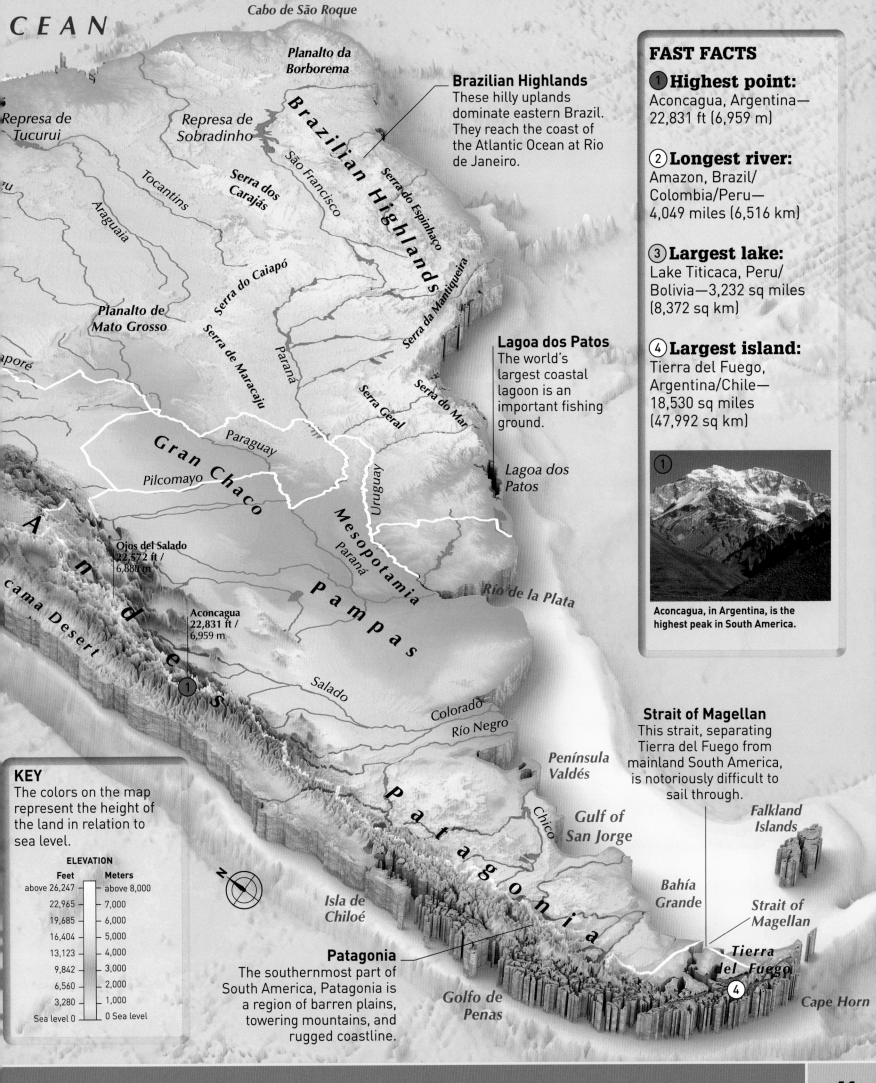

CEAN

Cabo de São Roque

Planalto da Borborema

Represa de Tucurui

Represa de Sobradinho

Brazilian Highlands
These hilly uplands dominate eastern Brazil. They reach the coast of the Atlantic Ocean at Rio de Janeiro.

Tocantins

Araguaia

Serra dos Carajás

São Francisco

Serrado Espinhaço

Brazilian Highlands

Serra da Mantiqueira

Serra do Caiapó

Planalto de Mato Grosso

Serra de Maracaju

Paraná

Serra Geral

Serra do Mar

Lagoa dos Patos
The world's largest coastal lagoon is an important fishing ground.

Lagoa dos Patos

aporé

Paraguay

Gran Chaco

Pilcomayo

Uruguay

Mesopotamia

Paraná

Ojos del Salado
22,572 ft / 6,880 m

cama Desert

A n d e s

Aconcagua
22,831 ft / 6,959 m

①

P a m p a s

Río de la Plata

Salado

Colorado

Río Negro

Península Valdés

Strait of Magellan
This strait, separating Tierra del Fuego from mainland South America, is notoriously difficult to sail through.

Chico

Gulf of San Jorge

Falkland Islands

Bahía Grande

Strait of Magellan

P a t a g o n i a

Isla de Chiloé

Patagonia
The southernmost part of South America, Patagonia is a region of barren plains, towering mountains, and rugged coastline.

Golfo de Penas

Tierra del Fuego

④

Cape Horn

FAST FACTS

① **Highest point:**
Aconcagua, Argentina—22,831 ft (6,959 m)

② **Longest river:**
Amazon, Brazil/Colombia/Peru—4,049 miles (6,516 km)

③ **Largest lake:**
Lake Titicaca, Peru/Bolivia—3,232 sq miles (8,372 sq km)

④ **Largest island:**
Tierra del Fuego, Argentina/Chile—18,530 sq miles (47,992 sq km)

①

Aconcagua, in Argentina, is the highest peak in South America.

KEY
The colors on the map represent the height of the land in relation to sea level.

ELEVATION

Feet	Meters
above 26,247	above 8,000
22,965	7,000
19,685	6,000
16,404	5,000
13,123	4,000
9,842	3,000
6,560	2,000
3,280	1,000
Sea level 0	0 Sea level

N

Fascinating facts

BIGGEST GLACIER

Brüggen Glacier, Chile —**488 sq miles (1,265 sq km) and 41 miles (66 km)**

Number of time zones **4**

Rio de Janeiro

 The world is split into 39 time zones. Most are set whole hours ahead or behind Coordinated Universal Time (UCT)—the time at the Greenwich Meridian in London, UK. Some, however, are whole hours plus 30 or 45 minutes ahead or behind UCT. Therefore, on this map, if it was 12:00 in London, it would be 09:00 in Rio de Janeiro, Brazil (3 hours behind UCT).

COUNTRY WITH THE MOST NEIGHBORS

Brazil (10)

French Guiana, **Suriname,** Guyana, **Venezuela,** Colombia, **Peru,** Bolivia, **Paraguay,** Argentina, **Uruguay**

Longest tunnels

 Railroad tunnel
Cuajone–El Sargento tunnel, Peru—9.1 miles (14.72 km)

 Road tunnel
Fernando Gomez Martinez tunnel, Colombia—2.86 miles (4.6 km)

Number of official languages **5**
Portuguese ▪ Spanish ▪ English ▪ Dutch ▪ French

Longest coastline

Brazil—**4,655 miles (7,491 km)**

Most active volcano
Villarrica, Chile

 **Busiest airport**

Biggest airport São Paulo-Guarulhos Airport, Brazil—passengers in 2015: **35.96 million**

Tallest:
Angel Falls, Venezuela —3,212 ft (979 m)

Largest (by volume): **Iguazú Falls, Brazil— Argentina—** 62,012 ft^3 (1,756 m^3) of water per second

Tallest buildings

Gran Torre
Santiago, Chile
984 ft (300 m)

Parque Central Complex, East Tower
Caracas, Venezuela
738 ft (225 m)

Parque Central Complex, West Tower
Caracas, Venezuela
738 ft (225 m)

Torre Colpatria
Bogotá, Colombia
643 ft (196 m)

Titanium La Portada
Santiago, Chile
636 ft (194 m)

Most visited cities (Visitors per year)

Lima, Peru
4.03 million

São Paulo, Brazil
2.3 million

Buenos Aires, Argentina
2.02 million

Rio de Janeiro, Brazil
1.37 million

Bogotá, Colombia
1.26 million

South America's extreme points

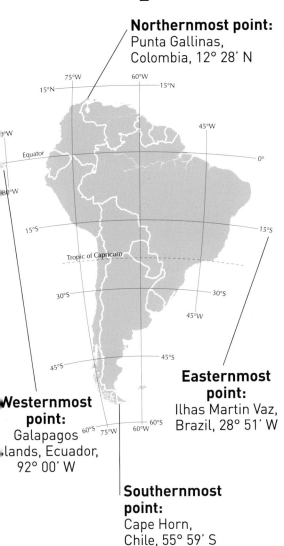

Northernmost point:
Punta Gallinas,
Colombia, 12° 28′ N

Easternmost point:
Ilhas Martin Vaz,
Brazil, 28° 51′ W

Westernmost point:
Galapagos
Islands, Ecuador,
92° 00′ W

Southernmost point:
Cape Horn,
Chile, 55° 59′ S

Longest bridge

Rio Niterói Bridge,
Guanabara Bay,
Brazil—**8.25 miles
(13.29 km)**

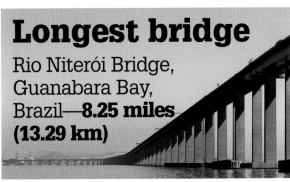

Lowest point

Laguna del Carbón,
Santa Cruz, Argentina—
-344 ft (-104.9 m)

This is the seventh-lowest point
on Earth's surface.

Landlocked countries 2—Bolivia and Paraguay

Highest mountains

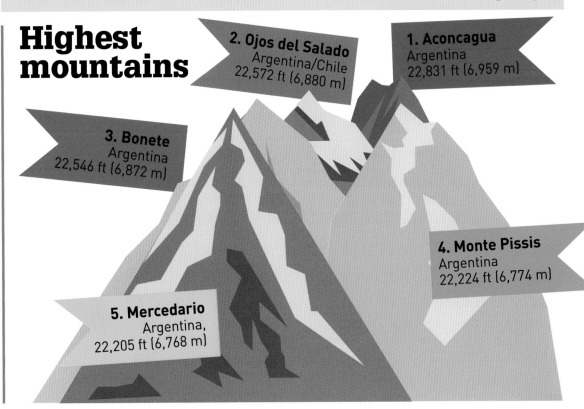

2. Ojos del Salado
Argentina/Chile
22,572 ft (6,880 m)

1. Aconcagua
Argentina
22,831 ft (6,959 m)

3. Bonete
Argentina
22,546 ft (6,872 m)

4. Monte Pissis
Argentina
22,224 ft (6,774 m)

5. Mercedario
Argentina,
22,205 ft (6,768 m)

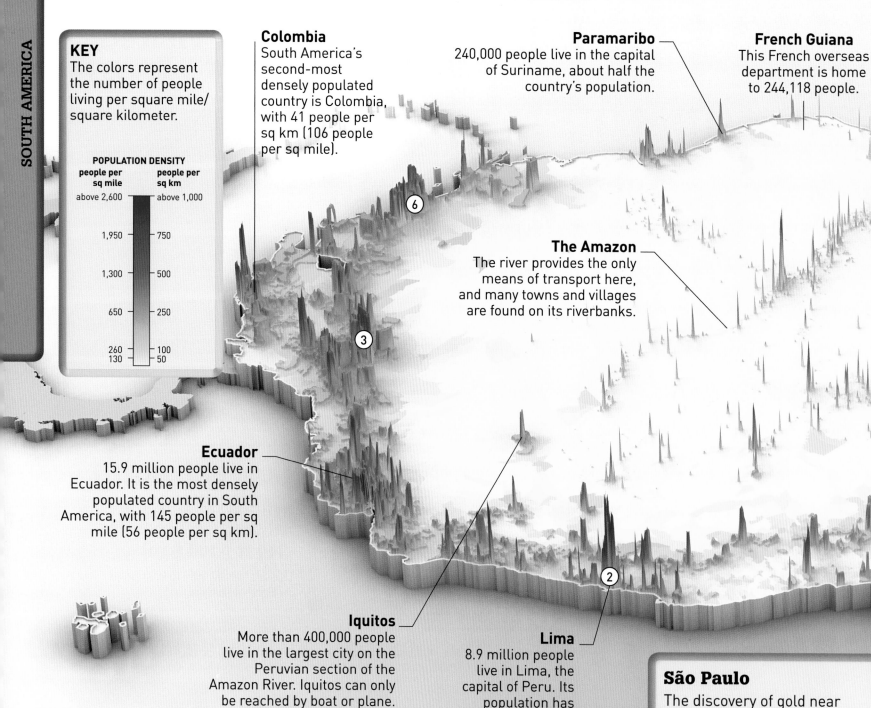

KEY
The colors represent the number of people living per square mile/ square kilometer.

POPULATION DENSITY

people per sq mile	people per sq km
above 2,600	above 1,000
1,950	750
1,300	500
650	250
260	100
130	50

Colombia
South America's second-most densely populated country is Colombia, with 41 people per sq km (106 people per sq mile).

Paramaribo
240,000 people live in the capital of Suriname, about half the country's population.

French Guiana
This French overseas department is home to 244,118 people.

The Amazon
The river provides the only means of transport here, and many towns and villages are found on its riverbanks.

Ecuador
15.9 million people live in Ecuador. It is the most densely populated country in South America, with 145 people per sq mile (56 people per sq km).

Iquitos
More than 400,000 people live in the largest city on the Peruvian section of the Amazon River. Iquitos can only be reached by boat or plane.

Lima
8.9 million people live in Lima, the capital of Peru. Its population has almost doubled since 1980.

São Paulo
The discovery of gold near São Paulo in the 1690s attracted settlers from around the world. Today, South America's largest city is a bustling business center, with a population of 12 million.

Tower blocks and modern architecture dominate downtown São Paulo.

Population

South America is highly urbanized, with the majority of its population living in cities such as Lima and Bogotá in the northwest, or São Paulo and Rio de Janeiro on the east coast of Brazil. By contrast, Amazonia, the Altiplano plateau, and Patagonia remain sparsely populated.

Brasília
Brazil's capital was planned from scratch, and was only finished in 1960. Today, it is home to 2.9 million people.

South America's largest cities

The list below is based on the number of people living inside a city's boundaries.

1. **São Paulo, Brazil—12 million**
2. **Lima, Peru—8.9 million**
3. **Bogotá, Colombia—7.9 million**
4. **Rio de Janeiro, Brazil—6.5 million**
5. **Santiago, Chile—5.5 million**
6. **Caracas, Venezuela—3.3 million**
7. **Buenos Aires, Argentina—3 million**
8. **Salvador, Brazil—2.902 million**
9. **Brasília, Brazil—2.9 million**
10. **Fortaleza, Brazil—2.6 million**

Rio de Janeiro, Brazil's second-largest city, was the country's capital until 1960.

Santa Cruz
The largest city in Bolivia is Santa Cruz, with a population of 1.4 million. It is one of the fastest growing cities in South America —its population has increased by a third in the past 10 years.

Chile
Most people in Chile live in the central region, home to the country's three largest cities: Santiago, Valparaíso, and Concepción.

Falkland Islands
Fewer than 3,000 people live on these islands, many of them working as sheep farmers. It is the least densely populated territory in South America.

IN TERMS OF BOTH ITS POPULATION AND SIZE.

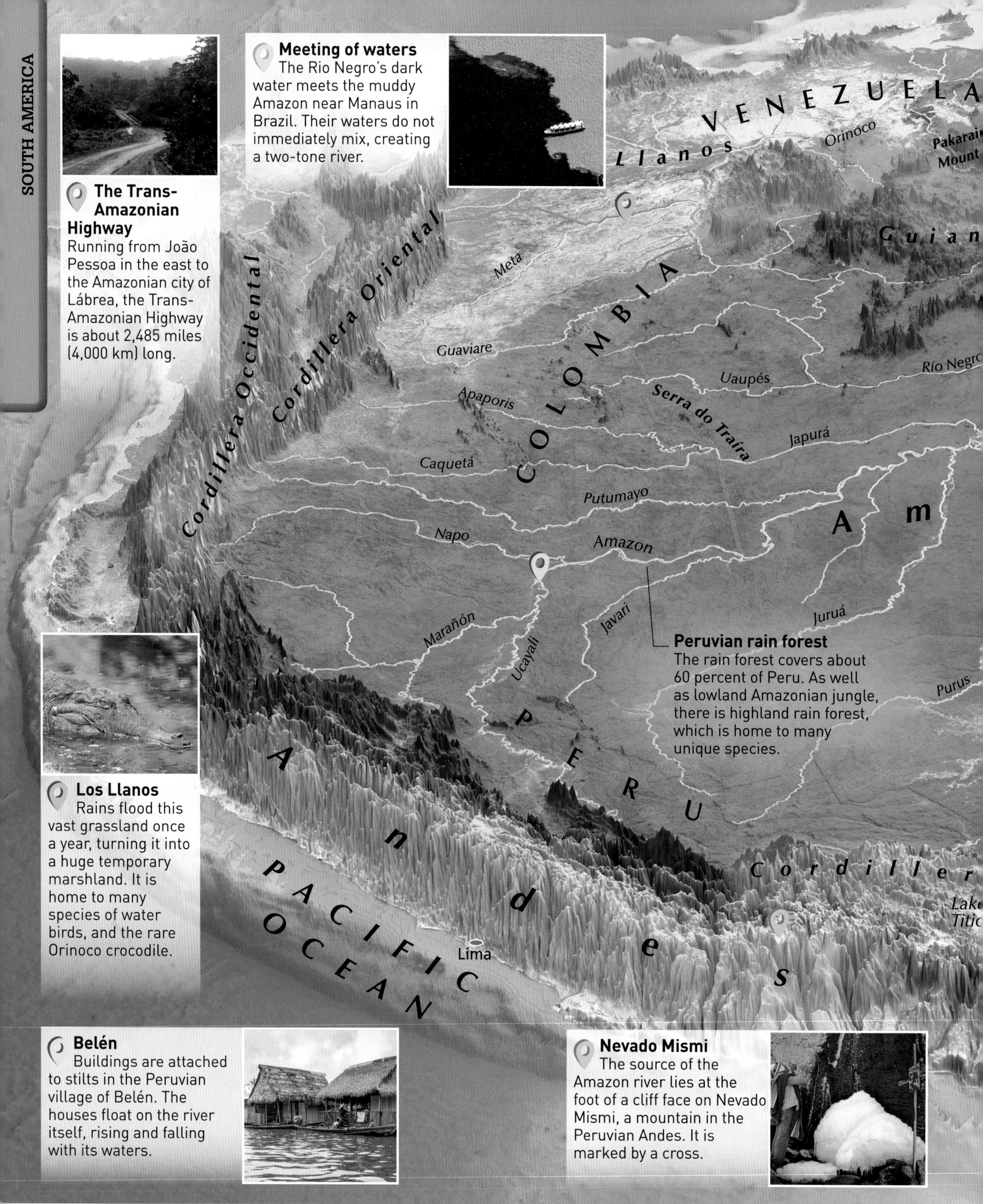
VENEZUELA
Llanos
Orinoco
Pakarai
Mount
Guian
Meta
COLOMBIA
Cordillera Oriental
Cordillera Occidental
Guaviare
Río Negro
Uaupés
Apaporis
Serra do Traíra
Japurá
Caquetá
Putumayo
Am
Napo
Amazon
Marañón
Javari
Juruá
Ucayali
Purus
PERU
Andes
PACIFIC OCEAN
Lima
Cordiller
Lake
Titic

The Trans-Amazonian Highway

Running from João Pessoa in the east to the Amazonian city of Lábrea, the Trans-Amazonian Highway is about 2,485 miles (4,000 km) long.

Meeting of waters

The Rio Negro's dark water meets the muddy Amazon near Manaus in Brazil. Their waters do not immediately mix, creating a two-tone river.

Peruvian rain forest

The rain forest covers about 60 percent of Peru. As well as lowland Amazonian jungle, there is highland rain forest, which is home to many unique species.

Los Llanos

Rains flood this vast grassland once a year, turning it into a huge temporary marshland. It is home to many species of water birds, and the rare Orinoco crocodile.

Belén

Buildings are attached to stilts in the Peruvian village of Belén. The houses float on the river itself, rising and falling with its waters.

Nevado Mismi

The source of the Amazon river lies at the foot of a cliff face on Nevado Mismi, a mountain in the Peruvian Andes. It is marked by a cross.

THE AMAZON BASIN RECEIVES AN AVERAGE 7.5 FT (2.3 M) OF

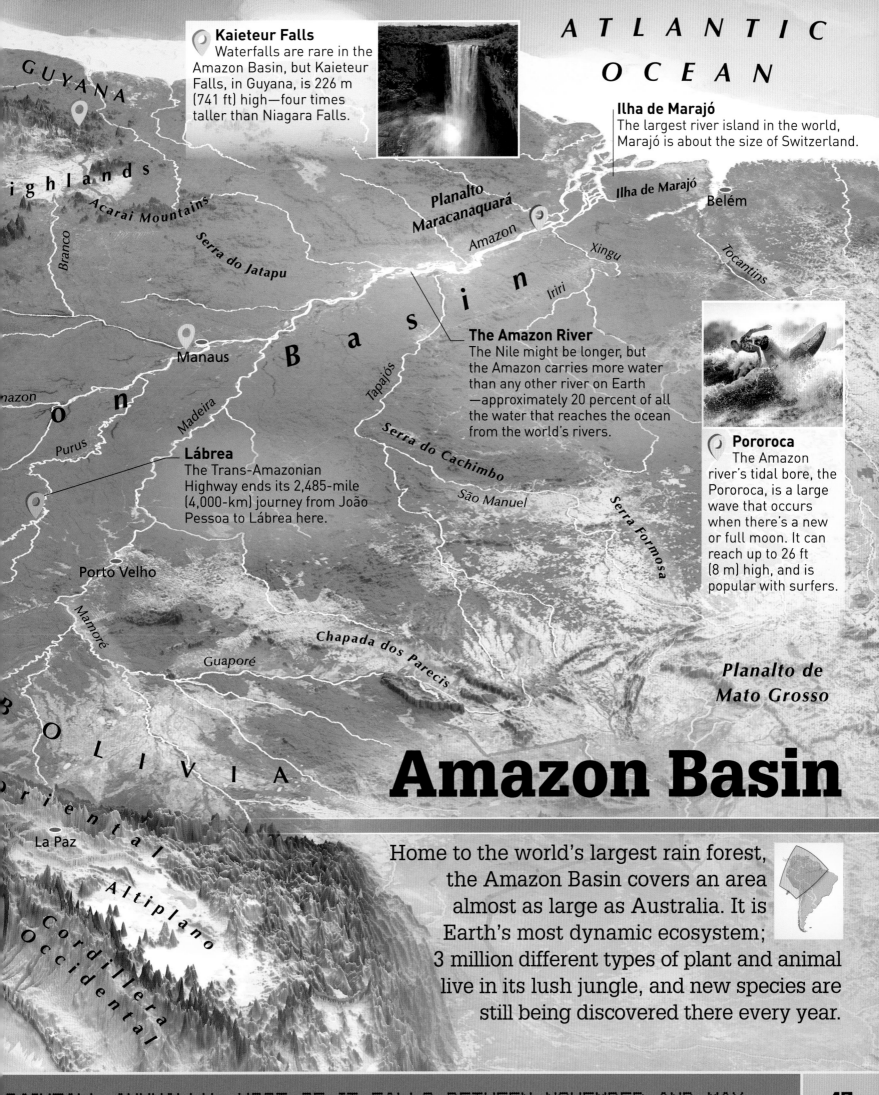

Kaieteur Falls
Waterfalls are rare in the Amazon Basin, but Kaieteur Falls, in Guyana, is 226 m (741 ft) high—four times taller than Niagara Falls.

ATLANTIC OCEAN

Ilha de Marajó
The largest river island in the world, Marajó is about the size of Switzerland.

GUYANA

ighlands

Acarai Mountains

Branco

Serra do Jatapu

Planalto Maracanaquará

Amazon

Ilha de Marajó

Belém

Xingu

Tocantins

Iriri

B a s i n

o n

Manaus

Tapajós

The Amazon River
The Nile might be longer, but the Amazon carries more water than any other river on Earth —approximately 20 percent of all the water that reaches the ocean from the world's rivers.

nazon

Madeira

Purus

Serra do Cachimbo

Lábrea
The Trans-Amazonian Highway ends its 2,485-mile (4,000-km) journey from João Pessoa to Lábrea here.

São Manuel

Serra Formosa

Pororoca
The Amazon river's tidal bore, the Pororoca, is a large wave that occurs when there's a new or full moon. It can reach up to 26 ft (8 m) high, and is popular with surfers.

Porto Velho

Mamoré

Chapada dos Parecis

Guaporé

Planalto de Mato Grosso

B O L I V I A

riental

Amazon Basin

La Paz

Altiplano

Cordillera Occidental

Home to the world's largest rain forest, the Amazon Basin covers an area almost as large as Australia. It is Earth's most dynamic ecosystem; 3 million different types of plant and animal live in its lush jungle, and new species are still being discovered there every year.

Angel Falls
At 3,212 ft (979 m), Angel Falls is the world's tallest waterfall—more than twice the height of the Empire State Building.

Presidential Palace,
Suriname

Coro historic town,
Venezuela

Angel Falls,
Venezuela

Teatro Amazonas,
Brazil

Castillo San Felipe de Barajas,
Colombia

Santa Barbara Church,
Colombia

San Agustín Archaeological Park,
Colombia

El Panecillo Statue,
Ecuador

Jesuit missions,
Bolivia

Machu Picchu,
Peru

Giant tortoise
11 species of giant tortoise live on the Galápagos Islands. Many live for more than 100 years.

Chan Chan,
Peru

Sacred city of Caral-Supe,
Peru

Wak'a Wallamarka,
Peru

Nazca Lines,
Peru

Tiwanaku,
Bolivia

Giant tortoise,
Galápagos

Chan Chan
The largest pre-Columbian city in the Americas, Chan Chan was built by the Chimu people in around 850 CE. Many of the city's walls have crumbled over time, but several statues have survived.

Nazca Lines
Hundreds of geometric patterns cover the Nazca Desert. About 70 of them are images of animals, but they can only be seen in full from an aircraft.

Christ the Redeemer
Looking down from the summit of Mount Corcovado onto Rio de Janeiro, Christ the Redeemer is one of the continent's best-loved landmarks. Finished in 1931, the 128-ft (39-m) tall statue took five years to build.

Famous landmarks

South America is home to an incredible wealth of cultural sites, ranging from the Inca ruins of Machu Picchu to the modern architecture of Brasília. It also boasts awe-inspiring natural wonders, such as Venezuela's Angel Falls and the glaciers of Chile and Argentina.

○ The giant statue of Jesus Christ towers over Brazil's second city, Rio de Janeiro.

THE CUEVA DE LAS MANOS IS A CAVE IN ARGENTINA COVERED WITH

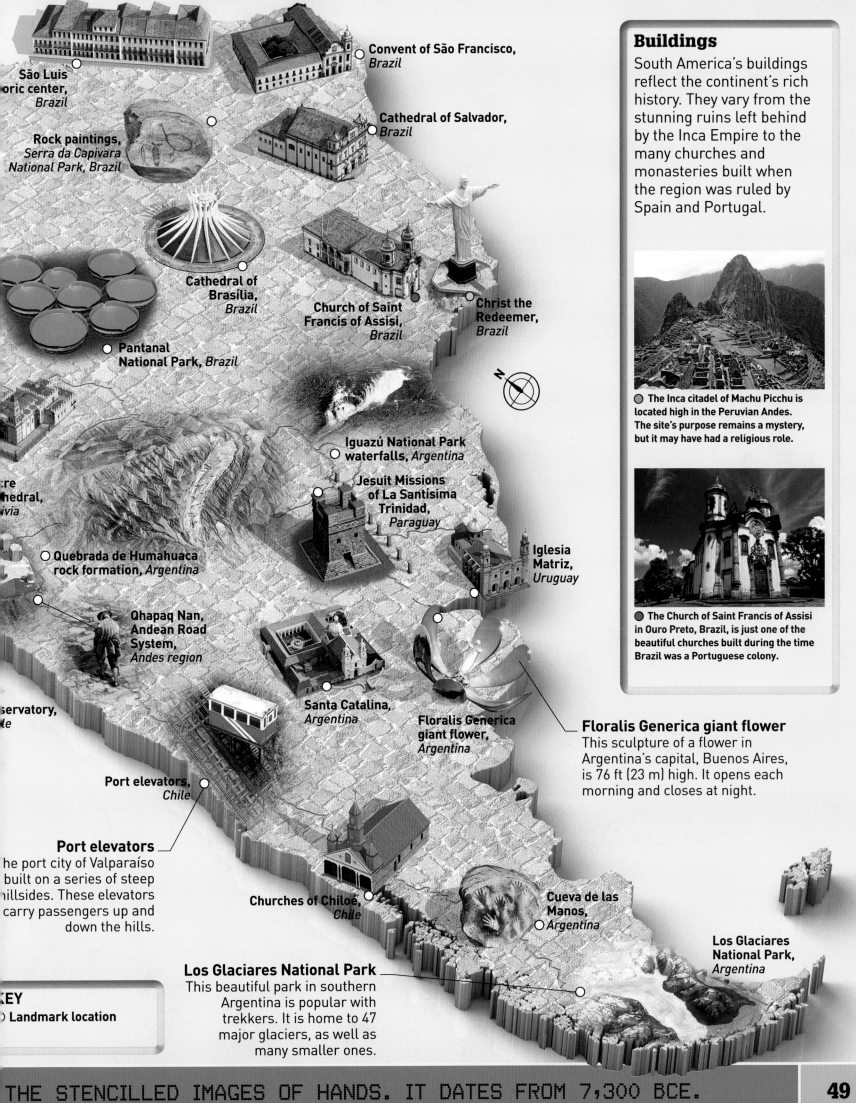

São Luis
oric center,
Brazil

Rock paintings,
*Serra da Capivara
National Park, Brazil*

Convent of São Francisco,
Brazil

Cathedral of Salvador,
Brazil

Cathedral of Brasília,
Brazil

Church of Saint Francis of Assisi,
Brazil

Christ the Redeemer,
Brazil

Pantanal National Park, *Brazil*

re
hedral,
ivia

○ **Quebrada de Humahuaca rock formation,** *Argentina*

Iguazú National Park waterfalls, *Argentina*

Jesuit Missions of La Santísima Trinidad, *Paraguay*

Iglesia Matriz, *Uruguay*

Qhapaq Nan, Andean Road System, *Andes region*

servatory,
e

Santa Catalina, *Argentina*

Floralis Generica giant flower, *Argentina*

Port elevators, *Chile*

Port elevators
he port city of Valparaíso built on a series of steep illsides. These elevators carry passengers up and down the hills.

Churches of Chiloé, *Chile*

Cueva de las Manos, *Argentina*

Los Glaciares National Park
This beautiful park in southern Argentina is popular with trekkers. It is home to 47 major glaciers, as well as many smaller ones.

Los Glaciares National Park, *Argentina*

Buildings
South America's buildings reflect the continent's rich history. They vary from the stunning ruins left behind by the Inca Empire to the many churches and monasteries built when the region was ruled by Spain and Portugal.

● The Inca citadel of Machu Picchu is located high in the Peruvian Andes. The site's purpose remains a mystery, but it may have had a religious role.

● The Church of Saint Francis of Assisi in Ouro Preto, Brazil, is just one of the beautiful churches built during the time Brazil was a Portuguese colony.

Floralis Generica giant flower
This sculpture of a flower in Argentina's capital, Buenos Aires, is 76 ft (23 m) high. It opens each morning and closes at night.

KEY
○ **Landmark location**

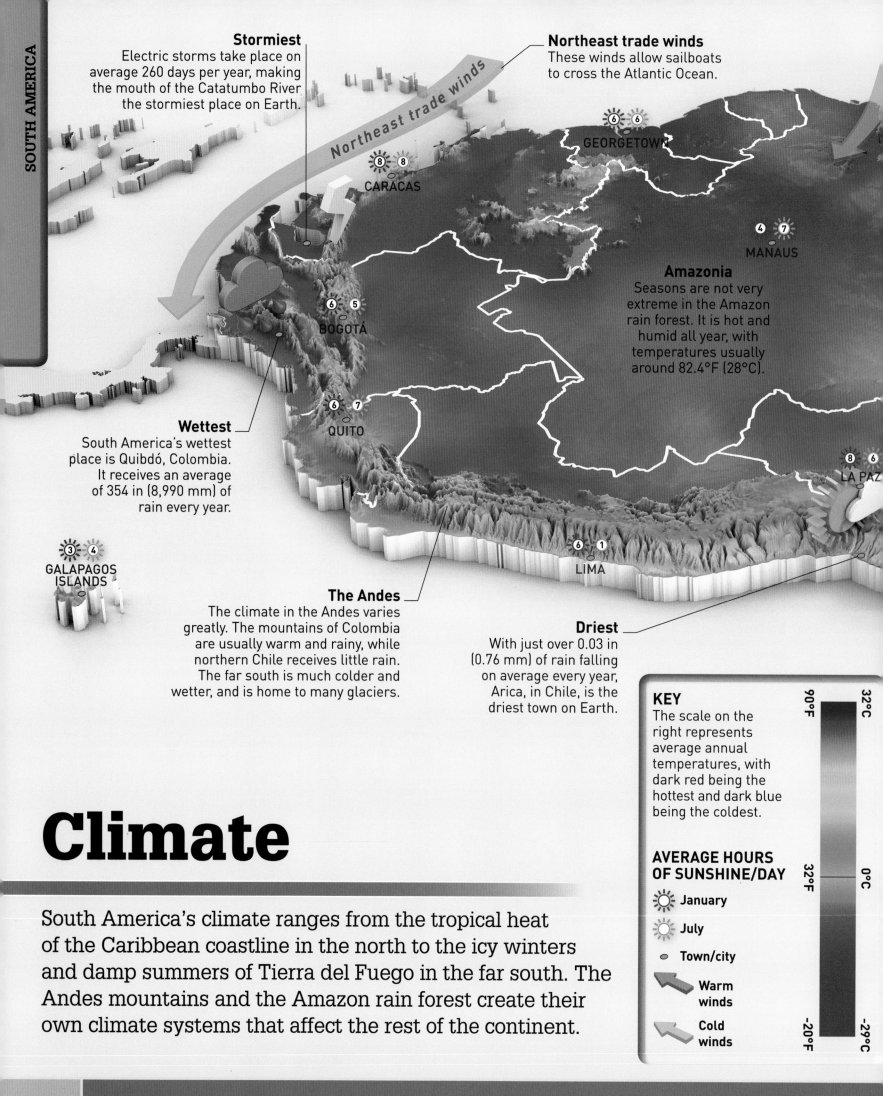

Stormiest
Electric storms take place on average 260 days per year, making the mouth of the Catatumbo River the stormiest place on Earth.

Northeast trade winds
These winds allow sailboats to cross the Atlantic Ocean.

Northeast trade winds

8 **8** CARACAS

6 **6** GEORGETOWN

4 **7** MANAUS

6 **5** BOGOTÁ

Amazonia
Seasons are not very extreme in the Amazon rain forest. It is hot and humid all year, with temperatures usually around 82.4°F (28°C).

6 **7** QUITO

8 **6** LA PAZ

Wettest
South America's wettest place is Quibdó, Colombia. It receives an average of 354 in (8,990 mm) of rain every year.

3 **4** GALAPAGOS ISLANDS

6 **1** LIMA

The Andes
The climate in the Andes varies greatly. The mountains of Colombia are usually warm and rainy, while northern Chile receives little rain. The far south is much colder and wetter, and is home to many glaciers.

Driest
With just over 0.03 in (0.76 mm) of rain falling on average every year, Arica, in Chile, is the driest town on Earth.

KEY
The scale on the right represents average annual temperatures, with dark red being the hottest and dark blue being the coldest.

90°F | 32°C
32°F | 0°C
-20°F | -29°C

AVERAGE HOURS OF SUNSHINE/DAY
☀ January
☀ July
⬭ Town/city
⬅ Warm winds
⬅ Cold winds

Climate

South America's climate ranges from the tropical heat of the Caribbean coastline in the north to the icy winters and damp summers of Tierra del Fuego in the far south. The Andes mountains and the Amazon rain forest create their own climate systems that affect the rest of the continent.

THERE ARE WEATHER STATIONS IN THE ATACAMA DESERT THAT

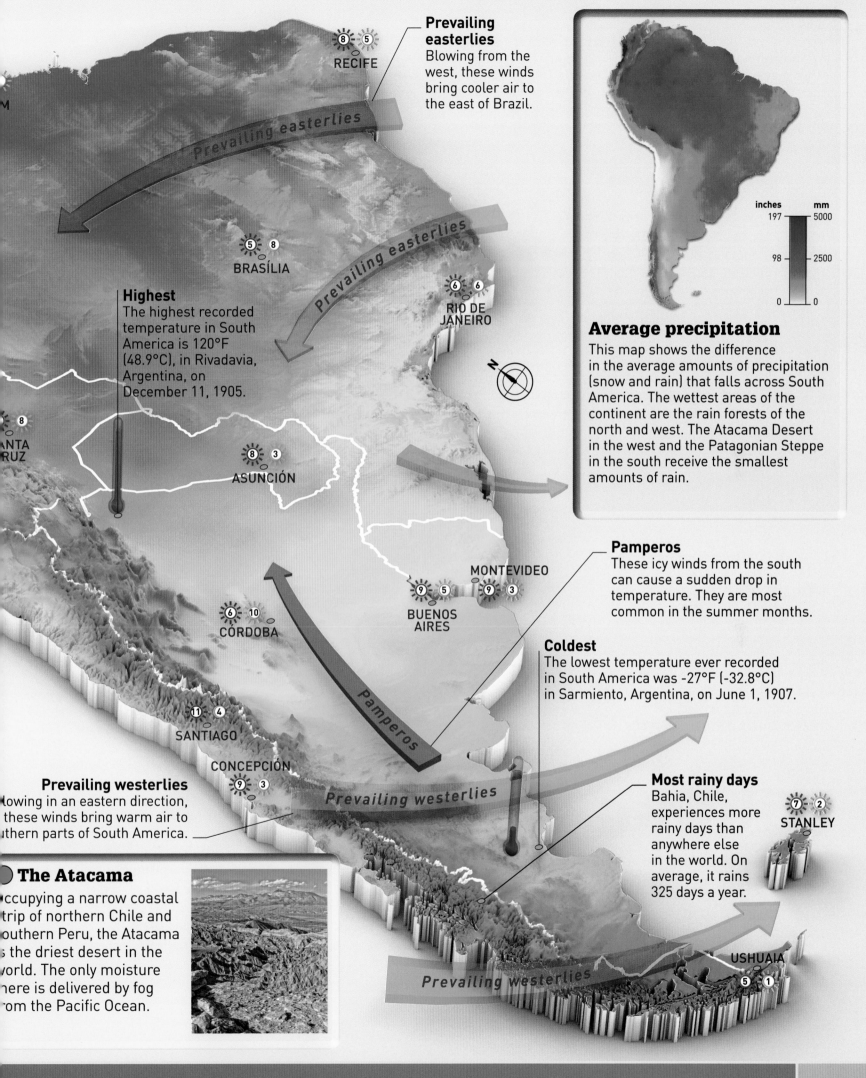

Prevailing easterlies
Blowing from the west, these winds bring cooler air to the east of Brazil.

Prevailing easterlies

RECIFE ☀8 ☀5

Prevailing easterlies

BRASÍLIA ☀5 ☀8

Highest
The highest recorded temperature in South America is 120°F (48.9°C), in Rivadavia, Argentina, on December 11, 1905.

RIO DE JANEIRO ☀6 ☀6

ANTA RUZ ☀8

ASUNCIÓN ☀8 ☀3

Average precipitation

This map shows the difference in the average amounts of precipitation (snow and rain) that falls across South America. The wettest areas of the continent are the rain forests of the north and west. The Atacama Desert in the west and the Patagonian Steppe in the south receive the smallest amounts of rain.

inches		mm
197		5000
98		2500
0		0

Pamperos
These icy winds from the south can cause a sudden drop in temperature. They are most common in the summer months.

MONTEVIDEO ☀9 ☀3

BUENOS AIRES ☀9 ☀5

CÓRDOBA ☀6 ☀10

Pamperos

Coldest
The lowest temperature ever recorded in South America was -27°F (-32.8°C) in Sarmiento, Argentina, on June 1, 1907.

SANTIAGO ☀11 ☀4

CONCEPCIÓN ☀9 ☀3

Prevailing westerlies
lowing in an eastern direction, these winds bring warm air to uthern parts of South America.

Prevailing westerlies

Most rainy days
Bahia, Chile, experiences more rainy days than anywhere else in the world. On average, it rains 325 days a year.

STANLEY ☀7 ☀2

The Atacama

ccupying a narrow coastal trip of northern Chile and outhern Peru, the Atacama s the driest desert in the orld. The only moisture here is delivered by fog rom the Pacific Ocean.

Prevailing westerlies

USHUAIA ☀5 ☀1

Common vampire bat
This bat drinks the blood of tapirs and cattle.

Goliath bird-eating spider
Despite its name, the world's largest spider prefers eating small rodents or toads.

Bull shark
This formidable hunter thrives in both freshwater and saltwater.

Hoatzin
Also known as the stinkbird. Its chick have "wing claws" for climbing throu branches.

Capuchin monkey
Intelligent and sociable, this monkey forages for food in the treetops.

Jaguar
The rain forest' largest killer is lone, nocturna hunter.

Spectacled caiman
A good swimmer, it hunts fish such as piranhas.

Bald uakari
This monkey's bright red face is seen as highly attractive in a mate.

Harpy eagle
This large raptor can snatch sloths and monkeys from trees.

Tiger shark
Coastal waters and estuaries are home to this dangerous shark.

Spectacled bear
The continent's only bear lives in mountain forests and eats fruit and nuts.

Ocelot
A nocturnal hunter, this small cat preys on rodents. It is also an excellent swimmer.

Puma
Found throughout the Americas, the puma thrives in deserts, prairies, and forests.

Great white shark
This dangerous predato can live for up to 70 year

Darwin's finches
This group of small birds helped Charles Darwin to develop his theory of evolution.

Wildlife

The grasslands, mountains, and rain forests of South America are home to an incredible variety of plant and animal species. This vast range of habitats contain many species of birds, mammals, and amphibians that are found nowhere else on Earth.

BIOMES
Tropical broadleaf forest is widespread in the north, before it gives way to temperate grasslands and temperate broadleaf forest in the south.

- Ice
- Temperate broadleaf forest
- Temperate grassland
- Mediterranean
- Tropical broadleaf forest
- Tropical dry broadleaf forest
- Mountain
- Desert
- Flooded grassland
- Mangrove

THE JAGUAR IS AN EXCELLENT SWIMMER AND HAS EVEN

Amazonian river dolphin
s long snout is used to explore the
ver bed and get between
tree roots.

Toucan
This bird rests its beak
on its back while sleeping.

Capybara
Riverbanks and
wetland areas
are home to this
giant rodent.

Poison-dart frog
Has a brightly colored
skin to warn predators
that it is poisonous.

Peccary
These piglike
creatures form
groups to fend
off enemies.

Red-bellied piranha
A school of these fish
can strip its prey to
bare bones in minutes.

Golden lion tamarin
This elegant monkey has
a beautiful mane and lives
in large family groups.

**Humpback
whale**
These ocean
giants sing in
order to attract
a mate.

Guanaco
e wild ancestor of
e llama is adapted
high-altitude life.

Armadillo
The only mammal to
have body armor, the
armadillo rolls itself
into a ball when
threatened.

Giant anteater
Huge front claws and a
long snout help the anteater
to raid termite nests.

Yellow anaconda
Rarely seen out of water,
this snake can grow up to
14.4 ft (4.4 m) in length.

Geoffroy's cat
This tiny feline is
an excellent climber
and preys on birds.

Darwin's rhea
When threatened, this
flightless bird flees
in a zigzag pattern.

Andean condor
With a wingspan of
more than 10 ft (3 m),
this bird can glide for
vast distances.

Southern sea lion
Squid and octopus
form much of this
agile hunter's diet.

Patagonian mara
This rodent rears its young
in communal burrows
on the grassland.

Southern right whale
Following years
of exploitation by
whalers, numbers are
steadily increasing.

Magellanic penguin
Only 26 in (65 cm)
tall, this penguin
hunts small fish.

Caracas
89 percent of Venezuela's population live in towns or cities, with 5.3 million people living in the country's capital, Caracas.

Guyana
Less than 30 percent of Guyana's population of 735,900 live in towns or citi[es]

Ecuador
Many people in Ecuador live in the Andean highland region known as La Sierra. Important cities here include Cuenca and the capital, Quito.

Guayaquil
More than 5 million people live in and around Ecuador's most populous city. It is an important port and business centre.

Lima
Nearly 10 million people live in the area in and around the Peruvian capital.

Almost **one half** of South America's population lives **in Brazil**.

By night

The brightly lit urban areas of Ecuador, Colombia, and Venezuela dominate the northwest of the continent. The cities of southeast Brazil, meanwhile, contrast sharply with the dark expanses of Amazonia, in which only occasional dots of light mark the rain forest's few settlements.

● **Manaus**
Located at the heart of the Amazon rain forest, Manaus, with a population of 2 million, is the largest city in Amazonia. This lively port made its wealth in the 19th century through the rubber trade.

The opera house in Manaus is one of the grandest buildings in Amazonia.

Salvador
The largest city in the north east of Brazil, Salvador has a population of 2.901 million.

Brazil
More than 80 million people live in the urban areas that dominate Brazil's south east.

● **Buenos Aires**
Three million people live in the Argentinian capital. As well as being an important political and business center, Buenos Aires is known for its lively nightlife, and has a superb choice of theaters, restaurants, and music venues.

The Argentinian tango remains popular in the bars and cafés of Buenos Aires.

Porto Alegre
1.5 million people live in Brazil's 10th-largest city.

Uruguay
95.3 percent of Uruguay's population of 3.4 million live in towns or cities—the highest percentage of any South American country.

Comodoro Rivadavia
182,631 live in Comodoro Rivadavia, the most southerly city in South America with a population of more than 150,000.

Santiago
One third of Chile's population of 17.5 million live in the country's capital city.

KEY
Illuminated areas on the map reflect urban, built-up areas and roads, in contrast to rural regions.

■ Rural area

▨ Urban area

Patagonia
Fewer than 2 million people live in the southernmost part of the continent.

AFRICA

Africa from space
The Equator splits Africa between
the northern and southern
hemispheres. It is bordered by the
Mediterranean, the Red Sea, and
the Atlantic and Indian Oceans.

Algeria
Algeria is Africa's largest country, and more than 80 percent of it is made up of the Sahara Desert. Its main cities are all in the north.

EUROPE

Madeira
(to Portugal)

Canary Islands
(to Spain)

WESTERN
SAHARA
(occupied
by Morocco)

Mediterranean S

TUNIS
Constantine
ALGIERS
TUNISIA
TRIPOLI
Misratah
Benghazi

Tangier
Oran
Fès
RABAT
Casablanca
Marrakech
MOROCCO

L I B Y A

A L G E R I A

Laâyoune

N

MAURITANIA

NOUAKCHOTT

DAKAR
SENEGAL

BANJUL

GAMBIA

BISSAU

GUINEA-BISSAU

CONAKRY

GUINEA

FREETOWN

MONROVIA

SIERRA
LEONE   LIBERIA

Liberia
Claiming independence as early as 1847, it became a new home to many African-American former slaves.

M A L I

BAMAKO

N I G E R

Zinder

NIAMEY

OUAGADOUGOU

BURKINA
FASO

IVORY
COAST

GHANA

YAMOUSSOUKRO

ACCRA

Abidjan

LOMÉ

TOGO

BENIN

PORTO-NOVO

Ibadan

Lagos

Kano

N'DJAMÉ

Maroua

Moun

Garoua

N I G E R I A

ABUJA

CAMEROON

Douala   YAOUNDÉ

MALABO

EQUATORIAL
GUINEA

SÃO TOMÉ

LIBREVILLE

GABO

Port-Gentil

ANG
(Cal

CH

Nigeria
It is known as the "Giant of Africa" for its large population (186 million) and booming economy (the 20th largest in the world).

SÃO TOMÉ &
PRINCIPE

*ATLANTIC
OCEAN*

KEY
● Capital city
● Major city

Countries and borders

Africa's different kingdoms were brutally split up between European nations in the 19th century. After World War Two, struggle for independence, as well as civil wars, created new nations, re-drawn borders, and disputed territories.

FAST FACTS

Total land area:
11,712,409 sq miles
(30,335,000 sq km)

Total population:
1.1 billion

Number of countries: 53

Largest country:
Algeria—919,595 sq miles
(2,381,741 sq km)

Smallest country:
Seychelles—
176 sq miles (455 sq km)

**Largest country
population:**
Nigeria—186 million

ETHIOPIA IS THE ONLY COUNTRY IN AFRICA THAT HAS

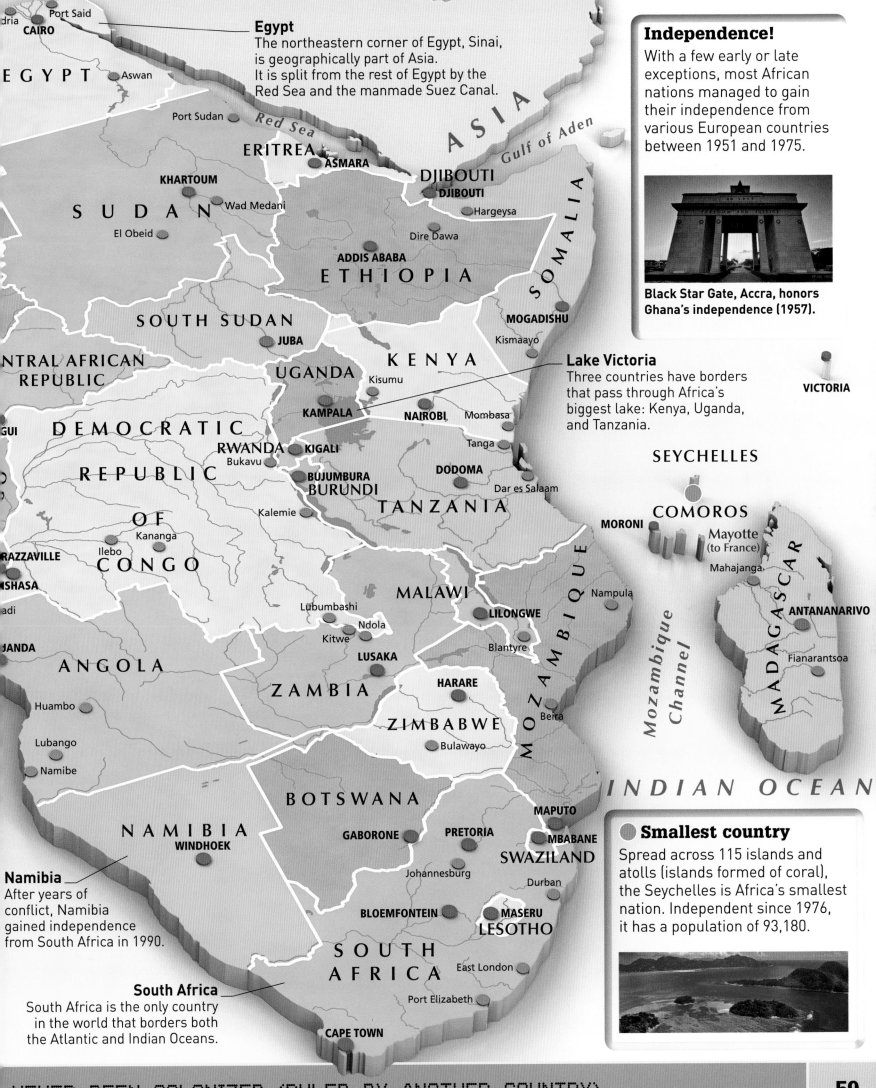

Egypt
The northeastern corner of Egypt, Sinai, is geographically part of Asia. It is split from the rest of Egypt by the Red Sea and the manmade Suez Canal.

ASIA

Red Sea

Gulf of Aden

dria
Port Said
CAIRO
EGYPT
Aswan

Port Sudan

ERITREA
ASMARA

DJIBOUTI
DJIBOUTI
Hargeysa

KHARTOUM
S U D A N
Wad Medani

El Obeid

Dire Dawa

S O M A L I A

ADDIS ABABA
E T H I O P I A

SOUTH SUDAN

MOGADISHU
Kismaayo

NTRAL AFRICAN REPUBLIC

JUBA

K E N Y A

GUI

UGANDA
Kisumu

Lake Victoria
Three countries have borders that pass through Africa's biggest lake: Kenya, Uganda, and Tanzania.

VICTORIA

D E M O C R A T I C

KAMPALA
NAIROBI
Mombasa

RWANDA
KIGALI
Bukavu

Tanga

R E P U B L I C

BUJUMBURA
BURUNDI

DODOMA
Dar es Salaam

SEYCHELLES

Independence!
With a few early or late exceptions, most African nations managed to gain their independence from various European countries between 1951 and 1975.

Black Star Gate, Accra, honors Ghana's independence (1957).

O F

Kalemie
T A N Z A N I A

COMOROS

MORONI
Mayotte (to France)

RAZZAVILLE
Kananga

Mahajanga

Ilebo
C O N G O

NSHASA

M A D A G A S C A R

ANTANANARIVO

M A L A W I
Nampula

JANDA

Lubumbashi
LILONGWE

Fianarantsoa

A N G O L A

Ndola
Kitwe
Blantyre

Mozambique Channel

Huambo

LUSAKA
Z A M B I A
M O Z A M B I Q U E

HARARE

Lubango

Z I M B A B W E

I N D I A N   O C E A N

Namibe

Beira

B O T S W A N A
Bulawayo

MAPUTO

Smallest country
Spread across 115 islands and atolls (islands formed of coral), the Seychelles is Africa's smallest nation. Independent since 1976, it has a population of 93,180.

N A M I B I A
WINDHOEK

GABORONE
PRETORIA
MBABANE
SWAZILAND

Johannesburg

Durban

Namibia
After years of conflict, Namibia gained independence from South Africa in 1990.

BLOEMFONTEIN
MASERU
LESOTHO

S O U T H   A F R I C A
East London

South Africa
South Africa is the only country in the world that borders both the Atlantic and Indian Oceans.

Port Elizabeth

CAPE TOWN

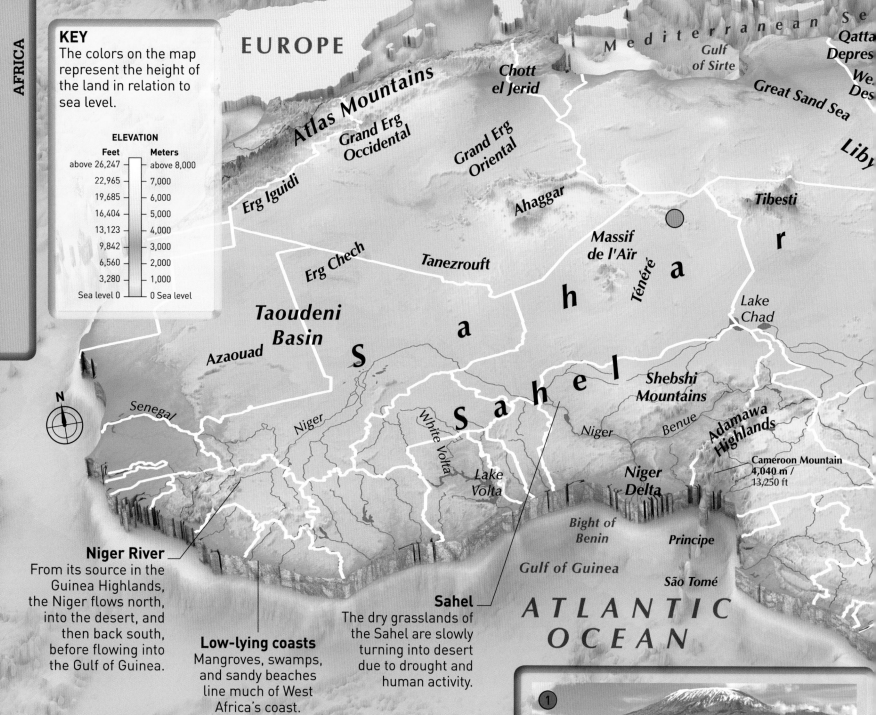

KEY
The colors on the map represent the height of the land in relation to sea level.

ELEVATION

Feet	Meters
above 26,247	above 8,000
22,965	7,000
19,685	6,000
16,404	5,000
13,123	4,000
9,842	3,000
6,560	2,000
3,280	1,000
Sea level 0	0 Sea level

Mediterranean Se

Qatta
Depres

Gulf
of Sirte

Great Sand Sea

We
Des

Liby

Atlas Mountains

Chott
el Jerid

Grand Erg
Occidental

Grand Erg
Oriental

Erg Iguidi

Ahaggar

Tibesti

Massif
de l'Aïr

r

Erg Chech

Tanezrouft

Ténéré

a

Taoudeni
Basin

h

Lake
Chad

Azaouad

S

a

Senegal

Niger

White Volta

S

Sahel

Shebshi
Mountains

Niger

Benue

Adamawa
Highlands

Lake
Volta

Niger
Delta

Cameroon Mountain
4,040 m /
13,250 ft

Bight of
Benin

Principe

Niger River
From its source in the Guinea Highlands, the Niger flows north, into the desert, and then back south, before flowing into the Gulf of Guinea.

Low-lying coasts
Mangroves, swamps, and sandy beaches line much of West Africa's coast.

Sahel
The dry grasslands of the Sahel are slowly turning into desert due to drought and human activity.

Gulf of Guinea

São Tomé

ATLANTIC OCEAN

Landscape

Africa has many extreme landscapes. Deserts spread across the north and south, while rain forests dominate the continent's tropical central and western parts. The land rises toward the east, culminating in the Ethiopian Highlands and the Great Rift Valley region, home to Africa's largest lakes and mountains.

FAST FACTS

① **Highest point:**
Kilimanjaro—19,341 ft (5,895 m)

② **Longest river:**
Nile—4,160 miles (6,695 km)

③ **Largest lake:**
Lake Victoria— 26,828 sq miles (69,484 sq km)

④ **Largest island:**
Madagascar— 229,345 sq miles (594,000 sq km)

A S I A

Delta

Nile

Eastern Desert

Lake Nasser

Nubian Desert

②

Nile

Red Sea

Blue Nile

White Nile

Ethiopian Highlands
This high plateau contains peaks of over 14,764 ft (4,500 m) and is home to Lake Tana, source of the Blue Nile.

Lake Tana

Ethiopian Highlands

Gulf of Aden

Horn of Africa

Ogaden

Shebeli

⬤ **Sahara Desert**
The world's largest hot desert, the Sahara spreads over 3,600,000 sq miles (9,200,000 sq km). It features huge dunes, arid gravel plains, craggy mountains, and old volcanoes, as well as a few oases.

Sudd

Massif des Bongo

bangi

Uele

Lake Albert

Lake Turkana

Juba

Kilimanjaro
5,895 m /
19,341 ft

Kilimanjaro
Africa's highest mountain is a long-extinct volcano. Its famous ice and snow cap is getting smaller every year.

Seychelles

C o n g o

Congo

Lake Victoria

Great Rift Valley

③

①

Pemba

Zanzibar

B a s i n

Great Rift Valley

Lake Tanganyika

Comoro Islands

Cuango

kwilu

Kasai

Mitumba Range

Lake Nyasa

④

M a d a g a s c a r

Cunene

Bié Plateau

Muchinga Escarpment

Victoria Falls

Zambezi

Lundi

Okavango Delta
Seasonal flooding fills this large inland delta. Water drains into the Kalahari Desert, not the sea.

Okavango Delta

Ntwetwe Pan

Limpopo

② **Nile River**
At 4,160 miles (6,695 km), the Nile is the world's longest river. It has two main tributaries, the Blue and White Niles, which join in Khartoum, Sudan, before the river flows through Egypt.

Kalahari Basin

Kalahari Desert

N a m i b   D e s e r t

Orange River

Great Karoo

Drakensberg

Namib Desert
The extremely dry Namib Desert includes the Namib Sand Sea—giant coastal dunes up to 985 ft (300 m) high, that are often swept in dense fogs.

Cape of Good Hope

Fascinating facts

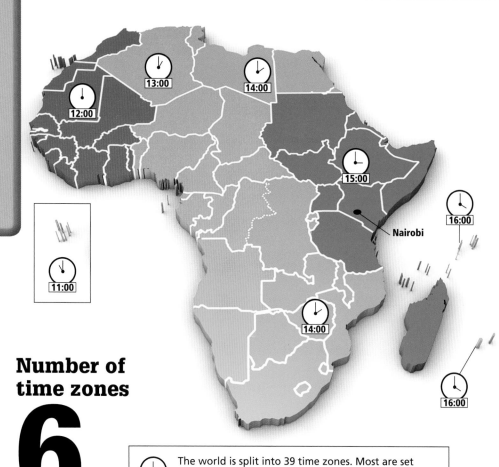

12:00
13:00
14:00
15:00
16:00
Nairobi
11:00
14:00
16:00

Number of time zones

6

12:00 The world is split into 39 time zones. Most are set whole hours ahead or behind Coordinated Universal Time (UCT)—the time at the Greenwich Meridian in London, UK. Some, however, are whole hours plus 30 or 45 minutes ahead or behind UCT. Therefore, on this map, if it was 12:00 in London, it would be 15:00 in Nairobi, Kenya (3 hours ahead of UCT).

COUNTRIES WITH THE MOST NEIGHBORS

Tanzania (8)
Burundi, **Democratic Republic of Congo**, Kenya, **Malawi**, Mozambique, **Rwanda**, Uganda, **Zambia**

Zambia (8)
Angola, **Botswana,** Democratic Republic of Congo, **Malawi**, Mozambique **Namibia**, Tanzania, **Zimbabwe**

LONGEST BRIDGE
6th October Bridge, Cairo, Egypt— 12.7 miles (20.5 km)

16 LANDLOCKED COUNTRIES
Botswana ▪ **Burkina Faso** ▪ Burundi ▪ **Central African Republic** ▪ Chad ▪ **Ethiopia** ▪ Lesotho ▪ **Malawi** ▪ Mali ▪ **Niger** ▪ Rwanda ▪ **South Sudan** ▪ Swaziland ▪ **Uganda** ▪ Zambia ▪ **Zimbabwe**

Tallest bridge
Bloukrans Bridge, Nature's Valley, Western Cape, South Africa—709 ft (216 m)

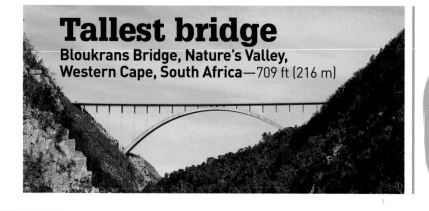

Number of languages spoken
more than
2,000

LAKES

Largest: **Lake Victoria**, Uganda / Tanzania / Kenya— 26,828 sq miles (69,484 sq km)

Deepest: **Lake Tanganyika**, Burundi / Democratic Republic of Congo / Tanzania / Zambia—4,823 ft (1,470 m) deep

WATERFALLS

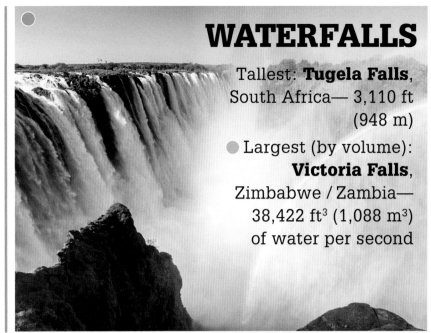

Tallest: **Tugela Falls**, South Africa— 3,110 ft (948 m)

Largest (by volume): **Victoria Falls**, Zimbabwe / Zambia— 38,422 ft^3 (1,088 m^3) of water per second

LONGEST COASTLINE Madagascar—3,000 miles (4,828 km)

✈ **Busiest airport** O.R. Tambo International, Johannesburg, South Africa— **19.164 million passengers per year**

Longest railroad line
The Blue Train, Pretoria–Cape Town, South Africa— 994 miles (1,600 km)

Longest subway system
Cairo Metro, Egypt— 48 miles (78 km)

AFRICA'S EXTREME POINTS

Northernmost point:
Jalta, Tunisia
37° 31′ N

Easternmost point:
Raas Xaafuun, Somalia
51° 24′ E

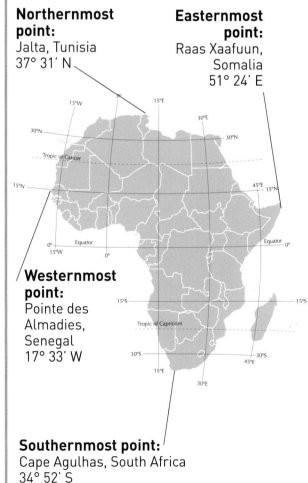

Westernmost point:
Pointe des Almadies, Senegal
17° 33′ W

Southernmost point:
Cape Agulhas, South Africa
34° 52′ S

Most visited cities (Visitors per year)

Johannesburg, S. Africa
3.6 million

Cairo, Egypt
1.5 million

Cape Town, S. Africa
1.4 million

Casablanca, Morocco
1.1 million

Durban, S. Africa
0.8 million

Most active volcano
Nyamuragira, **Democratic Republic of Congo**

LOWEST POINT
Lake 'Assal, Djibouti— 512 ft (156 m) below sea level

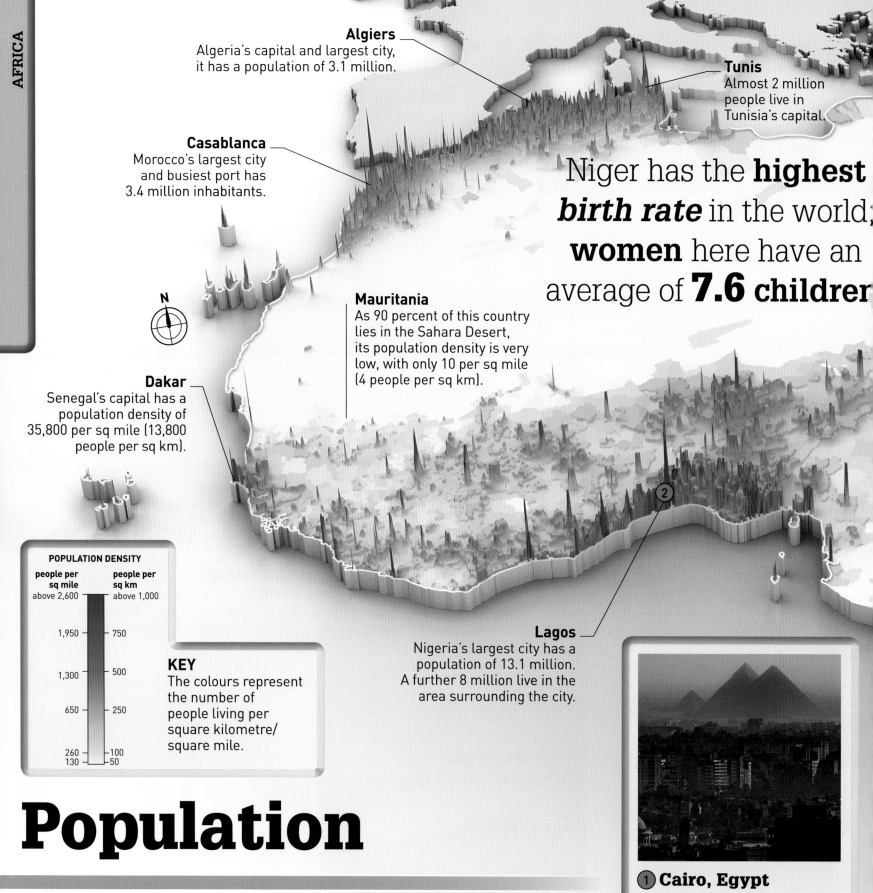

Algiers
Algeria's capital and largest city, it has a population of 3.1 million.

Tunis
Almost 2 million people live in Tunisia's capital.

Casablanca
Morocco's largest city and busiest port has 3.4 million inhabitants.

Niger has the **highest birth rate** in the world; **women** here have an average of **7.6 children**

Mauritania
As 90 percent of this country lies in the Sahara Desert, its population density is very low, with only 10 per sq mile (4 people per sq km).

Dakar
Senegal's capital has a population density of 35,800 per sq mile (13,800 people per sq km).

POPULATION DENSITY

people per sq mile	people per sq km
above 2,600	above 1,000
1,950	750
1,300	500
650	250
260	100
130	50

KEY
The colours represent the number of people living per square kilometre/ square mile.

Lagos
Nigeria's largest city has a population of 13.1 million. A further 8 million live in the area surrounding the city.

Population

Africa, the birthplace of our earliest human ancestors, is the second-most populous continent in the world (after Asia). But because the continent is so large, its average population density is low—only half that of Europe. In reality, some regions are very crowded, while others, like the Sahara, are almost deserted.

① Cairo, Egypt
Founded in ancient times and Egypt's capital since 1168, Cairo is Africa's largest city, with 18.7 million inhabitants. Greater Cairo sprawls in all directions, and includes the famous pyramids at Giza.

THE WORLD'S FIRST HOMININS (EARLY HUMANS) APPEARED IN

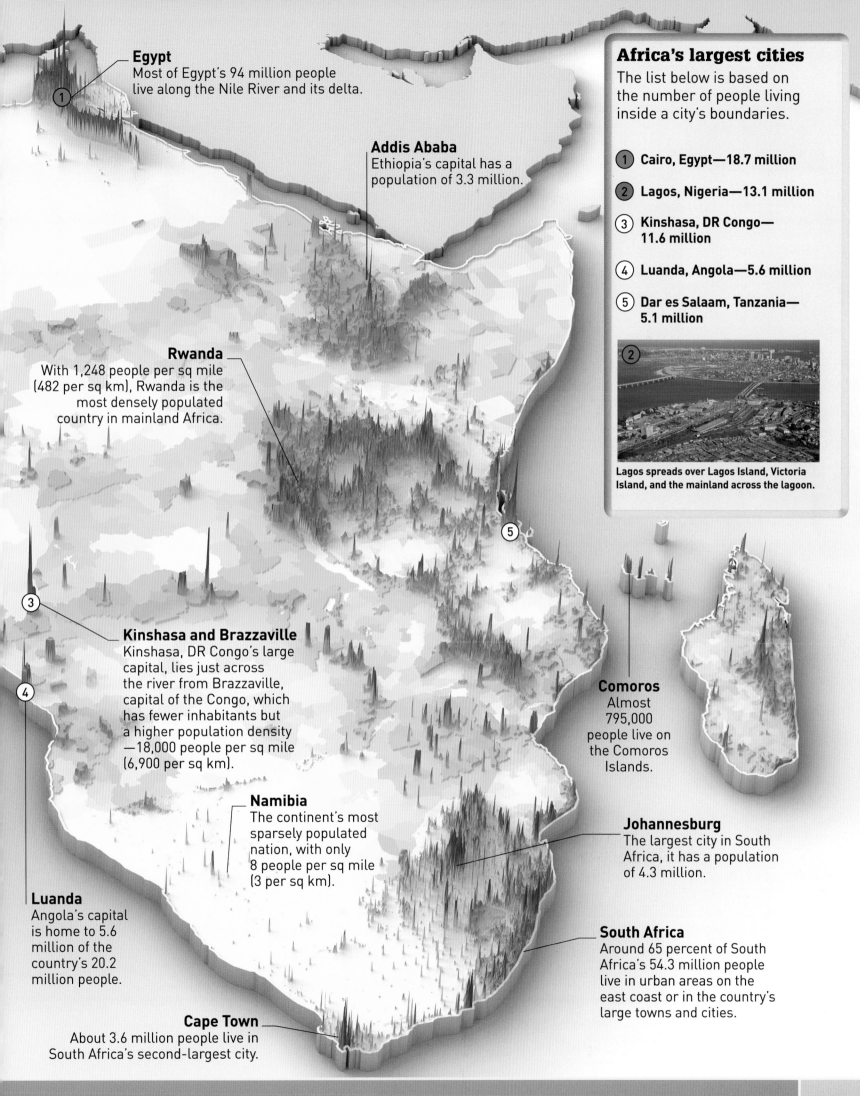

Egypt
Most of Egypt's 94 million people live along the Nile River and its delta.

Addis Ababa
Ethiopia's capital has a population of 3.3 million.

Rwanda
With 1,248 people per sq mile (482 per sq km), Rwanda is the most densely populated country in mainland Africa.

Kinshasa and Brazzaville
Kinshasa, DR Congo's large capital, lies just across the river from Brazzaville, capital of the Congo, which has fewer inhabitants but a higher population density —18,000 people per sq mile (6,900 per sq km).

Namibia
The continent's most sparsely populated nation, with only 8 people per sq mile (3 per sq km).

Luanda
Angola's capital is home to 5.6 million of the country's 20.2 million people.

Cape Town
About 3.6 million people live in South Africa's second-largest city.

Comoros
Almost 795,000 people live on the Comoros Islands.

Johannesburg
The largest city in South Africa, it has a population of 4.3 million.

South Africa
Around 65 percent of South Africa's 54.3 million people live in urban areas on the east coast or in the country's large towns and cities.

Africa's largest cities

The list below is based on the number of people living inside a city's boundaries.

1 **Cairo, Egypt—18.7 million**

2 **Lagos, Nigeria—13.1 million**

3 **Kinshasa, DR Congo— 11.6 million**

4 **Luanda, Angola—5.6 million**

5 **Dar es Salaam, Tanzania— 5.1 million**

Lagos spreads over Lagos Island, Victoria Island, and the mainland across the lagoon.

Red Sea
Formed when the African and Arabian plates split apart, and still widening, this salty sea can reach over 30°C (86°F). Its coral reefs are teeming with fish.

Rwenzori Mountains
The snow-capped peaks of this range in the Western Rift Valley include Mount Stanley, Africa's third highest mountain at 16,762 ft (5,109 m).

Ethiopian Highlands

Ahmar Mountains

ETHIOPIA

Mēga Escarpm

SOUTH SUDAN

Lake Turkana

Cherangany Hills

Victoria Nile

Lake Kyoga

UGANDA

Sese Islands

Lake Victoria

Ukerewe Island

Lake Albert

Rubondo Island

Lake Victoria
Africa's largest lake lies on the plateau located between the Great Rift Valley's eastern and western branch. At its widest, it measures 209 miles (337 km) across.

Lake Edward

RWANDA

Western Rift Valley
The western branch of the Great Rift Valley is characterized by deep lakes and high mountain ranges.

Lake Kivu

BURUNDI

G r e a t R i f t V a l l e y

Lake Tanganyika

Lake Tanganyika
The longest of the Rift Valley's many lakes, Tanganyika is also the world's second deepest lake, at 4,710 ft (1,436 m).

IN THE FUTURE, THE LAND EAST OF THE RIFT WILL FORM A NEW

The Great Rift Valley

Afar Triangle
This extremely hot, low-lying, molten-rock desert is where the rifts between the Arabian, African, and Somalian plates meet.

Horn of Africa

The Great Rift Valley is a growing rift between three of Earth's plates. This split, causing earthquakes, volcanic eruptions, and a changing landscape, began around 25 million years ago. It runs for approximately 3,700 miles (6,000 km) from the Middle East to Mozambique, but its most famous section is found in northeast Africa.

Kirinaga
At 17,057 ft (5,199 m), this is Africa's second-highest peak.

KENYA

Ngorogoro Crater

Great Rift Valley

Usambara Mountains

Pemba

Zanzibar

Masai Steppe

rengeti Plain

Lake Eyasi

Ngorogoro Crater
The Ngorogoro is an old volcanic crater, home to wildebeests, zebras, rhinos, and lions.

Gombe

Kilimanjaro
Africa's highest mountain reaches 19,341 ft (5,895 m).

Lake Natron
Like most of the Eastern Rift Valley lakes, the shallow water at Lake Natron is very salty and full of algae—making it a perfect breeding spot for flamingoes.

TANZANIA

Shama

Livingstone Mountains

Lake Rukwa

Lake Nyasa
Southernmost of the Rift Valley's lakes, Nyasa contains around 1,000 types of cichlid, a small, colorful fish.

ZAMBIA

CONTINENT AS THE SPLIT GETS GREATER AND FINALLY BREAKS OFF.

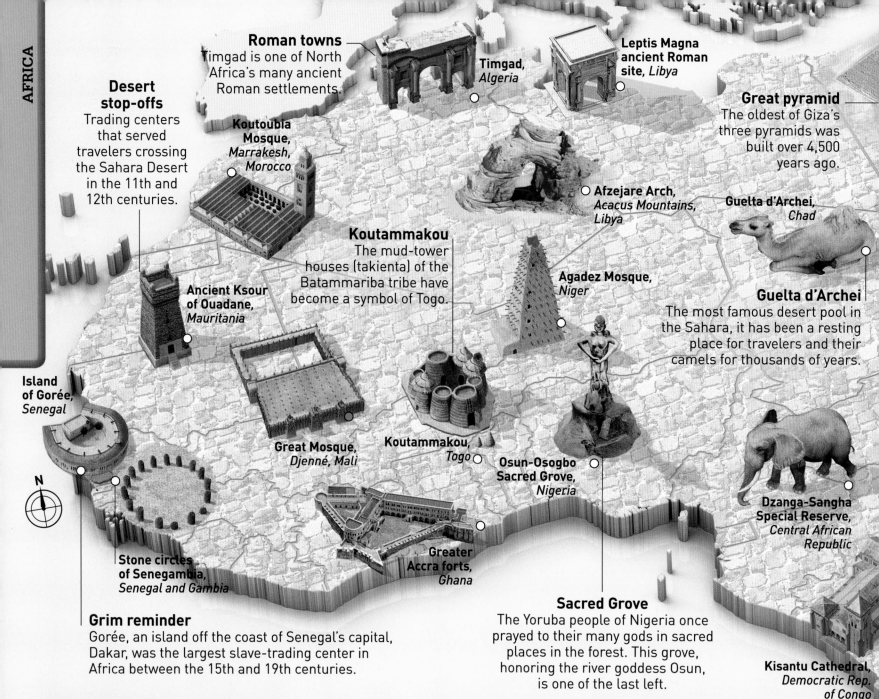

Roman towns
Timgad is one of North Africa's many ancient Roman settlements.

Timgad, *Algeria*

Leptis Magna ancient Roman site, *Libya*

Great pyramid
The oldest of Giza's three pyramids was built over 4,500 years ago.

Desert stop-offs
Trading centers that served travelers crossing the Sahara Desert in the 11th and 12th centuries.

Koutoubia Mosque, *Marrakesh, Morocco*

Afzejare Arch, *Acacus Mountains, Libya*

Guelta d'Archei, *Chad*

Koutammakou
The mud-tower houses (takienta) of the Batammariba tribe have become a symbol of Togo.

Agadez Mosque, *Niger*

Guelta d'Archei
The most famous desert pool in the Sahara, it has been a resting place for travelers and their camels for thousands of years.

Ancient Ksour of Ouadane, *Mauritania*

Island of Gorée, *Senegal*

Great Mosque, *Djenné, Mali*

Koutammakou, *Togo*

Osun-Osogbo Sacred Grove, *Nigeria*

Dzanga-Sangha Special Reserve, *Central African Republic*

Stone circles of Senegambia, *Senegal and Gambia*

Greater Accra forts, *Ghana*

Grim reminder
Gorée, an island off the coast of Senegal's capital, Dakar, was the largest slave-trading center in Africa between the 15th and 19th centuries.

Sacred Grove
The Yoruba people of Nigeria once prayed to their many gods in sacred places in the forest. This grove, honoring the river goddess Osun, is one of the last left.

Kisantu Cathedral, *Democratic Rep. of Congo*

Famous landmarks

Africa boasts breathtaking natural beauty and ancient archeological wonders. It is home to the rich wildlife of the Serengeti and the thunderous waters of Victoria Falls. Towering minarets, ancient pyramids, and monumental mud-brick architecture reflect the continent's rich cultural history.

● Great Mosque, Djenné
Djenné was one of the great cities of the rich Mali Empire, one of Africa's medieval kingdoms, and its mosque was a famous center of learning. Built of sun-baked bricks made of sand and earth, it was reconstructed in 1907.

FISH RIVER CANYON IS AFRICA'S BIGGEST CANYON: 100 MILES (160 KM)

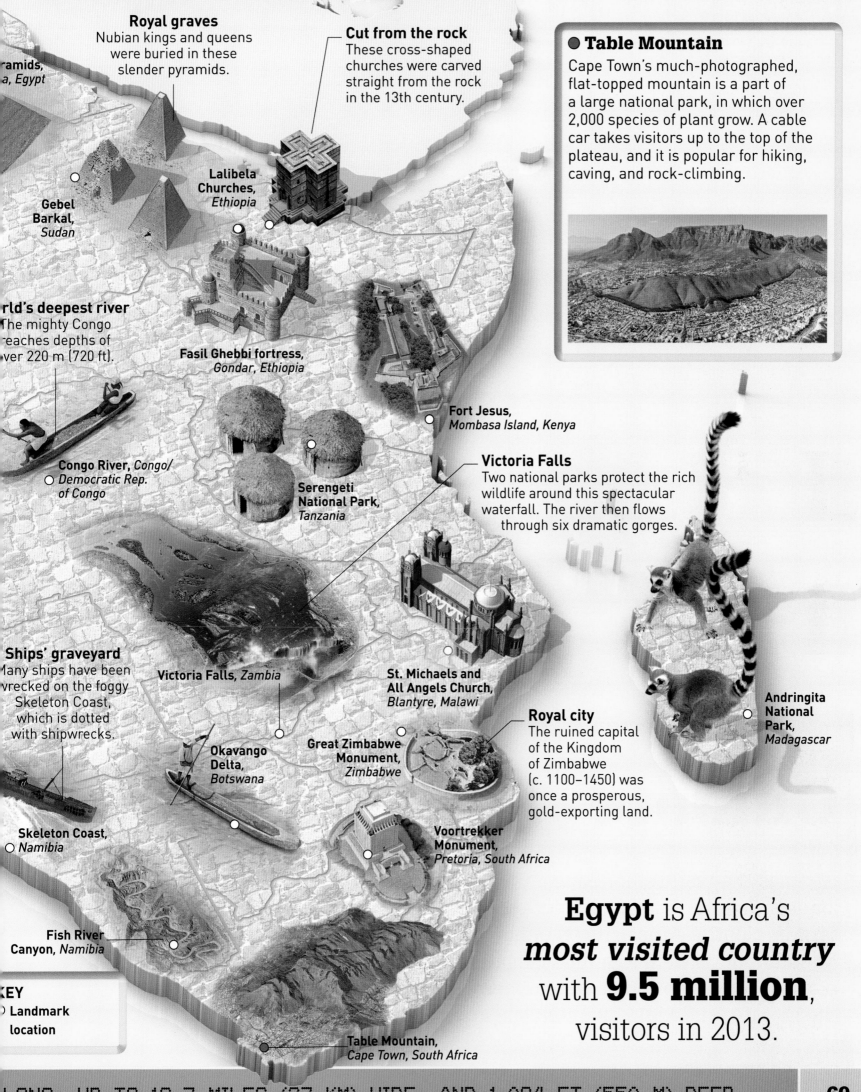

Royal graves
Nubian kings and queens were buried in these slender pyramids.

amids,
a, Egypt

Gebel Barkal, *Sudan*

Cut from the rock
These cross-shaped churches were carved straight from the rock in the 13th century.

Lalibela Churches, *Ethiopia*

● **Table Mountain**
Cape Town's much-photographed, flat-topped mountain is a part of a large national park, in which over 2,000 species of plant grow. A cable car takes visitors up to the top of the plateau, and it is popular for hiking, caving, and rock-climbing.

rld's deepest river
he mighty Congo eaches depths of ver 220 m (720 ft).

Fasil Ghebbi fortress, *Gondar, Ethiopia*

Congo River, *Congo/Democratic Rep. of Congo*

Fort Jesus, *Mombasa Island, Kenya*

Victoria Falls
Two national parks protect the rich wildlife around this spectacular waterfall. The river then flows through six dramatic gorges.

Serengeti National Park, *Tanzania*

Ships' graveyard
Many ships have been wrecked on the foggy Skeleton Coast, which is dotted with shipwrecks.

Victoria Falls, *Zambia*

St. Michaels and All Angels Church, *Blantyre, Malawi*

Andringita National Park, *Madagascar*

Royal city
The ruined capital of the Kingdom of Zimbabwe (c. 1100–1450) was once a prosperous, gold-exporting land.

Okavango Delta, *Botswana*

Great Zimbabwe Monument, *Zimbabwe*

Skeleton Coast, *Namibia*

Voortrekker Monument, *Pretoria, South Africa*

Fish River Canyon, *Namibia*

Egypt is Africa's *most visited country* with **9.5 million**, visitors in 2013.

KEY
Landmark location

Table Mountain, *Cape Town, South Africa*

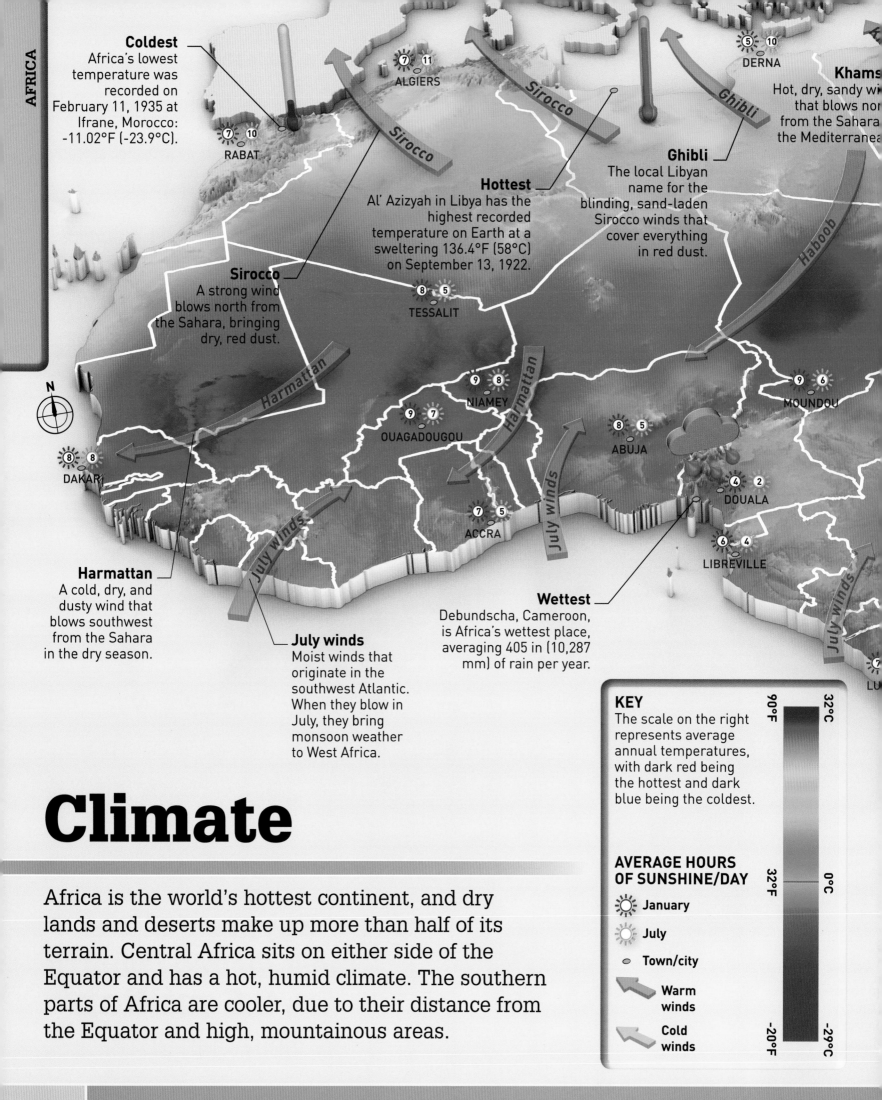

Coldest
Africa's lowest temperature was recorded on February 11, 1935 at Ifrane, Morocco: -11.02°F (-23.9°C).

ALGIERS

RABAT

DERNA

Khams
Hot, dry, sandy wi that blows nor from the Sahara the Mediterranea

Hottest
Al' Azizyah in Libya has the highest recorded temperature on Earth at a sweltering 136.4°F (58°C) on September 13, 1922.

Ghibli
The local Libyan name for the blinding, sand-laden Sirocco winds that cover everything in red dust.

Sirocco

Ghibli

Haboob

Sirocco
A strong wind blows north from the Sahara, bringing dry, red dust.

TESSALIT

Harmattan

NIAMEY

MOUNDOU

OUAGADOUGOU

ABUJA

DAKAR

DOUALA

July winds

ACCRA

LIBREVILLE

Harmattan
A cold, dry, and dusty wind that blows southwest from the Sahara in the dry season.

LU

July winds
Moist winds that originate in the southwest Atlantic. When they blow in July, they bring monsoon weather to West Africa.

Wettest
Debundscha, Cameroon, is Africa's wettest place, averaging 405 in (10,287 mm) of rain per year.

Climate

Africa is the world's hottest continent, and dry lands and deserts make up more than half of its terrain. Central Africa sits on either side of the Equator and has a hot, humid climate. The southern parts of Africa are cooler, due to their distance from the Equator and high, mountainous areas.

KEY
The scale on the right represents average annual temperatures, with dark red being the hottest and dark blue being the coldest.

90°F   32°C

AVERAGE HOURS OF SUNSHINE/DAY

☼ January

☼ July

○ Town/city

⬅ Warm winds

⬅ Cold winds

32°F   0°C

-20°F   -29°C

STORMS HAVE CARRIED SAND FROM THE SAHARA DESERT AS

Sunniest
Aswan, Egypt, is Africa's sunniest place, enjoying an average of 10.6 hours of sunshine per day.

Driest
Wadi Halfa, Sudan, is Africa's driest place, receiving just 0.1 in (2.54 mm) per year.

Haboob
Strong winds blow south from the Sahara during winter, causing fierce sand storms.

South Africa
As with most countries at this latitude in the southern hemisphere, the coldest days are from May to July, while summer falls from December to February.

Haboob

KHARTOUM ⑨ ☀11

DJIBOUTI ☀8 8

ADDIS ABABA ☀9 2

MOGADISHU ☀9 ☀7

NAIROBI ☀9 4

KISANGANI ☀7 5

DAR ES SALAAM ☀8 8

MZUZU ☀5 ☀7

ANTANANARIVO ☀7 5

LUSAKA ☀5 9

HARARE ☀6 9

WINDHOEK ☀9 10

JOHANNESBURG ☀9 9

DURBAN ☀9 9

CAPE TOWN ☀11 6

BANGO

Average precipitation

inches	mm
197	5,000
98	2,500
0	0

Scarce rain in the north has helped create the Sahara Desert; the south receives very little rainfall, too. In contrast, Central Africa's rain forests are drenched in more than 157.5 in (4,000 mm) of rain per year. Snow falls in the mountains of Morocco, South Africa, and, more rarely, East Africa.

Hot spot
Dallol, in Ethiopia's Danakil Desert, has the world's highest average temperature: 94°F (34.4°C). The area's few lakes are salt-encrusted and full of sulfur.

Dromedary camel
The Arabian camel has a single hump, which stores fat that the body converts into energy and water.

Deathstalker scorpion
This venomous arachnid feeds at night and lives in cool, shady burrows.

Nile crocodile
An aggressive reptile that surprise-attacks from submerged hiding places.

Ruppell's vulture
Has a powerful, hooked bill for ripping flesh and crushing bone from animal carcasses.

Spotted hyena
Can see in the dark and lives, hunts, and scavenges in female-led groups.

African rock python
Non-venomous but highly aggressive, this is one of the largest snake species, growing up to 23 ft (7 m) in length.

Chimpanzee
Lives in a community and eats mainly fruit and leaves.

N

African bush elephant
The largest land animal, this elephant lives in grasslands, tropical forests, and semideserts.

Lemon shark
This shark favors warm, shallow waters, and uses sensors (called electroreceptors) to detect hidden prey on the ocean floor.

Hippopotamus
This grass-eater is a fast runner, and spends much of its day in the water to cool off.

Whale shark
The largest fish in the world, this shark grows up to 65.6 ft (20 m) and feeds on tiny organisms, such as plankton and krill.

Wildlife

No safari of Africa is complete without seeing the big five—elephant, lion, buffalo, rhino, and leopard—but the African continent is also home to an incredible variety of other animals. Many of these are exclusive to their region, such as the lemur, which can only be found in Madagascar.

BIOMES
Africa is dominated by tropical and subtropical grasslands, jungles of tropical broadleaf forest, and dry desert regions.

- Mediterranean
- Tropical broadleaf forest
- Tropical dry broadleaf forest
- Tropical/subtropical grassland
- Mountain
- Desert
- Flooded grassland
- Mangrove

Giraffe
Its long legs and neck make it easy to reach leaves at the tops of trees, but hard to bend down to drink.

African wild dog
Hunts in packs to bring down large prey, such as wildebeest.

Serval
Long back legs help this cat jump to snatch birds in flight.

Eastern gorilla
The largest of the primates, it eats mainly fruit and leaves.

African buffalo
Formidably strong with curled horns, females and young live in herds for safety.

Ostrich
The largest bird and fastest two-legged runner in the world.

Aye aye
One of around 50 species of lemur in Madagascar, it uses its long, thin middle finger to scrape out grubs from trees.

Leopard
An incredibly strong cat that can drag large prey up trees to eat.

Lion
The only big cat that lives in groups, its roar can be heard up to 5 miles (8 km) away.

Black rhinoceros
A two-horned rhino with a pointed upper lip that plucks leaves and fruit from bushes.

Warthog
A long-legged pig with four sharp tusks used for defense and foraging.

Cheetah
The fastest animal on Earth, it can run at speeds of up to 60 mph (100 km/h).

Black mamba
A highly venomous snake that reveals the black inside its mouth when threatened.

Tiger shark
A savage scavenger of immense bulk that eats anything it can find in the ocean.

Meerkat
Groups work together to look out for predators while foraging for food.

Springbok
Small, speedy antelope that springs high into the air when startled.

Great white shark
This shark is a fierce predator that surprises prey by attacking it from below.

THESE EXIST NOWHERE ELSE ON EARTH AND MANY ARE ENDANGERED.

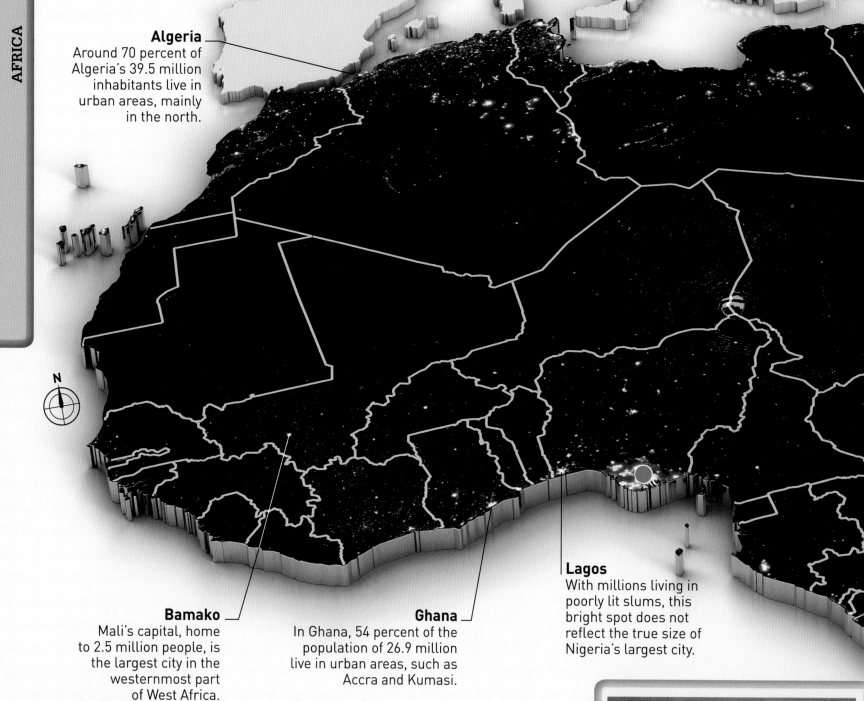

Algeria
Around 70 percent of
Algeria's 39.5 million
inhabitants live in
urban areas, mainly
in the north.

N

Bamako
Mali's capital, home
to 2.5 million people, is
the largest city in the
westernmost part
of West Africa.

Ghana
In Ghana, 54 percent of the
population of 26.9 million
live in urban areas, such as
Accra and Kumasi.

Lagos
With millions living in
poorly lit slums, this
bright spot does not
reflect the true size of
Nigeria's largest city.

By night

The speed at which cities grow in population
is very high in Africa. But here, not all densely
populated places show up at night—poorer areas
do not have street lights, lit-up store windows,
or even electric indoor lights. Most dark areas,
however, are desert, jungle, or savanna.

● **Niger Delta oil fields**
Much of the strong glow in
Nigeria's Niger Delta comes from
the many oil fields, with their
open gas flares, big refineries,
and busy ports.

SOUTH SUDAN HAS THE FASTEST-GROWING POPULATION OF ANY

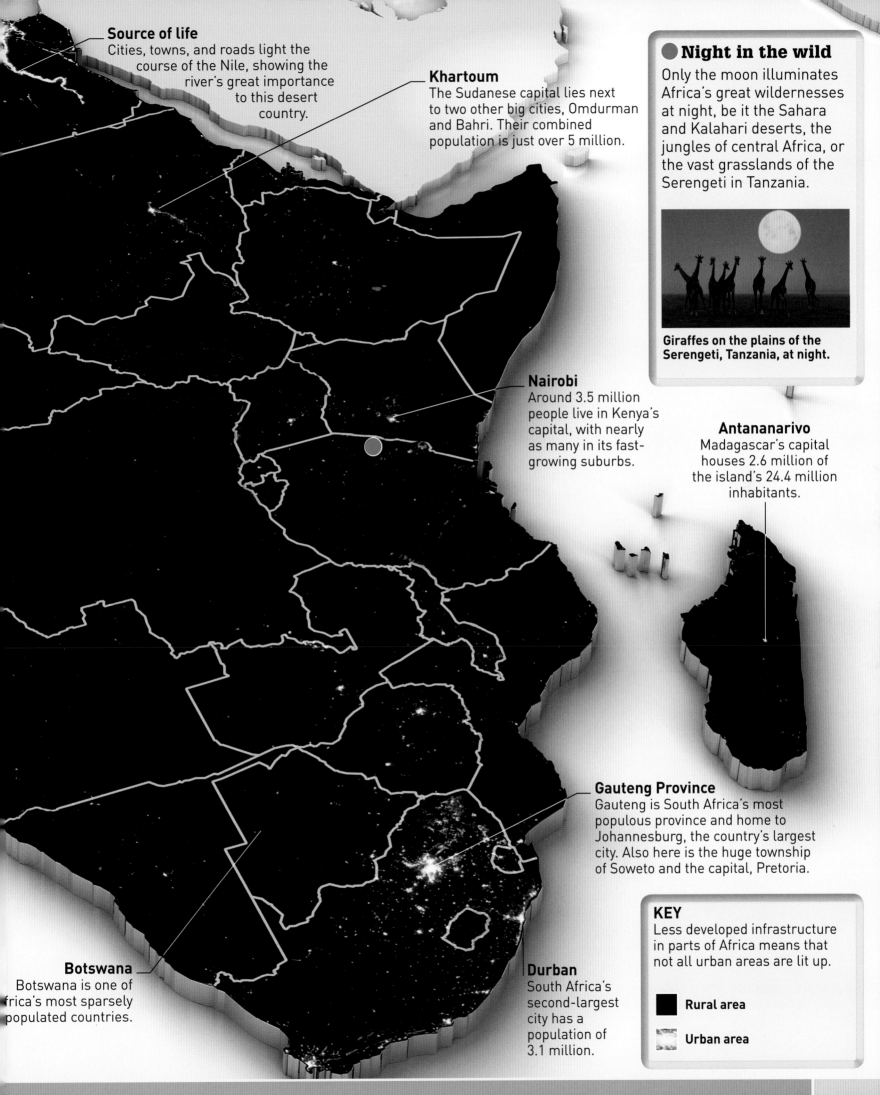

Source of life
Cities, towns, and roads light the course of the Nile, showing the river's great importance to this desert country.

Khartoum
The Sudanese capital lies next to two other big cities, Omdurman and Bahri. Their combined population is just over 5 million.

● Night in the wild
Only the moon illuminates Africa's great wildernesses at night, be it the Sahara and Kalahari deserts, the jungles of central Africa, or the vast grasslands of the Serengeti in Tanzania.

Giraffes on the plains of the Serengeti, Tanzania, at night.

Nairobi
Around 3.5 million people live in Kenya's capital, with nearly as many in its fast-growing suburbs.

Antananarivo
Madagascar's capital houses 2.6 million of the island's 24.4 million inhabitants.

Gauteng Province
Gauteng is South Africa's most populous province and home to Johannesburg, the country's largest city. Also here is the huge township of Soweto and the capital, Pretoria.

KEY
Less developed infrastructure in parts of Africa means that not all urban areas are lit up.

■ Rural area

▨ Urban area

Botswana
Botswana is one of Africa's most sparsely populated countries.

Durban
South Africa's second-largest city has a population of 3.1 million.

EUROPE

Europe from space
The European continent lies in the northern hemisphere and has an eastern land border with Asia. The distinctive "boot" of Italy is clearly visible in this image.

Countries and borders

The borders of European countries have changed many times over history, as conquering armies advanced and defeated ones retreated. In the 20th century, two world wars shook the continent, and conflict and political change continue to shape the continent's borders.

United Kingdom
It is formed of England, Scotland, Wales, and Northern Ireland.

Faroe Islands (to Denmark)

Andorra
The small principality was formed in is bordered by France to the north and by Spain to the south.

Gibraltar (to UK)

Norwegian Sea

North Sea

ATLANTIC OCEAN

British Isles

Bay of Biscay

Corsica

Sardinia

Balearic Islands

Mediterranea

FAST FACTS

Total land area:
4,053,300 sq miles
(10,498,000 sq km)

Total population:
743 million

Number of countries: 46

Largest country:
Russian Federation (European section) —
1,527,350 sq miles
(3,955,818 sq km)

Smallest country:
Vatican City—0.17 sq miles (0.44 sq km)

Largest country population:
Russian Federation (European section)—
110 million

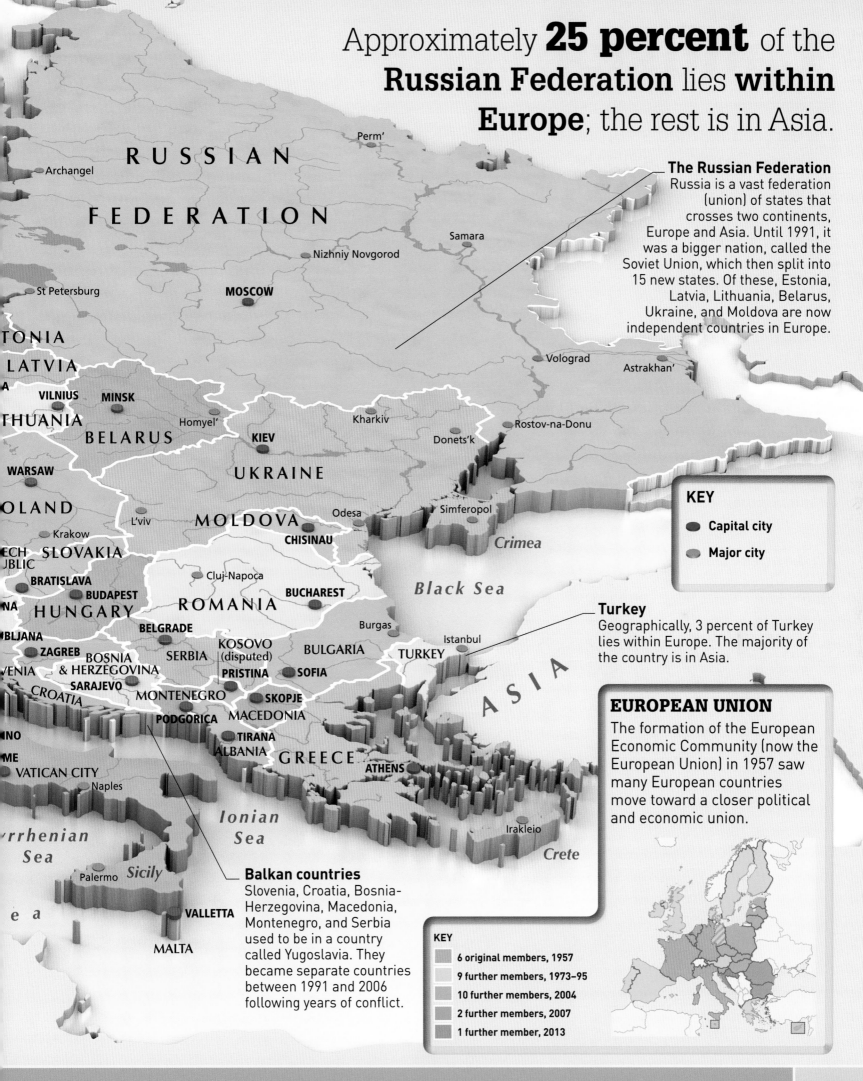

Approximately **25 percent** of the **Russian Federation** lies **within Europe**; the rest is in Asia.

The Russian Federation
Russia is a vast federation (union) of states that crosses two continents, Europe and Asia. Until 1991, it was a bigger nation, called the Soviet Union, which then split into 15 new states. Of these, Estonia, Latvia, Lithuania, Belarus, Ukraine, and Moldova are now independent countries in Europe.

KEY
- Capital city
- Major city

Turkey
Geographically, 3 percent of Turkey lies within Europe. The majority of the country is in Asia.

EUROPEAN UNION
The formation of the European Economic Community (now the European Union) in 1957 saw many European countries move toward a closer political and economic union.

KEY
- 6 original members, 1957
- 9 further members, 1973–95
- 10 further members, 2004
- 2 further members, 2007
- 1 further member, 2013

Balkan countries
Slovenia, Croatia, Bosnia-Herzegovina, Macedonia, Montenegro, and Serbia used to be in a country called Yugoslavia. They became separate countries between 1991 and 2006 following years of conflict.

RUSSIAN FEDERATION

Archangel
Perm'
Samara
Nizhniy Novgorod
St Petersburg
MOSCOW
Volograd
Astrakhan'
TONIA
LATVIA
A
VILNIUS
MINSK
THUANIA
Homyel'
Kharkiv
BELARUS
KIEV
Donets'k
Rostov-na-Donu
WARSAW
UKRAINE
OLAND
L'viv
MOLDOVA
Odesa
Simferopol
Crimea
Krakow
CHISINAU
ECH
SLOVAKIA
JBLIC
Cluj-Napoca
Black Sea
BRATISLAVA
BUCHAREST
NA
BUDAPEST
ROMANIA
HUNGARY
Turkey
BLJANA
BELGRADE
Burgas
Istanbul
ZAGREB
KOSOVO
BULGARIA
TURKEY
VENIA
BOSNIA
(disputed)
SERBIA
& HERZEGOVINA
PRISTINA
SOFIA
ASIA
SARAJEVO
CROATIA
MONTENEGRO
SKOPJE
NO
PODGORICA
MACEDONIA
TIRANA
ME
ALBANIA
GREECE
VATICAN CITY
Naples
ATHENS
rrhenian
Ionian
Sea
Irakleio
Sea
Sea
Crete
Palermo
Sicily
VALLETTA
e a
MALTA

Landscape

Despite its small size, the continent of Europe has an incredibly diverse landscape. To the northwest, east, and south, it is enclosed by mountains. In between, lies the North European Plain, which stretches 2,485 miles (4,000 km) from eastern England to the Ural Mountains in Russia.

FAST FACTS

① Highest point:
Mount Elbrus, Russia—18,510 ft (5,642 m)

② Longest river:
Volga, Russia—2,291 miles (3,688 km)

③ Largest lake:
Lake Ladoga, Russia—7,100 sq miles (18,390 sq km)

④ Largest island:
Britain (England, Wales, and Scotland)—88,745 sq miles (229,848 sq km)

Novaya Zemlya

Barents Sea

Kola Peninsula

Kölen

Gulf of Bothnia

Iceland

ATLANTIC OCEAN

Norwegian Sea

Vänern

Faroe Islands

Shetland Islands

Vättern

Outer Hebrides

Orkney Islands

Jutland

Baltic Sea

North Sea

Ireland

Britain ④

British Isles

English Channel

Seine

Mont Blanc 15,780 ft / 4,808 m

Alps

Loire

Rhône

Appennines

Bay of Biscay

Pyrenees

Corsica

Douro

Ebro

Sardinia

Iberian Peninsula

Balearic Islands

Mediterranean

AFRICA

③

Europe's largest lake, Ladoga lies close to the city of St. Petersburg, in Russia.

EUROPE HAS A HIGHER RATIO OF COAST TO LANDMASS

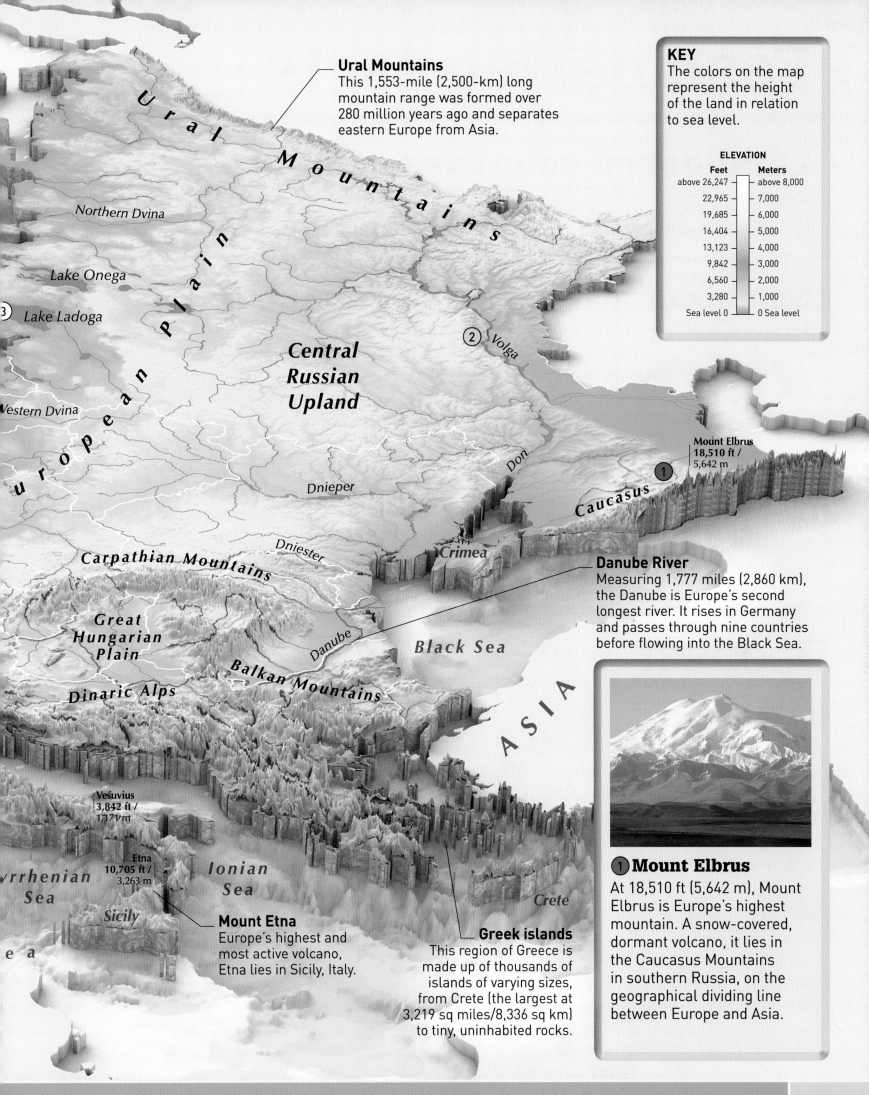

Ural Mountains
This 1,553-mile (2,500-km) long mountain range was formed over 280 million years ago and separates eastern Europe from Asia.

U r a l   M o u n t a i n s

Northern Dvina

Lake Onega

Lake Ladoga

Western Dvina

3

Central Russian Upland

2 *Volga*

E u r o p e a n   P l a i n

Dnieper

Don

Dniester

**Mount Elbrus
18,510 ft /
5,642 m**

1

Caucasus

Carpathian Mountains

Crimea

Great Hungarian Plain

Danube

Danube River
Measuring 1,777 miles (2,860 km), the Danube is Europe's second longest river. It rises in Germany and passes through nine countries before flowing into the Black Sea.

Balkan Mountains

Black Sea

Dinaric Alps

A S I A

**Vesuvius
3,842 ft /
1,171 m**

Tyrrhenian Sea

**Etna
10,705 ft /
3,263 m**

Ionian Sea

Crete

Sicily

Mount Etna
Europe's highest and most active volcano, Etna lies in Sicily, Italy.

Greek islands
This region of Greece is made up of thousands of islands of varying sizes, from Crete (the largest at 3,219 sq miles/8,336 sq km) to tiny, uninhabited rocks.

1 Mount Elbrus
At 18,510 ft (5,642 m), Mount Elbrus is Europe's highest mountain. A snow-covered, dormant volcano, it lies in the Caucasus Mountains in southern Russia, on the geographical dividing line between Europe and Asia.

Fascinating facts

Landlocked countries—14

Andorra ▪ Austria ▪ **Belarus** ▪ Czech Republic ▪ **Hungary** ▪ Liechtenstein ▪ **Luxembourg** ▪ Macedonia ▪ **Moldova** ▪ San Marino ▪ **Serbia** ▪ Slovakia ▪ **Switzerland** ▪ Vatican City

Number of languages

39

There are 39 official European languages and many more regional languages and dialects.

Helsinki

12:00
13:00
14:00
15:00
16:00
17:00

Number of time zones

6

12:00 The world is split into 39 time zones. Most are set whole hours ahead or behind Coordinated Universal Time (UCT)—the time at the Greenwich Meridian in London, UK. Some, however, are whole hours plus 30 or 45 minutes ahead or behind UCT. Therefore, on this map, if it was 12:00 in London, it would be 14:00 in Helsinki, Finland (2 hours ahead of UCT).

Deepest lake

Hornindalsvattnet, Norway—
1,686 ft (514 m)

Fastest train

Europe's fastest train is the **Frecciarossa 1000** in **Italy**, which can reach speeds of up to **249 mph (400 km/h)**

Tallest buildings

Federation Tower
Moscow, Russia
1,226 ft (373.7 m)

OKO: South Tower
Moscow, Russia
1,162 ft (354.1 m)

Mercury City Tower
Moscow, Russia
1,112 ft (338.8 m)

The Shard
London, United Kingdom
1,016 ft (309.6 m)

Eurasia
Moscow, Russia

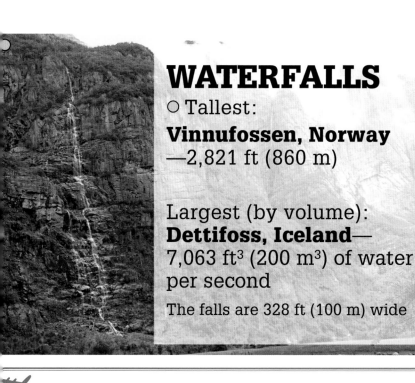

WATERFALLS

○ Tallest:
Vinnufossen, Norway
—2,821 ft (860 m)

Largest (by volume):
Dettifoss, Iceland—
7,063 ft³ (200 m³) of water
per second

The falls are 328 ft (100 m) wide

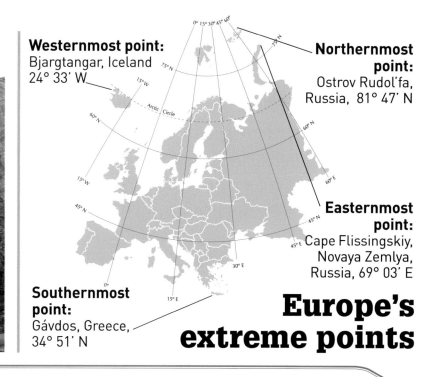

Westernmost point:
Bjargtangar, Iceland
24° 33' W

Northernmost point:
Ostrov Rudol'fa,
Russia, 81° 47' N

Easternmost point:
Cape Flissingskiy,
Novaya Zemlya,
Russia, 69° 03' E

Southernmost point:
Gávdos, Greece,
34° 51' N

Europe's extreme points

✈ **Busiest airport** Heathrow Airport, London, UK: **74,985 million passengers per year**

Largest tunnels

Railroad tunnel
Gotthard Base Tunnel,
Switzerland—
35.5 miles (57.09 km)

Subway line
Serpukhovsko line,
Moscow, Russia—
25.8 miles (41.5 km)

Road tunnel
Laerdal, Norway
—15.2 miles
(24.53 km)

Longest bridge
Vasco da Gama,
Lisbon, Portugal
10.68 miles (17.185 km)

Biggest glacier

Severny Island ice cap—
northern island of the Novaya
Zemlya archipelago in Russia
—7,915 sq miles (20,500 sq km)

Longest coastline

Norway
15,626 miles (25,148 km)

Most active volcano
Mount Etna, Italy

Highest mountains

1. Mount Elbrus
Russia
18,510 ft (5,642 m)

2. Dychtau
Russia
17,073 ft (5,204 m)

3. Mont Blanc
France
15,774 ft (4,808 m)

4. Dafourspitze
Switzerland
15,203 ft (4,634 m)

5. Zumsteinspitze
Switzerland
14,970 ft (4,563 m)

Tallest bridge

Millau Viaduct, France—
bridge deck is **886 ft
(270 m)** above the ground

Population

Murmansk, Russia
The largest city north of the Arctic Circle. It has 299,000 inhabitants.

Europe is the world's second-most densely populated continent (after Asia), with an average of 188 per sq mile (73 people per sq km). The majority of Europe's population live in the northern half of the continent.

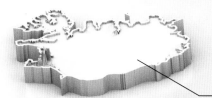

Iceland
This island of volcanoes and icy wilderness has the lowest population density in Europe— 8 people per sq mile (3 people per sq km).

Norway
Scandinavia's most sparsely populated country, with 42 people per sq mile (16 people per sq km).

Netherlands
With a population of 17 million, this is one of Europe's most densely populated nations, at 1,060 per sq mile (409 people per sq km).

Madrid
Population density in Spain's capital is 14,000 per sq mile (5,390 people per sq km), almost as high as that of London.

Monaco
The small principality is the world's mos densely populat nation, with 39,6 per sq mile (15,2 people per sq kr

Europe's largest cities

The list below is based on the number of people living inside a city's boundaries.

1. **Istanbul, Turkey— 14.7 million**
2. **Moscow, Russia—12.3 million**
3. **London, United Kingdom— 8.7 million**
4. **St. Petersburg, Russia— 5.2 million**
5. **Berlin, Germany—3.6 million**
6. **Madrid, Spain—3.1 million**
7. **Kiev, Ukraine—2.9 million**
8. **Rome, Italy—2.87 million**
9. **Paris, France—2.2 million**
10. **Minsk, Belarus—1.9 million**

(9)

The Eiffel Tower dominates the skyline of Paris, France's most populous city.

OF THE WORLD'S 10 MOST DENSELY POPULATED LOCATIONS, FOUR

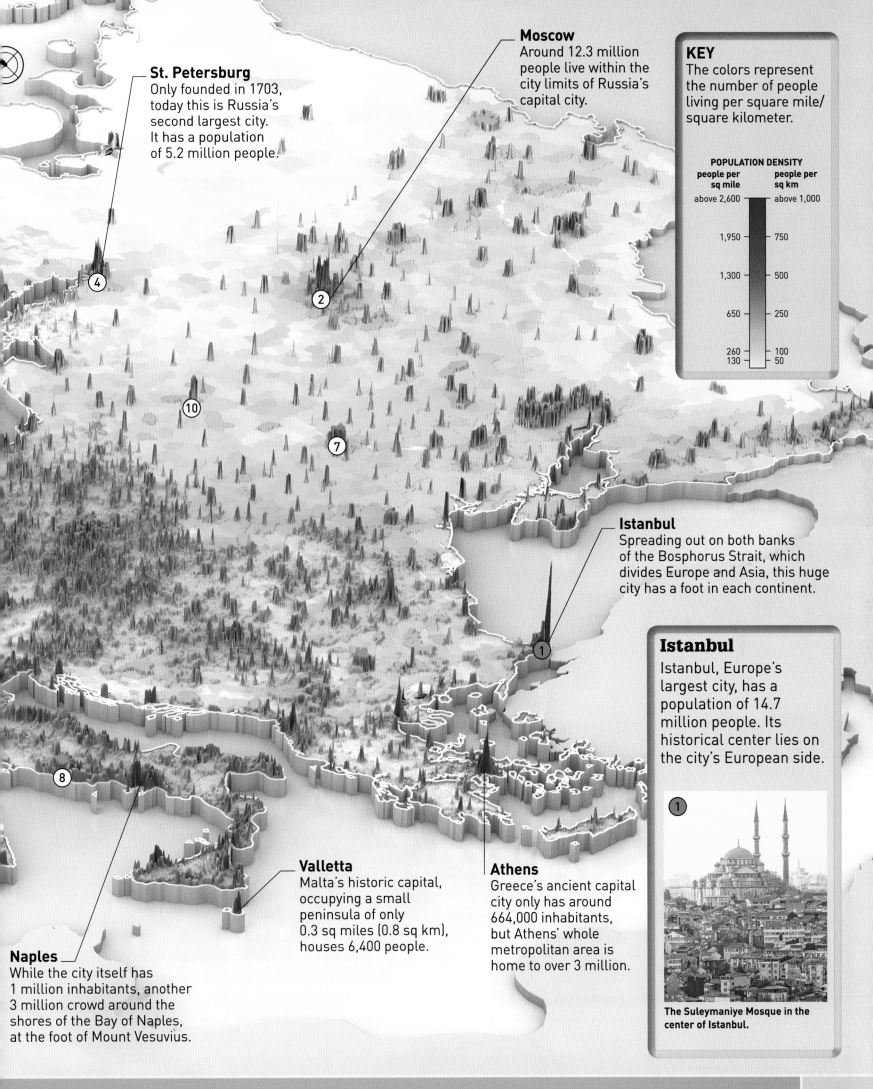

St. Petersburg
Only founded in 1703, today this is Russia's second largest city. It has a population of 5.2 million people.

(4)

Moscow
Around 12.3 million people live within the city limits of Russia's capital city.

(2)

(10)

(7)

POPULATION DENSITY

people per sq mile	people per sq km
above 2,600	above 1,000
1,950	750
1,300	500
650	250
260	100
130	50

Istanbul
Spreading out on both banks of the Bosphorus Strait, which divides Europe and Asia, this huge city has a foot in each continent.

(1)

Istanbul
Istanbul, Europe's largest city, has a population of 14.7 million people. Its historical center lies on the city's European side.

(1)

The Suleymaniye Mosque in the center of Istanbul.

(8)

Valletta
Malta's historic capital, occupying a small peninsula of only 0.3 sq miles (0.8 sq km), houses 6,400 people.

Athens
Greece's ancient capital city only has around 664,000 inhabitants, but Athens' whole metropolitan area is home to over 3 million.

Naples
While the city itself has 1 million inhabitants, another 3 million crowd around the shores of the Bay of Naples, at the foot of Mount Vesuvius.

(MONACO, GIBRALTAR, THE VATICAN CITY, AND MALTA) ARE IN EUROPE.

Highest road
At 9,068 ft (2,764 m), Col de l'Iseran, France, is only accesible by car in summer. Tour de France cyclists have struggled over it several times.

Biggest glacier
The Aletsch glacier, Switzerland, measures over 2,950 ft (900 m) at its thickest, and is 45 sq miles (117 sq km) in size, but it is melting every year.

Mont Blanc
On the border between France and Italy, the "white mountain" is topped by a permanent cap of snow and ice. A road tunnel runs through its base.

A
Lepont

BERN

SWITZERLAND

Pennine Alps

Lake Geneva

Geneva

Po

Turin

Southernmost Alps
The Maritime Alps straddle the France-Italy border and run all the way down to the sea.

Cottian Alps

Maritime Alps

F r e n c h   A l p s

F R A N C E

Artificial lake
The Lac Serre-Ponçon, one of Europe's biggest artificial lakes, was created from 1955–61 to prevent flooding. It covers 10.8 sq miles (28 sq km) and is up to 295 ft (90 m) deep.

French Alps
This range sits within France and contains Mont Blanc.

THE ALPS ARE HOME TO 14 MILLION PEOPLE AND 120 MILLION

GERMANY

Munich

AUSTRIA

S

lps

Dolomites

Dolomites, Italy
This mountain range is characterized by spectacular limestone rocks that rise vertically from the valley floor.

Piave

Brenta   Venice

Gulf of Venice

Adige

Po

Reno

Lake Garda

Mincio

Bologna

Maggiore

Milan

Adda

Po

Appenines
These mountains run the length of Italy, and most of the country's rivers have their source here.

P o   V a l l e y

Ticino

Po

I T A L Y

A p p e n i n e s

Po River
Beginning in the Cottian Alps, the mighty Po River is fed by several smaller rivers coming down from the Pennine and Lepontine Alps and the Dolomites.

Genoa

Gulf of Genoa

M e d i t e r r a n e a n   S e a

Lake Garda
At 142 sq miles (367 sq km), Garda is the largest of Italy's great Alpine lakes. It reaches a depth of 1,135 ft (346 m) at its narrow northern end.

The Alps

The Alps are the highest and most extensive mountain range in western Europe. Shaped like a crescent, they stretch across eight countries for 750 miles (1,200 km) and are 125 miles (200 km) wide at their broadest point. Over 100 peaks are in excess of 13,123 ft (4,000 m), the highest of which is Mont Blanc, on the France-Italy border.

HIGHEST PEAKS
With the exception of Mont Blanc, the Alps' highest peaks are all located in Switzerland.

Mont Blanc 15,774 ft (4,808 m)

Monte Rosa 15,203 ft (4,634 m)

Dom 14,911 ft (4,545 m)

Weisshorn 14,783 ft (4,506 m)

Matterhorn 14,692 ft (4,478 m)

Famous landmarks

From prehistoric monuments and Roman ruins to medieval town centers, Gothic cathedrals, and Baroque palaces, Europe has a wealth of architectural treasures from across the ages. Some of its most famous landmarks are natural formations, often protected as national parks.

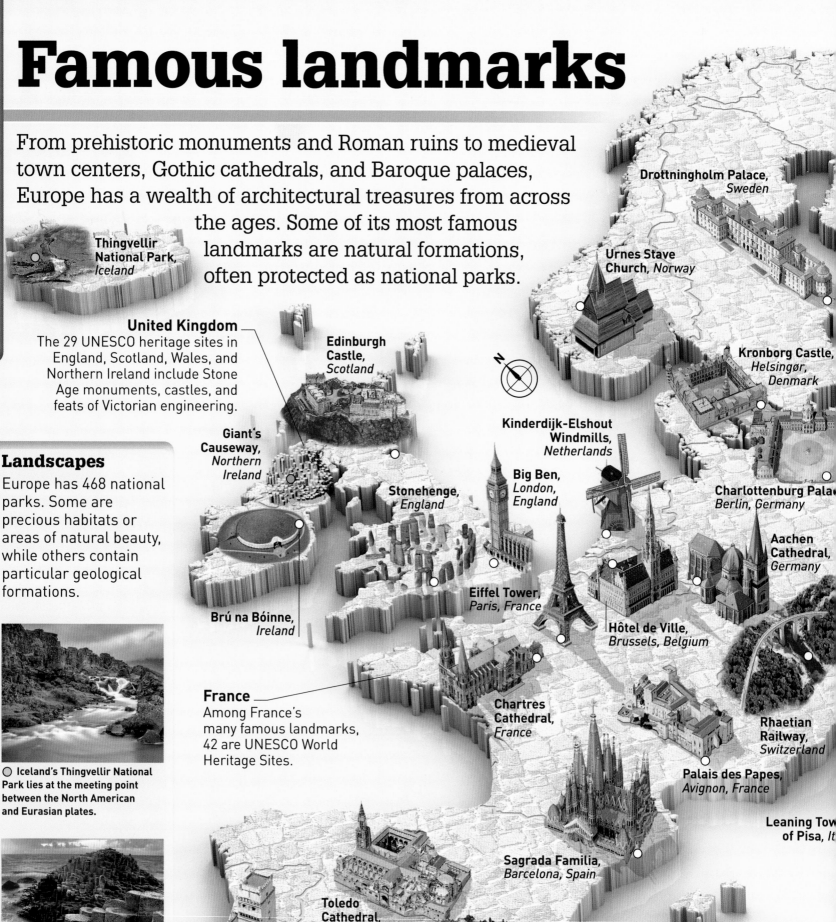

Thingvellir National Park, *Iceland*

Drottningholm Palace, *Sweden*

Urnes Stave Church, *Norway*

United Kingdom
The 29 UNESCO heritage sites in England, Scotland, Wales, and Northern Ireland include Stone Age monuments, castles, and feats of Victorian engineering.

Edinburgh Castle, *Scotland*

Kronborg Castle, *Helsingør, Denmark*

Kinderdijk-Elshout Windmills, *Netherlands*

Big Ben, *London, England*

Charlottenburg Pala *Berlin, Germany*

Giant's Causeway, *Northern Ireland*

Stonehenge, *England*

Aachen Cathedral, *Germany*

Landscapes

Europe has 468 national parks. Some are precious habitats or areas of natural beauty, while others contain particular geological formations.

Brú na Bóinne, *Ireland*

Eiffel Tower, *Paris, France*

Hôtel de Ville, *Brussels, Belgium*

○ Iceland's Thingvellir National Park lies at the meeting point between the North American and Eurasian plates.

France
Among France's many famous landmarks, 42 are UNESCO World Heritage Sites.

Chartres Cathedral, *France*

Rhaetian Railway, *Switzerland*

Palais des Papes, *Avignon, France*

Leaning Tow of Pisa, *It*

Sagrada Familia, *Barcelona, Spain*

Toledo Cathedral, *Spain*

● Giant's Causeway, Northern Ireland, is made of basalt columns in different formations, some like giant honeycombs.

Moorish Alhambra
Many of Spain's landmarks show the country's Arabic heritage, such as the Alhambr palace and gardens in Granad

Torre de Belem, *Lisbon, Portugal*

Alhambra, *Granada, Spain*

OF EUROPE'S MANY LANDMARKS, 453 ARE DESIGNATED UNESCO WORLD

Onion-dome churches
Onion domes top many churches in central and eastern Europe, the most famous of which is the colorful St. Basil's Cathedral in Moscow.

St. Isaac's Cathedral, *St. Petersburg, Russia*

Petjävesi Wooden Church, *Finland*

St. Basil's Cathedral, *Moscow, Russia*

St. Nicholas' Church, *Tallinn, Estonia*

Vilnius Cathedral, *Vilnius, Lithuania*

Mir Castle Complex, *Belarus*

St. Sophia Cathedral, *Kiev, Ukraine*

France is the *most visited* country in the world, with over **85 million** tourists per year.

Historic Center of Riga, *Latvia*

Historic Center of Krakow, *Poland*

gue thedral, ech ublic

Levoča, *Prešov Region, Slovakia*

Struve Geodetic Arc, *Rudi, Moldova*

Stephansdom Quarter, *Vienna, Austria*

Matthias Church, *Budapest, Hungary*

Wooden Churches of Maramureş, *Romania*

Stari Ras and Sopoćani, *Serbia*

Prehistoric Dwellings, *Ljubljansko Barje, Slovenia*

Old Bridge, *Mostar, Bosnia & Herz*

Rila Monastery, *Bulgaria*

Buildings
Europe's architectural landmarks, whether in ruins, reconstructed, or in their original glory, all tell fascinating tales of the continent's history and its people.

Palace of Diocletian, *Split, Croatia*

Parthenon, *Athens, Greece*

Butrint, *Chaonia, Albania*

Meteora, *Greece*

Colosseum, *Rome, Italy*

The historic city center of Riga, Latvia, is a mix of fine medieval buildings and some of the world's best Art Nouveau architecture.

Pompeii, *Italy*

Kotor Old Town, *Montenegro*

Duomo, *Florence, Italy*

Church of St. John at Kaneo, *Ohrid, Macedonia*

Valley of Temples, *Agrigento, Italy*

Ancient Greek ruins
The Valley of the Temples in Agrigento, Sicily, is one of many ancient Greek sites dotted around the Mediterranean.

Meteora, Greece, features a breathtaking group of monasteries perched on vertical cliffs. Only six of the original 24 remain today.

KEY
○ Landmark location

Climate

Europe's climate varies from subtropical in the south to polar in the north. Western and northwestern parts have a mild, generally humid climate, while central and eastern Europe has a humid climate with cool summers.

Polar easterlies
Prevailing winds that bring dry, cold air southward from the North Pole.

Polar easterlies

Prevailing westerlies
Blowing in a northeastern direction, these winds bring warm air to western parts of Europe.

Prevailing westerlies

Prevailing westerlies

Prevailing westerlies

Cloudiest
Glasgow, in the United Kingdom, is Europe's cloudiest city. It averages only 1,203 hours of sunshine a year.

Mistral
A strong, cold wind that blows hardest in winter and spring.

Sirocco winds
Hot air from Africa creates storms over the sea, bringing cloud, fog, and rain to northern Mediterranean locations.

Hottest
The highest temperature recorded in Europe is 122°F (50°C), in Seville, Spain, on August 4, 1881.

Föhn

Mistral

Sirocco

Sirocco

REYKJAVÍK ① ⑤

FAROE ISLANDS ⓪ ④

GLASGOW ② ⑤

HELS ①

STOCKHOLM ① ⑩

OSLO ① ⑦

COPENHAGEN ① ⑧

BERLIN ① ⑦

PRA ②

AMSTERDAM ① ⑥

LONDON ② ⑥

BRUSSELS ② ⑥

LUXEMBOURG ① ⑦

PARIS ② ⑧

BERN ② ⑦

VADUZ ② ⑥

MILAN ② ⑩

LYON ② ⑧

MONACO ⑤ ⑪

BORDEAUX ③ ⑨

BARCELONA ③ ⑨

CAGLIA ④ ①

MADRID ⑤ ⑮

LISBON ⑤ ⑬

ON JULY 7, 1889, 8.1 IN (205.7 MM) OF RAIN FELL AT THE CITY

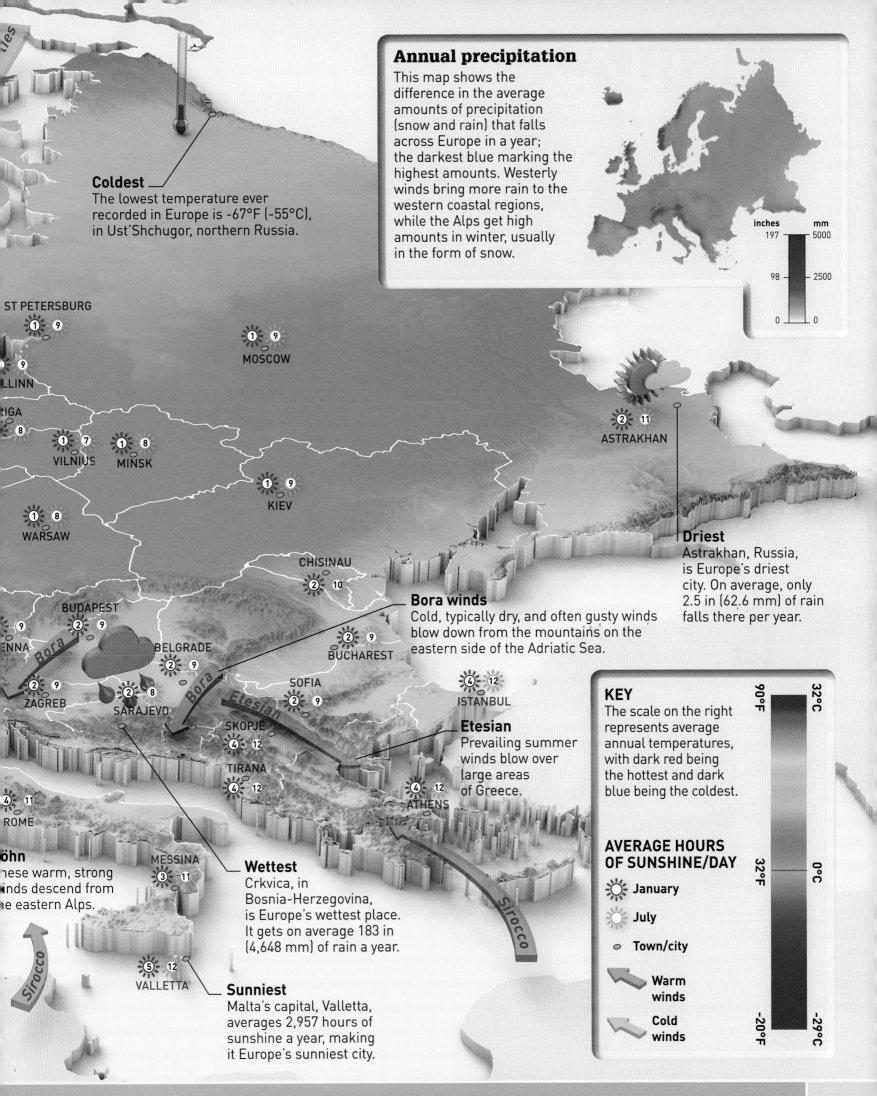

Annual precipitation

This map shows the difference in the average amounts of precipitation (snow and rain) that falls across Europe in a year; the darkest blue marking the highest amounts. Westerly winds bring more rain to the western coastal regions, while the Alps get high amounts in winter, usually in the form of snow.

inches   mm
197   5000

98   2500

0   0

Coldest
The lowest temperature ever recorded in Europe is -67°F (-55°C), in Ust'Shchugor, northern Russia.

ST PETERSBURG
① 9

① 9
MOSCOW

② 11
ASTRAKHAN

9
LLINN

9
IGA

8

① 7
VILNIUS

① 8
MINSK

① 9
KIEV

① 8
WARSAW

② 10
CHISINAU

Driest
Astrakhan, Russia, is Europe's driest city. On average, only 2.5 in (62.6 mm) of rain falls there per year.

Bora winds
Cold, typically dry, and often gusty winds blow down from the mountains on the eastern side of the Adriatic Sea.

9
BUDAPEST
② 9

② 9
ENNA

② 9
BELGRADE
② 9

② 9
BUCHAREST

② 9
② 8
ZAGREB
SARAJEVO

② 9
SOFIA
② 9

④ 12
ISTANBUL

④ 12
SKOPJE

Etesian
Prevailing summer winds blow over large areas of Greece.

④ 12
TIRANA

④ 12
ATHENS

④ 11
ROME

öhn
nese warm, strong inds descend from he eastern Alps.

③ 11
MESSINA

Wettest
Crkvica, in Bosnia-Herzegovina, is Europe's wettest place. It gets on average 183 in (4,648 mm) of rain a year.

⑤ 12
VALLETTA

Sunniest
Malta's capital, Valletta, averages 2,957 hours of sunshine a year, making it Europe's sunniest city.

KEY
The scale on the right represents average annual temperatures, with dark red being the hottest and dark blue being the coldest.

90°F   32°C

32°F   0°C

-20°F   -29°C

AVERAGE HOURS OF SUNSHINE/DAY

☀ January

☀ July

⬮ Town/city

➤ Warm winds

➤ Cold winds

Wildlife

In densely populated Europe there is not much wilderness left for animals to thrive in, but nature reserves and some species' ability to adapt mean that the continent's wildlife is still surprisingly varied.

Humpback whale
In winter, Arctic waters provide rich feeding grounds for these migrating whales.

Reindeer
Both male ar female reind have antlers

Eurasian lynx
Large padded paws prevent this big cat from sinking through the snow.

Arctic fox
Thick, white winter fur keeps this fox warm and camouflaged in snow and ice.

Moose
This giant of the forest is commonly seen in Scandinavia and the Baltic states.

Capercailli
A bird famous its spectacu courting ritua

Red deer
Scotland has its own subspecies of this large deer, which is common throughout the continent.

Roe deer
Small and graceful, this deer is widespread throughout Europe.

Irish hare
Modern farming practices threaten this shy, nocturnal creature.

Gray wolf
The largest of the dog family, wolves live in family packs in isolated, forested areas of Europe.

Basking shark
To feed, this gigantic shark simply keeps its mouth wide open as it swims.

Badger
Big groups live in setts (tunnels and underground chambers).

Pine marten
Hollow trees make good homes for this member of the weasel family.

Alpine marmot
These rodents hibernate in burrows for up to nine months.

Golden eagle
This huge raptor picks and patrols huge territories in less populated areas across Europe.

Pyrenean chamois
Close to extinction, as its skin was used for chamois gloves and polishing cloths, the numbers have recovered.

European bee eater
Male birds offer the best insect morsels to the female during courtship.

Barbary macaque
A 300-strong colony of Barbary macaques live on the Rock of Gibraltar.

Iberian lynx
Only around 400 remain of the endangered Spanish lynx.

EUROPE ONLY HAS ABOUT 260 SPECIES OF

Eurasian brown bear
Found in Scandinavia and eastern Europe, these omnivores love berries and fresh fish.

Changing habitats
Many of the forests that once covered most of Europe have been replaced by farmland, towns and villages, and roads. Wild animals lost their habitats and were hunted, many to near extinction, but today some protected species, such as the gray wolf, are slowly spreading again.

Wolverine
Incredibly fierce, this predator hunts in the tundra and northern forests.

White-tailed eagle
Once almost extinct, this enormous bird now soars across northern Europe.

Eurasian otter
This web-footed otter catches fish in lakes, rivers, and ponds all over Europe.

Red fox
Common across the European countryside, this opportunist now also thrives in cities.

European polecat
This hunter produces a stinky smell to defend its territory.

European bison
Hunted to near extinction in the 1920s, the bison has been reintroduced to the wild.

BIOMES
In the north, the wide tundra and dense boreal forests and taiga provide good shelter for hardy animals. The temperate forest and grasslands and dry, warm Mediterranean biomes of the rest of Europe make for great habitats for a variety of species, but many are threatened by the impact of human activity.

European wild cat
Striped, bushy-tailed, and larger than domestic cats, this rare species lives in southern and central forests.

Golden jackal
A hunter and scavenger, it has started to spread north and west from the Balkans.

Ice
Tundra
Boreal forest/Taiga
Temperate broadleaf forest
Temperate coniferous forest
Temperate grassland
Mediterranean
Desert

Wild boar
These large, bristly pigs are abundant in southern Europe.

Greater flamingo
Mudflats and coastal lagoons are home to these noisy, pink birds.

Common dolphin
These playful, sociable dolphins travel the Mediterranean in big groups.

Mediterranean monk seal
One of the world's most endangered sea mammals, this seal breeds in underwater caves.

By night

This image photo of Europe at night shows where people live. The west of the continent is densely populated; the north and east are relatively uninhabited.

Iceland
Reykjavík is almost the only bright spot, and is home to two-thirds of the country's population.

Scandinavia
The relatively small populations of the large Scandinavian countries are concentrated in the main southern coastal cities.

Northwest England
The triangle formed by the cities of Liverpool, Manchester, and Birmingham is densely populated.

Mega metropolitan area
Urban areas of Belgium, the Netherlands, Luxembourg, and Germany's Rhine-Ruhr form a continuous built-up zone.

London
Europe's third-largest city has a population density of 14,290 people per sq mile (5,518 per sq km).

● **Urban Monaco**
The small principality of Monaco, squeezed into an area of only 0.78 sq miles (2 sq km), is all city. Every one of its 30,581 inhabitants lives in an urban environment.

Paris
About 20 percent of France's 62.8 million inhabitants live in the Paris metropolitan area.

Industrial hub
Milan and Turin, two of Italy's major industrial and economic centres are home to a combined 6.57 million people.

Lisbon
Just over one-quarter (26.2 percent) of Portugal's 10.8 million inhabitants live in the metropolitan area of Lisbon.

Madrid
Madrid is Spain's largest metropolitan area and 6.3 million people live here.

ALBANIA IS THE COUNTRY WITH THE FASTEST GROWING

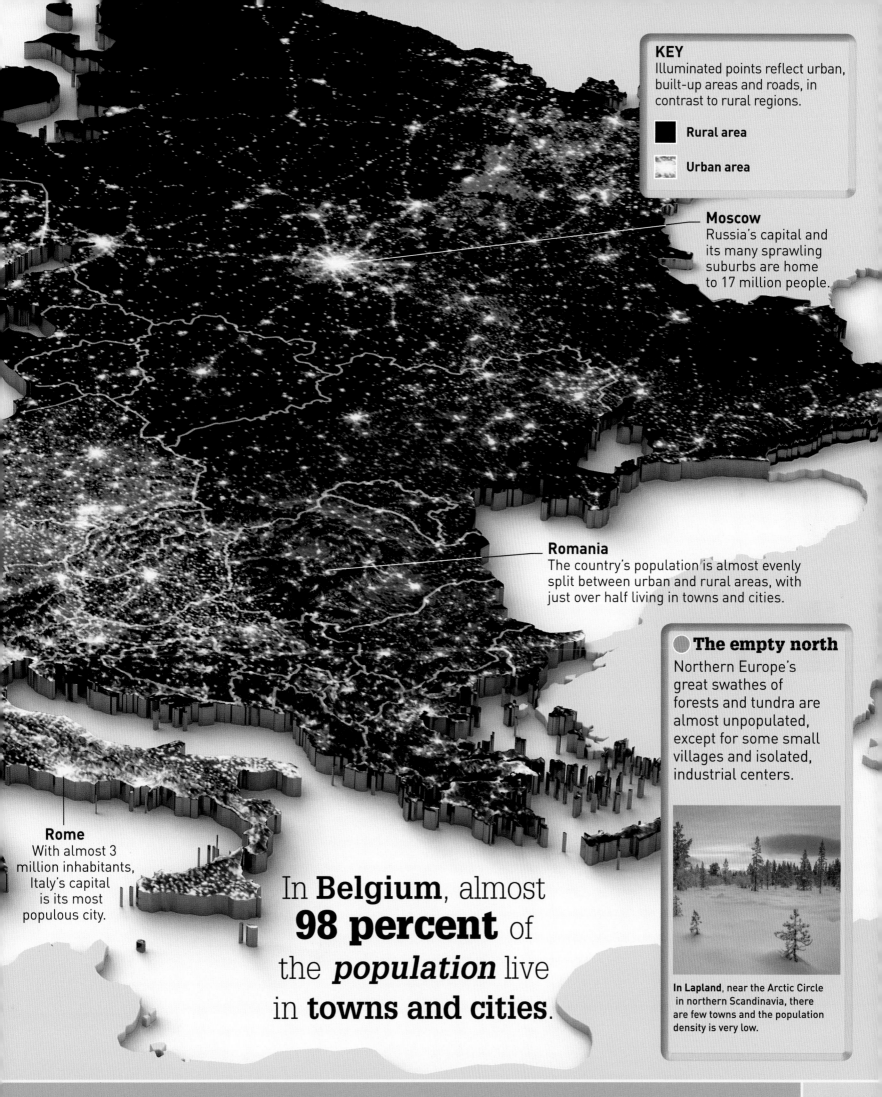

KEY
Illuminated points reflect urban, built-up areas and roads, in contrast to rural regions.

KEY
Illuminated points reflect urban, built-up areas and roads, in contrast to rural regions.

■ **Rural area**

▨ **Urban area**

Moscow
Russia's capital and its many sprawling suburbs are home to 17 million people.

Romania
The country's population is almost evenly split between urban and rural areas, with just over half living in towns and cities.

● The empty north
Northern Europe's great swathes of forests and tundra are almost unpopulated, except for some small villages and isolated, industrial centers.

In Lapland, near the Arctic Circle in northern Scandinavia, there are few towns and the population density is very low.

Rome
With almost 3 million inhabitants, Italy's capital is its most populous city.

In **Belgium**, almost **98 percent** of the *population* live in **towns and cities**.

ASIA

Mighty continent
Asia extends from the Arctic Ocean in the north to the Indian Ocean in the south, and from the Pacific Ocean in the east, to the Ural Mountains, the Suez Canal, the Bosphorus Strait, and the Caucasus Mountains in the west.

EUROPE

Mediterranean Sea

Russian Federation
Three-quarters of the Russian Federation, commonly known as Russia, lies in Asia, making it the continent's largest country.

AFRICA

Ural'sk
Yekaterin

ANKARA
TURKEY
Black Sea
Istanbul

CYPRUS
NICOSIA
GEORGIA
BEIRUT
LEBANON
Aleppo
ARMENIA
TBILISI
K A Z A K H S T A N

Israel
The State of Israel was established in 1948.

JERUSALEM
DAMASCUS
YEREVAN
AST
ISRAEL
SYRIA
Mosul
AZERBAIJAN
JORDAN
AMMAN
AZERB.
BAKU
Aktau
Kara

BAGHDAD
Caspian Sea
Dasoguz
Kyzylorda

SAUDI
ARABIA
IRAQ
TEHRAN
TURKMENISTAN
UZBEKISTAN
Shymkent
Jedda
Basra
ASHGABAT
TASHKENT
BISHKEK
Mecca
Mashhad
Samarqand
Al

RIYADH
KUWAIT
KUWAIT
IRAN
DUSHANBE
KYRGYZSTAN
BAHRAIN
MANAMA
Herat
TAJIKISTAN
QATAR
DOHA
KABUL
(claimed by Indi
UAE
Dubai
AFGHANISTAN
ISLAMABAD
SANA
ABU DHABI
Quetta
Peshawar
(administe
China, clai
by India)
YEMEN
MUSCAT
PAKISTAN
Lahore
(line of control)
Aden
OMAN
Gulf of Oman
Karachi
NEW DELHI
NEPAL
Gulf of Aden
Hyderabad
KATHMANDU

Arabian Sea
Ahmadabad
Jaipur
Kanpur

Bhopal
Patna
THIM

Mumbai
(Bombay)
Nagpur
I N D I A
BH

Hyderabad

Kolkata
(Calcutta)
BANGLA

MYANM
(BUR

Bangalore
Chennai
(Madras)
Bay of Bengal

Kochi
(Ra

India
With a population of 1.27 billion, India is the world's largest democracy.

MALE'
COLOMBO
SRI LANKA
SRI JAYEWARDENAPURA KOTTE
MALDIVES

Nicobar Islands
(to India)

*Andan
Sea*

I N D I A N

O C E A N

Med

Countries and borders

The vast continent of Asia includes two giant nations—China and India, each with a population of more than a billion people and with rapidly growing economies. To the north is the world's biggest country by area—the Russian Federation. To the west lie the countries of the Middle East, today the centre of the Islamic world.

Indonesia
The world's largest island nation, Indonesia is made up of more than 13,000 islands.

ARCTIC OCEAN

NORTH AMERICA

Kara Sea

Laptev Sea

East Siberian Sea

Bering Sea

Noril'sk

Anadyr'

RUSSIAN FEDERATION

Yakutsk

Magadan

Novosibirsk

Petropavlosk-Kamchatskiy

Sea of Okhotsk

Irkutsk

Ürümqi

Khabarovsk

ULAN BATOR

MONGOLIA

Harbin

Vladivostok

Sapporo

Lanzhou

BEIJING

NORTH KOREA

Sea of Japan (East Sea)

Sendai

CHINA

Dalian

Tianjin

Xi'an

Qingdao

SOUTH KOREA

PYONGYANG

SEOUL

SEJONG CITY

Busan

Hiroshima

Kyoto

TOKYO

Chengdu

Wuhan

Yellow Sea

Fukuoka

Osaka

Kunming

Guiyang

Shanghai

East China Sea

JAPAN

claimed by China)

Fuzhou

Japan
Japan is a major industrial power and has the world's fourth-largest economy.

AY PYI TAW

HANOI

Guangzhou

TAIPEI

Chiang Mai

VIENTIANE

Hong Kong

Gaoxiong

THAILAND

LAOS

VIETNAM

TAIWAN

BANGKOK

Da Nang

China
Relatively closed to the outside world until the 1970s, China now plays a major role on the world's political stage.

N

CAMBODIA

PHNOM PENH

Ho Chi Minh City

PHILIPPINES

Philippine Sea

KEY

🔴 Capital city

🔴 Major city

Gulf of Thailand

MANILA

PUR

AJAYA

GAPORE

MALAYSIA

BANDAR SERI BEGAWAN

South China Sea

BRUNEI

SINGAPORE

Cebu

Davao

PACIFIC

Dividing line
The western half of the island of New Guinea lies in Asia; the eastern half is in Australasia and Oceania.

N

O

OCEAN

JAKARTA

Java Sea

E

S

I

A

ng

Bandung

Semarang

Makassar

Jayapura

Surabaya

Flores Sea

DILI

EAST TIMOR

Timor Sea

Arafura Sea

SHARES BORDERS WITH THREE OTHER CONTINENTS.

Dead Sea
A salt lake bordering Israel, the West Bank, and Jordan. At 1,286 ft (392 m) below sea level, it is the lowest land point on Earth's surface.

West Siberian Plain
One of the largest plains in the world, it is a vast system of marshes.

EUROPE

Mediterranean Sea

Anatolia

Black Sea

Caucasus

AFRICA

Syrian Desert

Euphrates

Tigris

Caspian Sea ③

Aral Sea

Syr Darya

Amu Darya

Kara Kum

Ural Mo

We

Siber

Pla

Kirghiz Stepp

Lake Balk

Dead Sea -1,286 ft / -392 m

Red Sea

Arabian Peninsula

Persian Gulf

Zagros Mountains

Iranian Plateau

Hindu Kush

K2 28,251 ft / 8,611 m

Tien Shan

Takla Makan Desert

Kunlun Mount.

Ar Rub' al Khálí (Empty Quarter)

Gulf of Aden   Socotra

Gulf of Oman

Indus

Thar Desert

Mount Everest 29,029 ft / 8,848 m

Himalaya

Plat of T

Arabian Sea

Ganges

Brahm

FAST FACTS

① **Highest point:**
Mount Everest, Nepal/Tibet, China—29,029 ft (8,848 m)

② **Longest river:**
Yangtze, China—3,964 miles (6,380 km)

③ **Largest lake:**
Caspian Sea—143,243 sq miles (371,000 sq km)

④ **Largest island:**
Borneo—288,869 sq miles (748,168 sq km)

Borneo is the largest island in Asia, and the third-largest island in the world.

Western Ghats

Deccan

Eastern Ghats

Sri Lanka

Indian Shield
Its collision with the Eurasian Plate has created the Himalayas, the world's tallest mountain system.

Bay of Bengal

Andaman Islands

Andaman Sea

Nicobar Islands

INDIAN

OCEAN

Sum

Landscape

Asia covers approximately 30 percent of Earth's land area and makes up the eastern portion of the Eurasian supercontinent (with Europe lying to the west). It is made up of five different landscapes: mountain systems, plateaus, plains, steppes (large areas of unforested grassland), and deserts.

Indonesian islands
Indonesia is the most volcanic country in the world. It is home to 147 volcanoes, 76 of which are active.

Kara Sea

ns

Ob·

Yenisey

Central Siberian Plateau

Laptev Sea

Lena

S i b e r i a

Aldan

East Siberian Sea

Wrangel Island

Chukchi Sea

NORTH AMERICA

Bering Sea

Lena

Altai Mountains

Lake Baikal

Amur

Plateau of Mongolia

G o b i

Sakhalin

Sea of Okhotsk

Kamchatka

Khrebet Sikhote-Alin'

Kurile Islands

Hokkaido

Qilian Shan

Yellow River

Sea of Japan (East Sea)

Honshu

Mekong

Salween

Sichuan Pendi

Great Plain of China

Shandong Peninsula

Yellow Sea

Kyushu

Korea Strait

Shikoku

Japan
The country is made up of 6,852 islands, of which the largest is Honshu.

Yangtze
②

Xi Jiang

East China Sea

Taiwan Strait

Red River

Mekong

Hainan

Great Plain of China
This relatively flat area of land is one of the most densely populated regions in the world.

Taiwan

Ryukyu Islands

PACIFIC OCEAN

KEY
The colors on the map represent the height of the land in relation to sea level.

f Thailand

South China Sea

Ph

Luzon

Philippine Sea

Natuna Islands

Sunda   Islands

④ **Borneo**

Palawan

Celebes Sea

Mindanao

ELEVATION

Feet	Meters
above 26,247	above 8,000
22,965	7,000
19,685	6,000
16,404	5,000
13,123	4,000
9,842	3,000
6,560	2,000
3,280	1,000
Sea level 0	0 Sea level

eater

Celebes

Halmahera

Java Sea

Moluccas

Java

Flores Sea

Banda Sea

Seram

Flores

New Guinea

Lesser

Sunda Islands

Timor

Timor Sea

Arafura Sea

Fascinating facts

Number of time zones

16

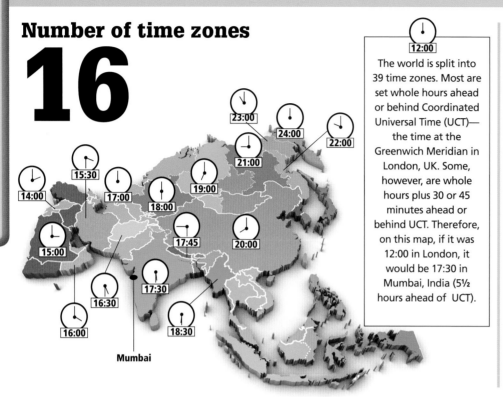

12:00

The world is split into 39 time zones. Most are set whole hours ahead or behind Coordinated Universal Time (UCT)— the time at the Greenwich Meridian in London, UK. Some, however, are whole hours plus 30 or 45 minutes ahead or behind UCT. Therefore, on this map, if it was 12:00 in London, it would be 17:30 in Mumbai, India (5½ hours ahead of UCT).

23:00 **24:00** **22:00**
15:30 **21:00**
14:00 **17:00** **19:00**
18:00
15:00 **17:45** **20:00**
16:30 **17:30**
16:00 **18:30**

Mumbai

13 Landlocked countries

Afghanistan ▪ Armenia ▪ Azerbaijan ▪ Belarus ▪ Bhutan ▪ Kazakhstan ▪ Kyrgyzstan ▪ Laos ▪ Mongolia ▪ Nepal ▪ Tajikistan ▪ Turkmenistan ▪ Uzbekistan

Fastest train
Shanghai Maglev Train, China— **267.2 mph (430 km/h)**

Longest tunnels

Railroad tunnel
Seikan Tunnel, Tsugaru Strait, Japan —33.5 miles (53.85 km)

Subway line
Guangzhou Metro Line 3, Guangzhou, China— 37.5 miles (60.4 km)

Road tunnel
Xishan Tunnel, Shanxi, China— 8.5 miles (13.6 km)

Longest coastline Indonesia— **33,999 miles (54,716 km)**

✈ **Busiest airport** Beijing International Airport, China— **90.203 million** passengers per year

Tallest buildings

Burj Khalifa Dubai, UAE 2,715 ft (828 m)

Shanghai Tower Shanghai, China 2,073 ft (632 m)

Makkah Royal Clock Tower Mecca, Saudi Arabia 1,971 ft (601 m)

Taipei 101 Taipei, Taiwan 1,670 ft (509 m)

Shanghai World Finance Centre Shanghai, China 1,614 ft (492 m)

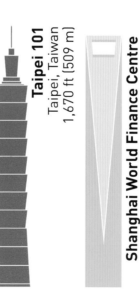

Biggest glacier
Fedchenko Glacier, Tajikistan— 48 miles (77 km) long
The Fedchenko Glacier is the longest glacier in the world outside of the polar regions

WATERFALLS

Tallest:
Hannoki Falls, Toyama, Japan—1,640 ft (500 m)

Largest (by volume):
Chutes de Khone, Laos—410,000 ft^3 (11,610 m^3) of water per second

Deepest lake

Lake Baikal, Russian Federation—
5,387 ft (1,642 m)

Lake Baikal is the deepest lake in the world

Most active volcano
Mount Merapi, Indonesia

Asia's extreme points

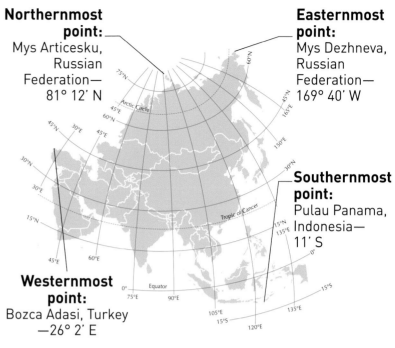

Northernmost point:
Mys Articesku, Russian Federation—81° 12' N

Easternmost point:
Mys Dezhneva, Russian Federation—169° 40' W

Southernmost point:
Pulau Panama, Indonesia—11' S

Westernmost point:
Bozca Adasi, Turkey—26° 2' E

Highest mountains

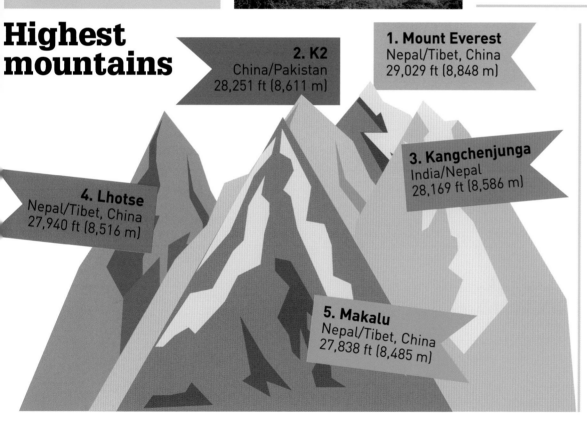

1. Mount Everest
Nepal/Tibet, China
29,029 ft (8,848 m)

2. K2
China/Pakistan
28,251 ft (8,611 m)

3. Kangchenjunga
India/Nepal
28,169 ft (8,586 m)

4. Lhotse
Nepal/Tibet, China
27,940 ft (8,516 m)

5. Makalu
Nepal/Tibet, China
27,838 ft (8,485 m)

Most visited cities (Visitors per year)

Bangkok, Thailand
18.24 million

Singapore
11.88 million

Kuala Lumpur, Malaysia
11.12 million

Seoul, South Korea
10.35 million

Hong Kong
8.66 million

Tallest bridge

Duge Beipan River Bridge, Liupanshui, Guizhou, China —**1,854 ft (535 m)**

The world's three tallest bridges are all in Asia:
- Duge Beipan River Bridge—1,854 ft (565 m)
- Sidu River Bridge—1,627 ft (496 m)
- Puli Bridge—1,591 ft (485 m)

Longest bridge Danyang–Kunshan Grand Bridge (Beijing–Shanghai high-speed railroad)
—**102.4 miles (164.8 km)**

This is the longest bridge of any type in the world

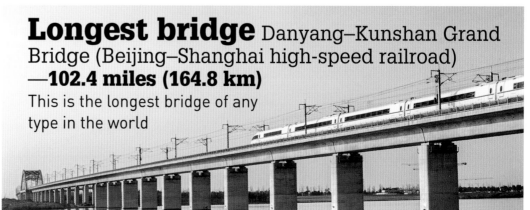

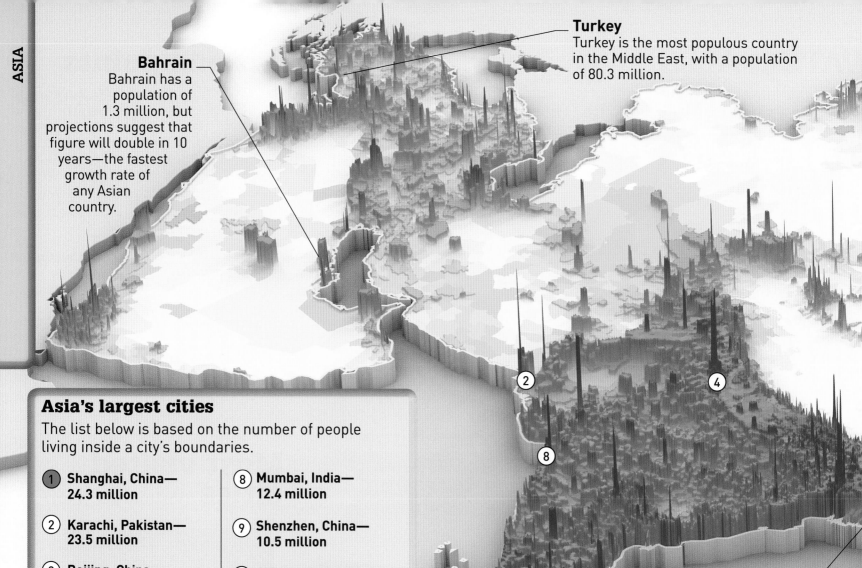

Bahrain
Bahrain has a population of 1.3 million, but projections suggest that figure will double in 10 years—the fastest growth rate of any Asian country.

Turkey
Turkey is the most populous country in the Middle East, with a population of 80.3 million.

Bangladesh
Of all the countries in the world with a population of over 100 million, Bangladesh has the highest population density —2,948 people per sq mile (1,138 per sq km).

India
India has the world's second-largest population (1.27 billion), but is expected to be the world's most populous country by 2028.

Asia's largest cities

The list below is based on the number of people living inside a city's boundaries.

1. **Shanghai, China—** 24.3 million
2. **Karachi, Pakistan—** 23.5 million
3. **Beijing, China—** 21.5 million
4. **Delhi, India—** 16.4 million
5. **Tianjin, China—** 15.2 million
6. **Tokyo, Japan—** 13.5 million
7. **Guangzhou, China—** 13.1 million
8. **Mumbai, India—** 12.4 million
9. **Shenzhen, China—** 10.5 million
10. **Jakarta, Indonesia—** 10.1 million

The bright lights and busy streets of Tokyo—Japan's largest city.

KEY
The colors represent the number of people living per square mile/ square kilometer.

POPULATION DENSITY

people per sq mile	people per sq km
above 2,600	above 1,000
1,950	750
1,300	500
650	250
260	100
130	50

Population

Asia contains some of the most populous regions on Earth. The plains of eastern China, the Ganges-Brahmaputra rivers in India, Japan, and the Indonesian island of Jakarta all have very high population densities. By contrast, Siberia and the Plateau of Tibet are virtually uninhabited.

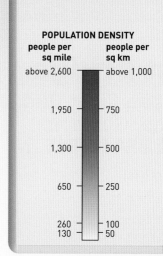

OVER HALF OF ASIA'S POPULATION OF 4.5 BILLION LIVES IN

Mongolia
The least densely populated country in Asia, with an average of 4 inhabitants per sq mile (2 people per sq km).

Almost **two-thirds** of the world's population live **in Asia**.

China
With a population of 1.37 billion people, China is home to approximately one-fifth of the world's population.

N

Shanghai

With a population of 24.3 million, Shanghai, China, located on the country's east coast, is the most populous city in the world.

Shanghai's Pudong district is on the banks of the Huangpu River.

Java
The Indonesian island is the world's most populous island—139.4 million people live there.

EITHER CHINA (31.35 PERCENT) OR INDIA (29.72 PERCENT).

Karakoram Range
This vast mountain range lies to the west of the Himalayas and contains the highest concentration of peaks over 26,247 ft (8,000 m) on Earth.

Kathmandu
The capital city of Nepal, Kathmandu has a population of 1.18 million people and is a gateway for tourism in the Himalayas.

Taklamakan Desert
A lifeless, sand-shifting desert, the famed Silk Road passed along its northern and southern fringes.

Mount Everest
Situated on the border between Nepal and Tibet, China, Mount Everest is the world's tallest mountain at 29, 029 ft (8,848 m).

The Ganges
The Ganges is the most sacred river of the Hindu religion. It rises in the Himalayas, and flows through India and Bangladesh to the Bay of Bengal.

Siwalik Range
An outer range of the Himalayas that extends more than 1,000 miles (1,600 km) from east to west.

Bhutan
The small Himalayan kingdom only opened its borders to foreigners in 1974.

Thimphu
At 8,688 ft (2,648 m), Thimphu, in Bhutan, is the third-highest capital city in the world, after La Paz (Bolivia) and Quito (Ecuador).

KYRGYZSTAN

TAJIKISTAN

Hindu Kush

Karakoram Range

Tarim He

Tarim Basin

Taklamakan Shamo

Kunlun Shan

Altu

Qingzang (Plateau o.

Gangdise Shan

H I M A L A Y A

Siwalik

Nepal Range

Delhi

Lucknow

I N D I A

Patna

Ganges

BHUTA

Brahmaputra

Padma

BANGLADESH

Dhaka

Bay of Bengal

THE HIMALAYAS ARE STILL RISING AT A RATE OF 0.25 IN (4 MM) PER

The Himalayas

The Himalayas is the world's highest mountain range. It runs in an arc 1,500 miles (2,400 km) long, spread across five countries: Pakistan, India, Nepal, Bhutan, and China. It is also the source of some of the region's major rivers, including the mighty Ganges and Brahmaputra rivers.

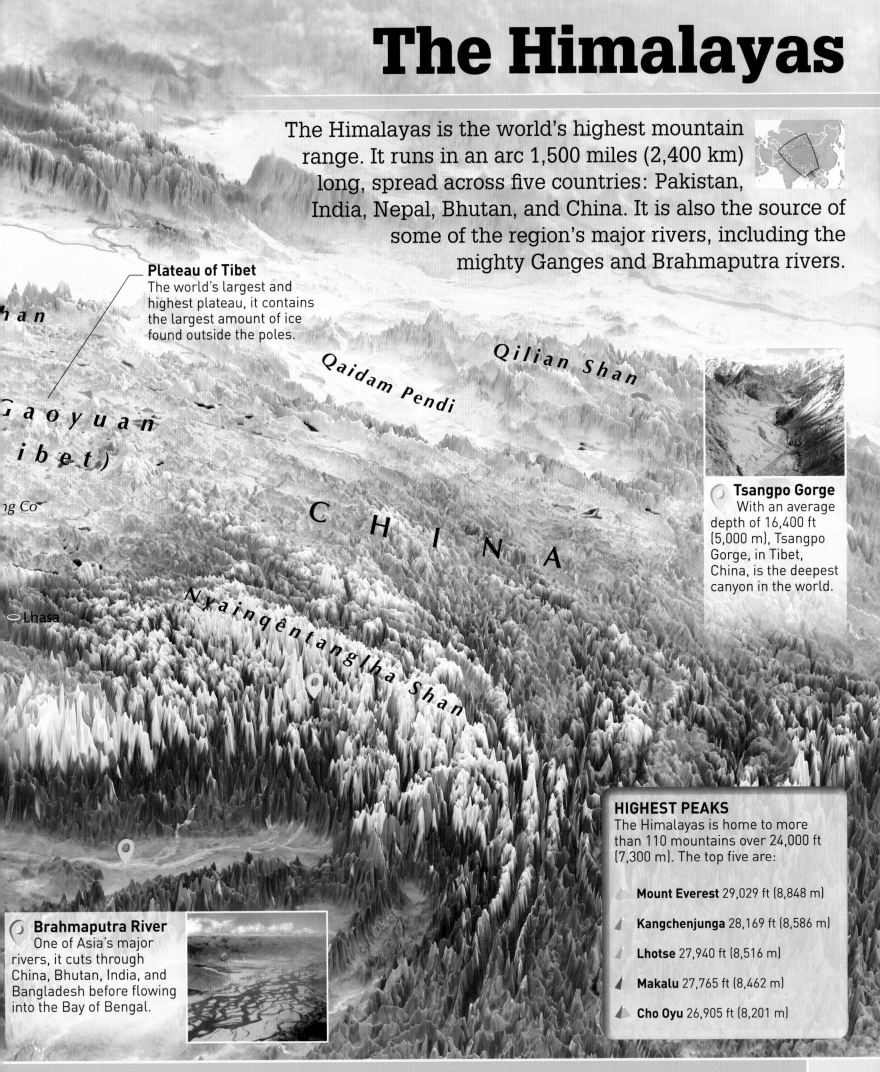

Plateau of Tibet
The world's largest and highest plateau, it contains the largest amount of ice found outside the poles.

...han

Gaoyuan
(ibet)

ng Co

Qaidam Pendi

Qilian Shan

CHINA

Lhasa

Nyainqêntanglha Shan

Tsangpo Gorge
With an average depth of 16,400 ft (5,000 m), Tsangpo Gorge, in Tibet, China, is the deepest canyon in the world.

HIGHEST PEAKS
The Himalayas is home to more than 110 mountains over 24,000 ft (7,300 m). The top five are:

Mount Everest 29,029 ft (8,848 m)

Kangchenjunga 28,169 ft (8,586 m)

Lhotse 27,940 ft (8,516 m)

Makalu 27,765 ft (8,462 m)

Cho Oyu 26,905 ft (8,201 m)

Brahmaputra River
One of Asia's major rivers, it cuts through China, Bhutan, India, and Bangladesh before flowing into the Bay of Bengal.

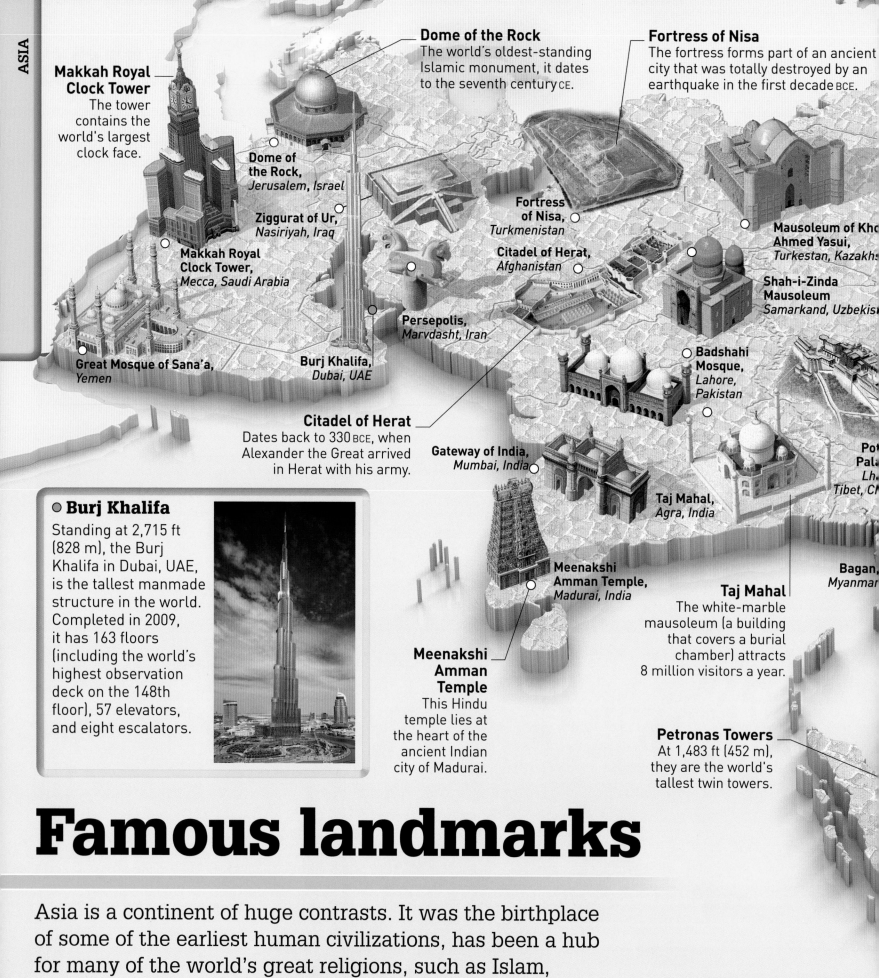

Makkah Royal Clock Tower
The tower contains the world's largest clock face.

Dome of the Rock
The world's oldest-standing Islamic monument, it dates to the seventh century CE.

Fortress of Nisa
The fortress forms part of an ancient city that was totally destroyed by an earthquake in the first decade BCE.

Dome of the Rock, *Jerusalem, Israel*

Ziggurat of Ur, *Nasiriyah, Iraq*

Makkah Royal Clock Tower, *Mecca, Saudi Arabia*

Fortress of Nisa, *Turkmenistan*

Citadel of Herat, *Afghanistan*

Mausoleum of Kho Ahmed Yasui, *Turkestan, Kazakhs*

Shah-i-Zinda Mausoleum *Samarkand, Uzbekis*

Great Mosque of Sana'a, *Yemen*

Persepolis, *Marvdasht, Iran*

Burj Khalifa, *Dubai, UAE*

Badshahi Mosque, *Lahore, Pakistan*

Citadel of Herat
Dates back to 330 BCE, when Alexander the Great arrived in Herat with his army.

Gateway of India, *Mumbai, India*

Po Pala *Lh Tibet, C*

Taj Mahal, *Agra, India*

● **Burj Khalifa**
Standing at 2,715 ft (828 m), the Burj Khalifa in Dubai, UAE, is the tallest manmade structure in the world. Completed in 2009, it has 163 floors (including the world's highest observation deck on the 148th floor), 57 elevators, and eight escalators.

Meenakshi Amman Temple, *Madurai, India*

Taj Mahal
The white-marble mausoleum (a building that covers a burial chamber) attracts 8 million visitors a year.

Bagan, *Myanmar*

Meenakshi Amman Temple
This Hindu temple lies at the heart of the ancient Indian city of Madurai.

Petronas Towers
At 1,483 ft (452 m), they are the world's tallest twin towers.

Famous landmarks

Asia is a continent of huge contrasts. It was the birthplace of some of the earliest human civilizations, has been a hub for many of the world's great religions, such as Islam, Hinduism, and Buddhism, and, today, is the site of some of the world's most amazing modern architecture.

KEY
○ Landmark location

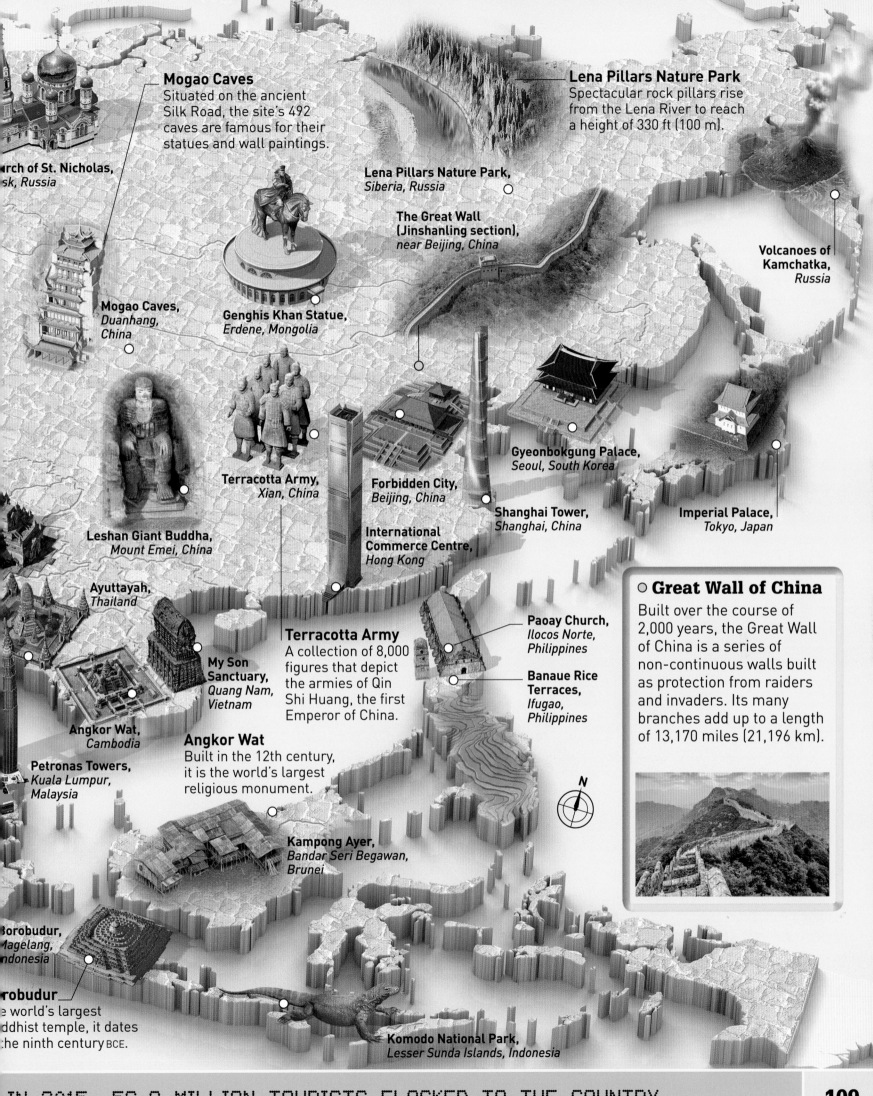

Mogao Caves
Situated on the ancient Silk Road, the site's 492 caves are famous for their statues and wall paintings.

Lena Pillars Nature Park
Spectacular rock pillars rise from the Lena River to reach a height of 330 ft (100 m).

rch of St. Nicholas,
sk, *Russia*

Lena Pillars Nature Park,
Siberia, Russia

The Great Wall (Jinshanling section),
near Beijing, China

Volcanoes of Kamchatka,
Russia

Mogao Caves,
Duanhang, China

Genghis Khan Statue,
Erdene, Mongolia

Terracotta Army,
Xian, China

Forbidden City,
Beijing, China

Gyeonbokgung Palace,
Seoul, South Korea

Imperial Palace,
Tokyo, Japan

Leshan Giant Buddha,
Mount Emei, China

Shanghai Tower,
Shanghai, China

International Commerce Centre,
Hong Kong

Ayuttayah,
Thailand

Terracotta Army
A collection of 8,000 figures that depict the armies of Qin Shi Huang, the first Emperor of China.

Paoay Church,
Ilocos Norte, Philippines

○ **Great Wall of China**
Built over the course of 2,000 years, the Great Wall of China is a series of non-continuous walls built as protection from raiders and invaders. Its many branches add up to a length of 13,170 miles (21,196 km).

My Son Sanctuary,
Quang Nam, Vietnam

Banaue Rice Terraces,
Ifugao, Philippines

Angkor Wat,
Cambodia

Angkor Wat
Built in the 12th century, it is the world's largest religious monument.

Petronas Towers,
Kuala Lumpur, Malaysia

N

Kampong Ayer,
Bandar Seri Begawan, Brunei

Borobudur,
Magelang,
ndonesia

robudur
e world's largest
ddhist temple, it dates
he ninth century BCE.

Komodo National Park,
Lesser Sunda Islands, Indonesia

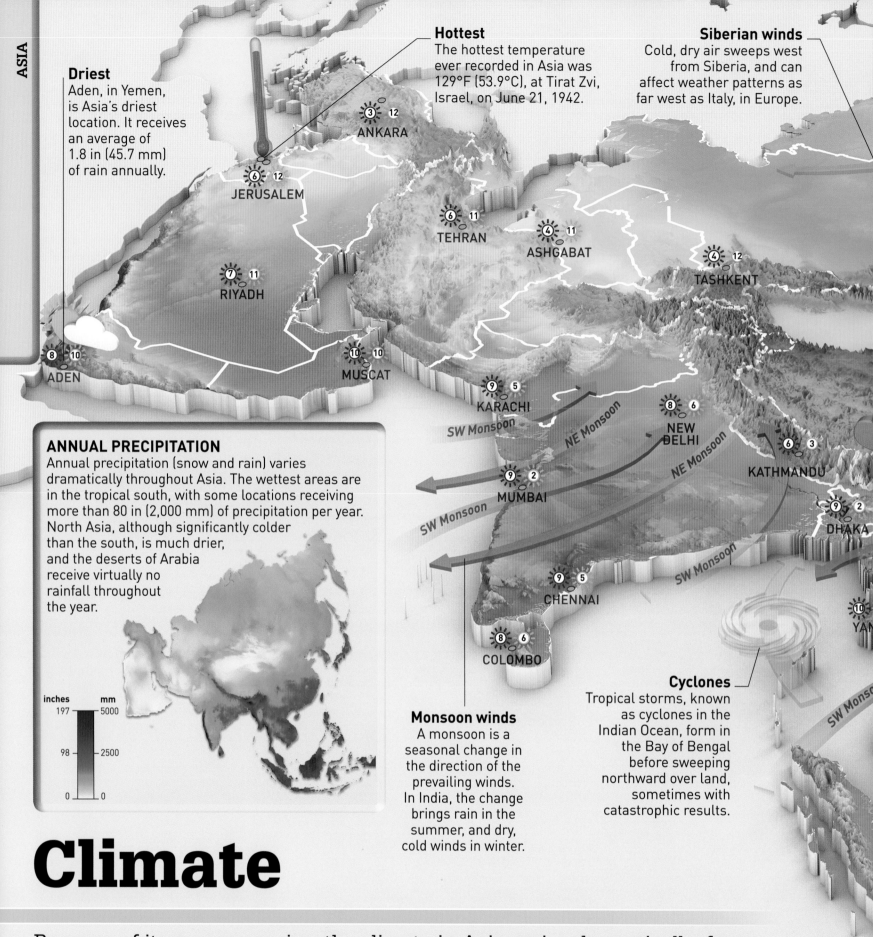

Driest
Aden, in Yemen, is Asia's driest location. It receives an average of 1.8 in (45.7 mm) of rain annually.

Hottest
The hottest temperature ever recorded in Asia was 129°F (53.9°C), at Tirat Zvi, Israel, on June 21, 1942.

Siberian winds
Cold, dry air sweeps west from Siberia, and can affect weather patterns as far west as Italy, in Europe.

ANKARA

JERUSALEM

TEHRAN

ASHGABAT

TASHKENT

RIYADH

ADEN

MUSCAT

KARACHI

NEW DELHI

KATHMANDU

SW Monsoon

NE Monsoon

NE Monsoon

MUMBAI

SW Monsoon

DHAKA

CHENNAI

SW Monsoon

COLOMBO

YAN

SW Monsoon

ANNUAL PRECIPITATION
Annual precipitation (snow and rain) varies dramatically throughout Asia. The wettest areas are in the tropical south, with some locations receiving more than 80 in (2,000 mm) of precipitation per year. North Asia, although significantly colder than the south, is much drier, and the deserts of Arabia receive virtually no rainfall throughout the year.

inches	mm
197	5000
98	2500
0	0

Monsoon winds
A monsoon is a seasonal change in the direction of the prevailing winds. In India, the change brings rain in the summer, and dry, cold winds in winter.

Cyclones
Tropical storms, known as cyclones in the Indian Ocean, form in the Bay of Bengal before sweeping northward over land, sometimes with catastrophic results.

Climate

Because of its enormous size, the climate in Asia varies dramatically, from the polar cold of the north, to the dry, desert environments of the southwest and center, and the hot, humid conditions of the tropical south. The continent is home to some of the coldest, hottest, driest, and wettest places on Earth.

LIFE IN ASIA IS CRITICALLY DEPENDENT ON MONSOON RAINS. A WEAK

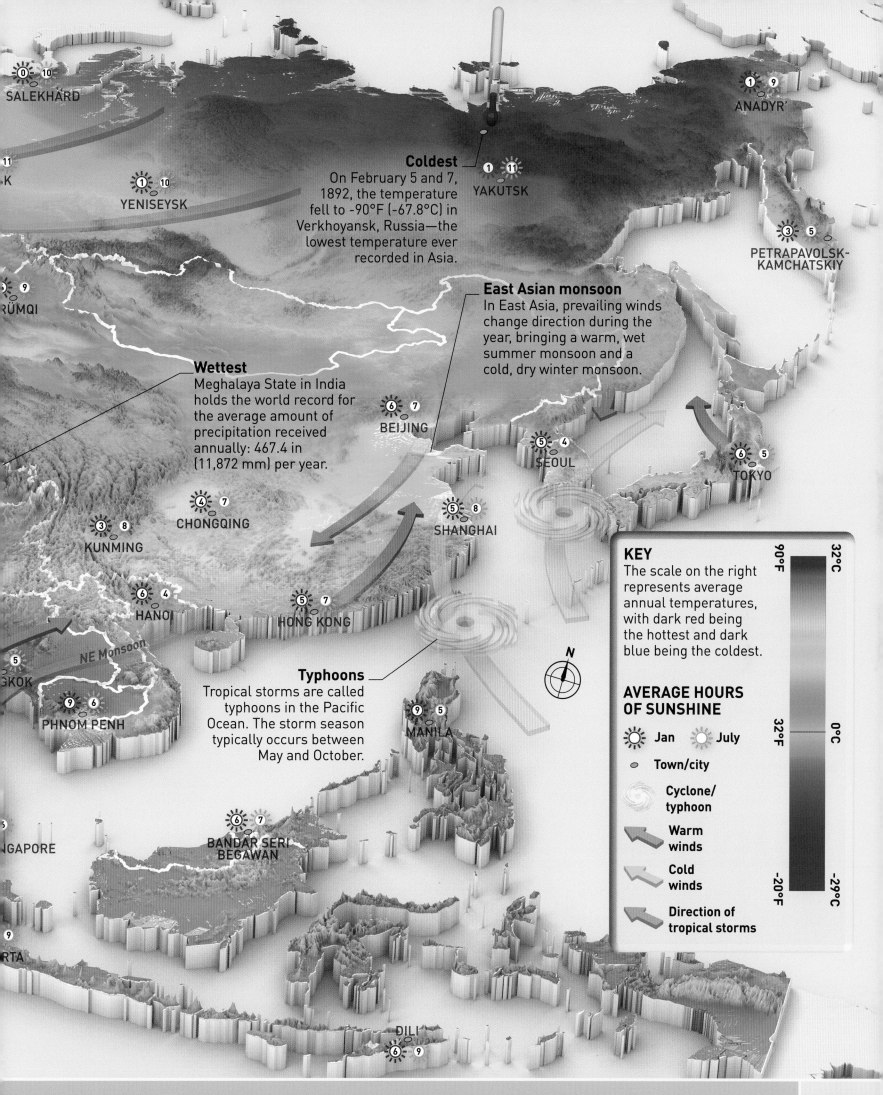

SALEKHARD · 0 · 10

ANADYR' · 1 · 9

YENISEYSK · 1 · 10

Coldest
On February 5 and 7, 1892, the temperature fell to -90°F (-67.8°C) in Verkhoyansk, Russia—the lowest temperature ever recorded in Asia.

YAKUTSK · 1 · 11

PETRAPAVOLSK-KAMCHATSKIY · 3 · 5

ÜRÜMQI · 9

East Asian monsoon
In East Asia, prevailing winds change direction during the year, bringing a warm, wet summer monsoon and a cold, dry winter monsoon.

Wettest
Meghalaya State in India holds the world record for the average amount of precipitation received annually: 467.4 in (11,872 mm) per year.

BEIJING · 6 · 7

SEOUL · 5 · 4

TOKYO · 6 · 5

CHONGQING · 4 · 7

KUNMING · 3 · 8

SHANGHAI · 5 · 8

KEY
The scale on the right represents average annual temperatures, with dark red being the hottest and dark blue being the coldest.

HANOI · 6 · 4

HONG KONG · 5 · 7

NE Monsoon

GKOK · 5

PHNOM PENH · 9 · 6

Typhoons
Tropical storms are called typhoons in the Pacific Ocean. The storm season typically occurs between May and October.

MANILA · 9 · 5

N

90°F / 32°C

32°F / 0°C

AVERAGE HOURS OF SUNSHINE

☀ Jan   ☀ July

⬭ Town/city

🌀 Cyclone/ typhoon

➡ Warm winds

➡ Cold winds

-20°F / -29°C

➡ Direction of tropical storms

BANDAR SERI BEGAWAN · 6 · 7

NGAPORE · 9

RTA

DILI · 6 · 9

Dromedary camel
This single-humped camel can travel up to 100 miles (160 km) a day in the desert without water.

Iranian wolf
Lives in a variety of habitats, from arid deserts to lush forests.

Snow leopard
A large cat that can live at altitudes of up to 14,800 ft (4,500 m). Also known as an "ounce."

Siberian musk deer
During the breeding season, males grow fangs instead of antlers.

Arabian leopard
An opportunistic hunter that lives in mountainous areas.

Bactrian camel
A two-humped camel native to the steppes of Central Asia.

Tibetan fox
A small fox, it is only found on the Plateau of Tibet.

Water buffalo
First domesticated in India 5,000 years ago, it is widespread throughout South Asia.

Bengal tiger
A powerful, nocturnal hunter that preys on large mammals.

BIOMES
The vast continent of Asia is home to virtually every habitat on Earth.

- Ice
- Tundra
- Boreal forest/Taiga
- Temperate coniferous forest
- Temperate broadleaf forest
- Temperate grassland
- Tropical coniferous forest
- Tropical broadleaf forest
- Tropical dry broadleaf forest
- Tropical/sub-tropical grassland
- Mountain
- Desert
- Mangrove

Asian elephant
Slightly smaller than its African counterpart, it is identified by its smaller, rounder ears.

Asian golden cat
An elusive forest predator that preys on small mammals and birds.

Gharial
One of the longest of all living crocodilians, measuring up to 20.5 ft (6.25 m) in length.

Siamang
The largest of the gibbons, it has a throat pouch that can be inflated to the size of its head.

Wildlife

From east to west, the continent of Asia stretches almost halfway around the world. As such, it contains a vast array of habitats, from Arctic tundra and high, cold plateaus, to barren deserts and damp, lush rain forests. The continent's array of wildlife is as vast and varied as the landscape itself.

Sumatran rhinoceros
The smallest of the rhinoceroses, it is one of the world's most endangered species.

MORE PEOPLE DEPEND ON THE WORLD'S 130 MILLION WATER

Polar bear
The largest land carnivore in the world, it is only found in the Arctic.

Arctic fox
Incredibly hardy animal is common throughout the Arctic region.

Baikal seal
Only found in Lake Baikal, Siberia, it is the only true seal that lives exclusively in freshwater.

Steller's sea eagle
Weighing up to 20 lb (9 kg), it is the heaviest eagle in the world.

Giant panda
The rarest member of the bear family, 99 percent of its diet is bamboo.

Siberian tiger
The largest of the tiger species, it can grow up to 13 ft (4 m) in length.

Japanese macaque
The world's most northern-living primate, it is also known as the "snow monkey."

Yak
Similar to the American bison, it is adapted to living at altitude.

King cobra
Reaching lengths of up to 18 ft (5.5 m), it is the world's longest venomous snake.

Deforestation
The world's third-largest area of tropical rainforest lies in Southeast Asia, but the region is experiencing deforestation at a faster rate than anywhere else on Earth. This has a devastating effect on both the region's wildlife and the global climate.

Dhole
A highly social animal well known for its vocal calls.

Clouded leopard
Named for the distinctive clouded spots on its coat, it is an excellent climber.

Proboscis monkey
Its large, fleshy nose is used to attract mates.

Bornean orangutan
The most intelligent of the primates, its name translates as "man of the forest."

Philippine crocodile
A freshwater crocodile, it has a broad snout and thick, bony plates on its body.

Borneo—56 percent of the island's forests were cut down between 1985 and 2001.

Komodo dragon
The world's largest lizard, it can consume 80 percent of its bodyweight in a single meal.

BUFFALO THAN ON ANY OTHER DOMESTICATED ANIMAL ON EARTH.

KEY
Illuminated areas on the map reflect urban, built-up areas and roads, in contrast to rural regions.

▪ **Rural area**

▫ **Urban area**

Trans-Siberian Railway
Bright lights mark a dotted line across Siberia, showing the route of the Trans-Siberian Railway.

Arabian Peninsula
A large portion of the Arabian Peninsula is an area of desert known as the "Empty Quarter."

Oman
This country had the fastest rate of urbanization in Asia over the past five years (8.54 percent).

● **Hong Kong**
Hong Kong has a population of 7.35 million, making it the 21st largest city in Asia, but the city is the fourth most densely populated territory on Earth, with a staggering 17,294 inhabitants per sq mile (6,682 per sq km).

India
Home to 1.27 billion people, but only 32.7 percent of the population live in towns or cities.

Indus Valley
This river valley in northern Pakistan is home to some of the country's largest cities, including Lahore and Islamabad.

Bangkok
Almost one-sixth of Thailand's 68.2 million people live in or around the country's capital, Bangkok.

Singapore
One of three territories in Asia —along with Hong Kong and Macau—in which the entire population live in an urban environment.

By night

This satellite image of Asia at night shows how the continent's huge population is concentrated in small pockets of land. India, northern China, the southern Korean peninsula, and Japan are densely populated, whereas Siberia and Central Asia are virtually empty.

Tokyo-Yokohama
38 million people
live in and around
the cities of Tokyo
and Yokohama.

North Korea
Almost 61 percent of North
Korea's population of 25.1 million
live in an urban environment, but
electricity shortages in the country
mean few lights shine at night.

Philippines
The National Capital
Region of the Philippines,
which includes Manila, the
country's capital, is home
to 12.9 million people.

Sri Lanka
Only 18.4 percent of
Sri Lanka's 22 million
population live in towns
and cities—the lowest
figure of any Asian country.

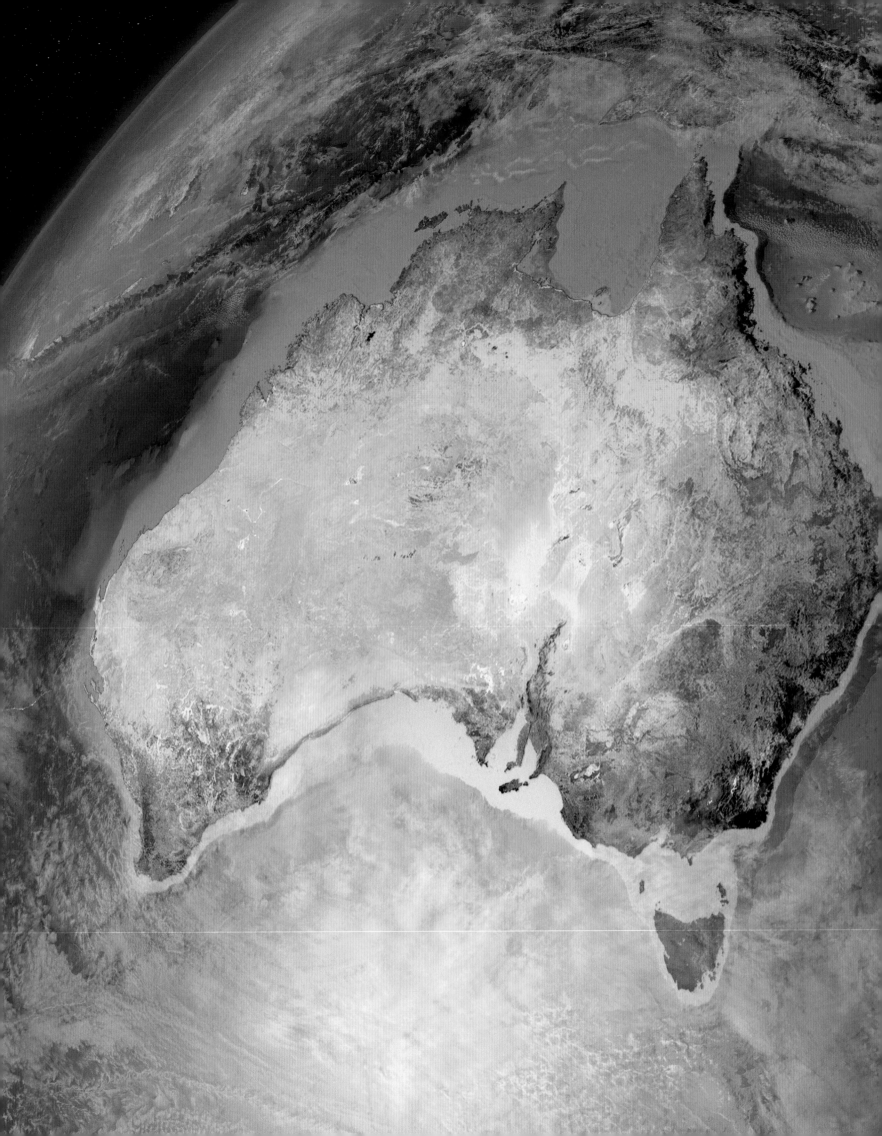

AUSTRALASIA & OCEANIA

Australasia & Oceania from space
Vast deserts dominate the interior of Australia, contrasting with the fertile southeast. To the north, dense forest covers much of New Guinea, while in the far south, the snowy peaks of New Zealand's mountains stand out clearly.

KEY
● Capital city   ● Major city

PACIFIC OCEAN

Wake
Island
(to US)

Marshall Islands
Conquered during World
War Two, these islands
belonged to the United
States until 1986.

MARSHALL
ISLANDS

MAJURO

Northern Mariana
Islands
(to US)

*Philippine
Sea*

HAGÅTÑA

Guam
(to US)

PALIKIR

TA

M I C R O N E S I A

K

NAURU

MELEKEOK

PALAU

*Bismarck
Sea*

HONIARA

SOLOMON
ISLANDS

PAPUA NEW GUINEA

*Solomon
Sea*

PORT MORESBY

VANUATU

ASIA

PORT

New Caledonia
One of the three groups
of islands in the Pacific
Ocean that are controlled
by France. The others are
French Polynesia and
Wallis and Futuna.

NO

Arafura Sea

*Coral
Sea*

Cairns

New Caledo
(to France)

*Gulf of
Carpentaria*

Townsville

*Joseph
Bonaparte
Gulf*

Darwin

QUEENSLAND

Brisbane

Lord Howe Is
(to Australia

*Timor
Sea*

NORTHERN

TERRITORY

Alice Springs

A U S T R A L I A

NEW
SOUTH WALES

Sydney

WESTERN

SOUTH AUSTRALIA

CANBERRA

AUSTRALIAN
CAPITAL TERRITORY

AUSTRALIA

Adelaide

VICTORIA
Melbourne

*Tasman
Sea*

*Great
Australian
Bight*

TASMANIA
Hobart

Perth

Australia
Canberra was chosen to be
Australia's capital city in
1908. The country is made
up of eight states.

N

THE BRITISH MONARCH, QUEEN ELIZABETH II, IS ALSO

Kiribati

This group of 33 tiny islands is spread over a vast area of the Pacific Ocean. Kiribati was a British colony from 1915 until it gained its independence in 1979.

● Nauru

The Republic of Nauru is the world's smallest island nation, with a total area of 8 sq miles (21 sq km) and a population of just 9,591. The oval-shaped island is surrounded by sandy beaches and a coral reef.

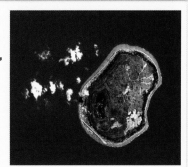

I B A T I

FUNAFITI
ATOLL

TUVALU

Tokelau
(to NZ)

Wallis and
Futuna
(to France)

MATA-
UTU

ÁPIA

PAGO
PAGO

SAMOA

American
Samoa
(to US)

K I R I B A T I

Cook
Islands
(to NZ)

PAPEETE

SUVA

NUKU'ALOFA

ALOFI
Niue
(to NZ)

AVARUA

French
Polynesia
(to France)

FIJI

TONGA

French Polynesia

Tahiti is the largest island in French Polynesia. Many people work in tourism and pearl-farming.

New Zealand

Most New Zealanders have European ancestors, but about 15 percent of the population belong to the Maori community. The Maoris arrived in New Zealand in about 1300.

Auckland

NEW
ZEALAND

WELLINGTON

Christchurch

-folk Island
Australia)

Countries and borders

Australasia is dominated by Australia and New Zealand, two former British colonies that, in recent years, have built new relations with other Pacific nations, such as Japan. Oceania includes the many islands of the Pacific Ocean, whose communities rely increasingly on tourism.

FAST FACTS

Total land area:
3,285,049 sq miles
(8,508,238 sq km)

Total population:
39.7 million

Number of countries: 14

Largest country:
Australia—
2,988,901 sq miles
(7,741,220 sq km)

Smallest country:
Nauru— 8.1 sq miles
(21 sq km)

Largest country population:
Australia—22.9 million

③ Lake Eyre

With an area of 3,700 sq miles (9,583 sq km), Lake Eyre is the largest lake in Australasia and Oceania. During the dry season, much of the lake evaporates, leaving behind a thick salt crust.

Lake Eyre sometimes turns pink because of a type of algae in the water.

Marshall Islands

A group of 34 scattered atolls (low-lying islands made of coral reefs) in the Pacific Ocean. The average height of each island is only 6.6 ft (2 m) above sea level.

New Guinea

The world's second-largest island after Greenland, New Guinea is dominated by the New Guinea Highlands.

Kimberley Plateau

Rocky gorges and sandstone hills dominate this isolated region of Western Australia.

Great Dividing Range

These mountains divide the fertile coastal plain from the dry interior.

Southern Alps

These young mountains are growing rapidly as the Australian and Pacific plates move toward one another.

Micr

Mariana Islands

Saipan

Guam

Yap

Babeldaob

Philippine Sea

Northern Mariana Islands

Chuuk

Caroline Islands

Bikini Atoll

Ratak Chain

Enewetak

Marshall Islands

Ralik Chain

Pohnpei

Kosrae

Tarawa

Nauru

M e l a n e s i

Mount Wilhelm **14,793 ft / 4,509 m**

Bismarck Archipelago

Admiralty Islands

New Ireland

Bismarck Sea

New Britain

Solomon Islands

Bougainville Island

Tungaru

Solomon Sea

New Georgia Islands

Santa Cruz Islands

Espiritu Santo

ASIA

New Guinea

①

④

Kikori

Fly

Louisiade Archipelago

Torres Strait

Arafura Sea

Cape York Peninsula

Coral Sea

Great Barrier Reef

New Caledo

Timor Sea

Joseph Bonaparte Gulf

Arnhem Land

Gulf of Carpentaria

Kimberley Plateau

Barkly Tableland

Tanami Desert

Fortescue

Ashburton

Great Sandy Desert

Macdonnell Ranges

Uluru **(Ayers Rock) 2,844 ft / 867 m**

Simpson Desert

Lake Eyre North

③

Lake Torrens

Flinders Ranges

Grey Range

Darling

Barwon

Lachlan

Great Dividing Range

Cape Byron

Lord Howe Island

Mount **Kosciuszko 7,310 ft / 2,228 m**

Gibson Desert

Great Victoria Desert

Lake Everard

Lake Gairdner

Murray

②

Australian Alps

Tasma Sea

Murchison

Nullarbor Plain

Great Australian Bight

Kangaroo Island

King Island

Furneaux Group

Tasmania

Darling Range

N

SOME OF THE OLDEST ROCKS ON EARTH—DATING BACK 4.4

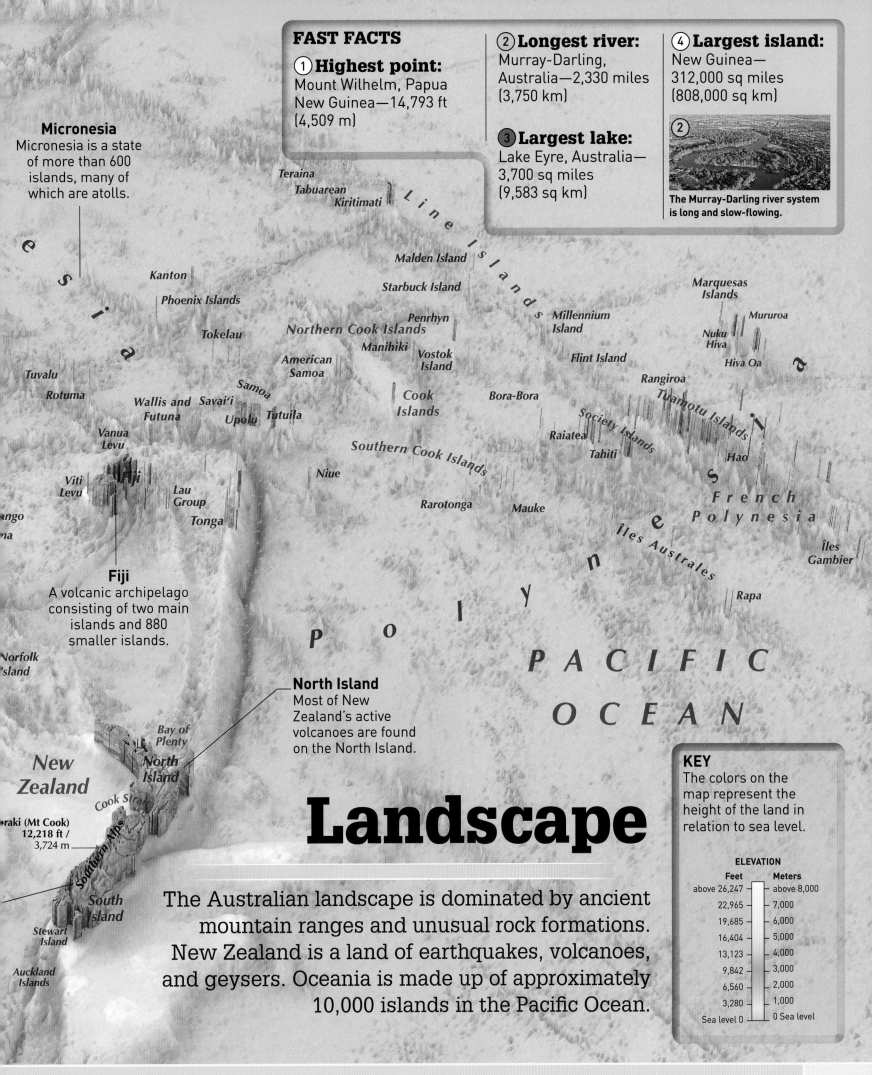

Micronesia
Micronesia is a state of more than 600 islands, many of which are atolls.

Teraina
Tabuarean
Kiritimati

Line Islands

Malden Island

Kanton
Starbuck Island

Phoenix Islands

Millennium Island

Marquesas Islands

Mururoa

Tokelau
Penrhyn

Nuku Hiva

Manihiki
Flint Island

Hiva Oa

Tuvalu

American Samoa
Vostok Island

Rangiroa

Rotuma

Samoa

Cook Islands
Bora-Bora

Tuamotu Islands

Wallis and Futuna
Savai'i
Upolu
Tutuila

Society Islands

Raiatea

Hao

Vanua Levu
Tahiti

Viti Levu
Fiji

Lau Group

Southern Cook Islands

Niue
French Polynesia

ango
na
Tonga
Rarotonga
Mauke
Îles Gambier

Rapa

Fiji
A volcanic archipelago consisting of two main islands and 880 smaller islands.

Îles Australes

Norfolk Island

P o l y n e s i a

North Island
Most of New Zealand's active volcanoes are found on the North Island.

PACIFIC

OCEAN

Bay of Plenty
North Island

New Zealand

Cook Str.

raki (Mt Cook)
12,218 ft / 3,724 m

Southern Alps

South Island

Landscape

Stewart Island

Auckland Islands

The Australian landscape is dominated by ancient mountain ranges and unusual rock formations. New Zealand is a land of earthquakes, volcanoes, and geysers. Oceania is made up of approximately 10,000 islands in the Pacific Ocean.

BILLION YEARS—HAVE BEEN FOUND IN WESTERN AUSTRALIA.

Fascinating facts

COUNTRY WITH THE MOST NEIGHBORS

 Papua New Guinea
1—Indonesia

LONGEST TUNNELS

 Railroad tunnel
Kaimai Tunnel, North Island, New Zealand—5.5 miles (8.85 km)

 Road tunnel
Airport Link, Brisbane, Australia—4.16 miles (6.7 km)

Number of time zones
11

The world is split into 39 time zones. Most are set whole hours ahead or behind Coordinated Universal Time (UCT) – the time at the Greenwich Meridian in London, UK. Some, however, are whole hours plus 30 or 45 minutes ahead or behind UCT. Therefore, on this map, if it was 12:00 in London, it would be 22:00 in Sydney, Australia (10 hours ahead of UCT).

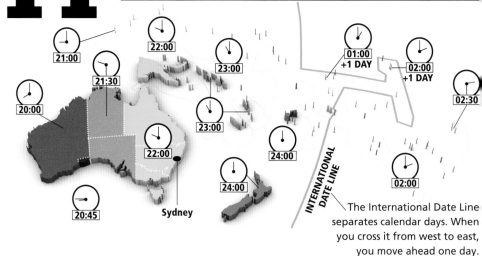

The International Date Line separates calendar days. When you cross it from west to east, you move ahead one day.

 ## Longest coastline
Australia—**16,006.5 miles (25,760 km)**

Busiest port
Port Hedland, Western Australia—**537,927 kilotons of cargo per year,** making it the eighth-busiest port in the world

Fastest train
Tilt Train, Australia—**130.5 mph (210 km/h)**

Q1 Gold Coast, Australia 1,060 ft (323 m)

Tallest buildings

Eureka Tower Melbourne, Australia 974 ft (297 m)

120 Collins Street Melbourne, Australia 869 ft (265 m)

101 Collins Street Melbourne, Australia 853 ft (260 m)

Prima Pearl Melbourne, Australia 833 ft (254 m)

 Busiest airport Sydney Airport, Sydney, Australia—**39.7 million passengers per year**

BRIDGES

Longest bridge: Macleay River Bridge, Australia — **2 miles (3.2 km)**

○ **Tallest bridge:** Mohaka Viaduct, Raupunga, New Zealand—**312 ft (95 m)**

WATERFALLS

Highest: **Browne Falls, New Zealand**— 2,744 ft (836 m)

Largest (by volume): **Huka Falls, Taupo, New Zealand**— 7,769 ft³ (220 m³) of water per second

LAKES

Largest lake: Lake Eyre, Australia— **3,700 sq miles (9,583 sq km)**

○ **Deepest lake:** Lake Hauroko, New Zealand—**1,516 ft (462 m)**

Most visited cities (Visitors per year)

Sydney, Australia
2.853 million

Melbourne, Australia
2.166 million

Auckland, NZ
1.965 million

Christchurch, NZ
1.732 million

Brisbane, Australia
1.066 million

Highest mountains

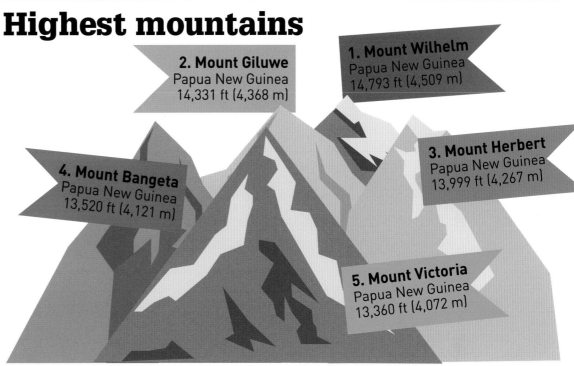

2. Mount Giluwe Papua New Guinea 14,331 ft (4,368 m)

1. Mount Wilhelm Papua New Guinea 14,793 ft (4,509 m)

3. Mount Herbert Papua New Guinea 13,999 ft (4,267 m)

4. Mount Bangeta Papua New Guinea 13,520 ft (4,121 m)

5. Mount Victoria Papua New Guinea 13,360 ft (4,072 m)

TALLEST VOLCANO

Mount Giluwe, Papua New Guinea—**14,331 ft (4,368 m)**

Australasia and Oceania's extreme points

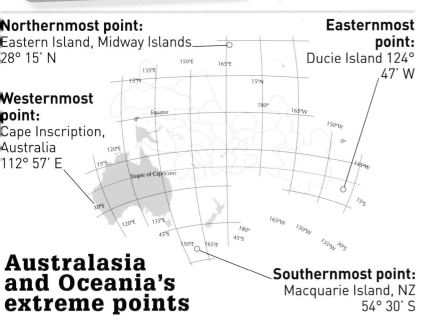

Northernmost point:
Eastern Island, Midway Islands 28° 15′ N

Westernmost point:
Cape Inscription, Australia 112° 57′ E

Easternmost point:
Ducie Island 124° 47′ W

Southernmost point:
Macquarie Island, NZ 54° 30′ S

BIGGEST GLACIER

Tasman Glacier, New Zealand— **17 miles (27 km) long, with an area of 39 sq miles (101 sq km)**

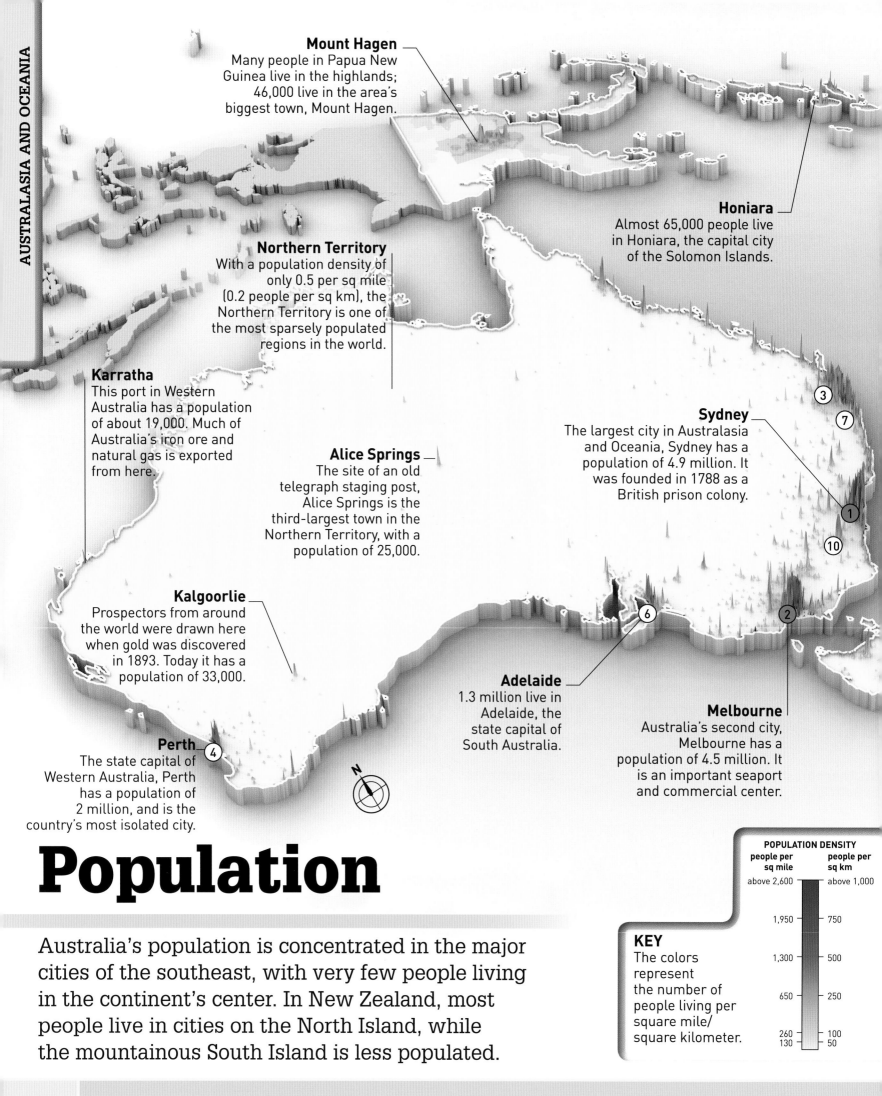

Mount Hagen
Many people in Papua New Guinea live in the highlands; 46,000 live in the area's biggest town, Mount Hagen.

Honiara
Almost 65,000 people live in Honiara, the capital city of the Solomon Islands.

Northern Territory
With a population density of only 0.5 per sq mile (0.2 people per sq km), the Northern Territory is one of the most sparsely populated regions in the world.

Karratha
This port in Western Australia has a population of about 19,000. Much of Australia's iron ore and natural gas is exported from here.

Sydney
The largest city in Australasia and Oceania, Sydney has a population of 4.9 million. It was founded in 1788 as a British prison colony.

Alice Springs
The site of an old telegraph staging post, Alice Springs is the third-largest town in the Northern Territory, with a population of 25,000.

Kalgoorlie
Prospectors from around the world were drawn here when gold was discovered in 1893. Today it has a population of 33,000.

Adelaide
1.3 million live in Adelaide, the state capital of South Australia.

Melbourne
Australia's second city, Melbourne has a population of 4.5 million. It is an important seaport and commercial center.

Perth
The state capital of Western Australia, Perth has a population of 2 million, and is the country's most isolated city.

Population

Australia's population is concentrated in the major cities of the southeast, with very few people living in the continent's center. In New Zealand, most people live in cities on the North Island, while the mountainous South Island is less populated.

POPULATION DENSITY

people per sq mile	people per sq km
above 2,600	above 1,000
1,950	750
1,300	500
650	250
260	100
130	50

KEY
The colors represent the number of people living per square mile/ square kilometer.

AUSTRALIA IS THE WORLD'S SIXTH-LARGEST COUNTRY

Fiji

Fiji has a population of 915,303. Its largest town is Nasinu, which is home to 87,000 people.

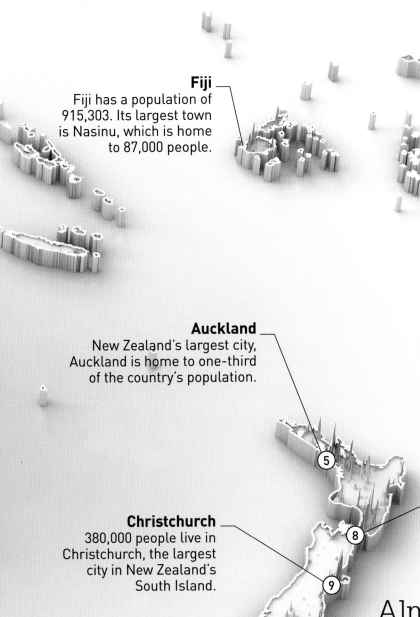

Auckland

New Zealand's largest city, Auckland is home to one-third of the country's population.

Christchurch

380,000 people live in Christchurch, the largest city in New Zealand's South Island.

Wellington

New Zealand's capital, Wellington has a population of 400,000 and is the country's second-largest city.

Australasia and Oceania's largest cities

The list below is based on the number of people living inside a city's boundaries.

1. **Sydney, Australia—4.9 million**
2. **Melbourne, Australia—4.5 million**
3. **Brisbane, Australia—2.3 million**
4. **Perth, Australia—2 million**
5. **Auckland, New Zealand—1.4 million**
6. **Adelaide, Australia—1.3 million**
7. **Gold Coast, Australia—530,000**
8. **Wellington, New Zealand—400,000**
9. **Christchurch, New Zealand—389,000**
10. **Canberra, Australia—380,000**

Melbourne is the capital city of the Australian state of Victoria.

Almost *one in three* Australians were born **outside** the country.

BY NIGHT

The brightly lit cities of southeastern Australia shine brightly, and Sydney, Melbourne, and Brisbane are easy to spot. In contrast, the country's interior is shrouded in darkness. Auckland and Wellington are two of the bright points on New Zealand's North Island, with only Christchurch standing out on South Island.

KEY

■ Rural area

▨ Urban area

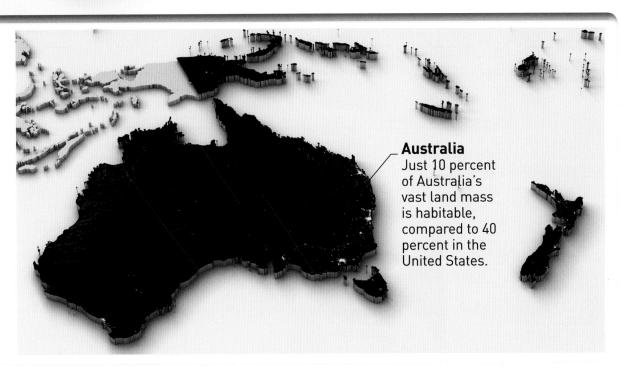

Australia

Just 10 percent of Australia's vast land mass is habitable, compared to 40 percent in the United States.

New Zealand

Almost one-third of New Zealand has been set aside as protected national park. Among its incredible range of landscapes are the towering peaks of the Southern Alps, and the geysers and hot springs of North Island.

Mount Aspiring National Park
Soaring peaks, alpine lakes, and dense forests make this one of the country's most beautiful national parks.

Fiordland National Park
Fourteen beautiful fjords cut their way through rugged mountain scenery in this remote wilderness. The fjords are home to fur seals, dolphins, and penguins.

Queenstown
One of the biggest tourist resorts in the South Island, Queenstown attracts lovers of extreme sports, such as bungee jumping and white-water rafting.

T a s m a n   S e a

S o u t h e

Livingstone Mountains

*La
Waka*

Queens

F i o r d l a n d   S o u t

Kepler Mountains

Lake Te Anau

Te Anau

Takitimu Mountains

Hunter Mountains

Kaherekoau Mts

Cameron Mts

Resolution Island

Te Waewae Bay

Southland
South Island's most southerly region is sparsely populated, with only 7.4 people per sq mile (2.9 people per sq km).

T a s m a n   S e a

Puysegur Point

Milford Sound
This 10-mile (16-km) long fjord is one of the highlights of the Fiordland National Park. The surrounding mountains are very popular with hikers.

Lake Te Anau
With a depth of up to 1,368 ft (417 m), Lake Te Anau contains the largest amount of freshwater in Australasia and Oceania. It is a popular destination for fishing and water sports.

A ROCK SLIDE IN 1991 TOOK 131 FT (40 M) FROM THE

Ruapehu
One of the most active volcanoes in New Zealand, Ruapehu is also a popular ski resort.

Franz Josef Glacier
This glacier descends from the Southern Alps into the lush forests 984 ft (300 m) above sea level.

Rotorua
The volcanic lake at Rotorua is surrounded by bubbling mud pools and hot springs. The Pohutu Geyser fires hot water 98.4 ft (30 m) into the air.

Pegasus Bay

Christchurch

Canterbury Plains

Canterbury Bight

A l p s

Lake Tekapo

Lake Pukaki

Dunstan Mountains

Hawkdun Range

Kakanui Mountains

tains

Garvie Mountains

Lammerlaw Range

Dunedin

Balclutha

C a t l i n s

Invercargill

Invercargill
New Zealand's southernmost city is home to 50,000 people.

Toetoes Bay

Ruapuke Island

The Catlins
This remote region is known for its rugged coastline and rolling, wooded hills.

Aoraki
New Zealand's highest mountain, Aoraki, is 12,218 ft (3,724 m) high. It is surrounded by eight of the country's largest glaciers.

F o v e a u x   S t r a i t

P A C I F I C

O C E A N

Codfish Island

Stewart Island

Shelter Point

Stewart Island
About 85 percent of New Zealand's third largest island is set aside as national park. Stewart Island is home to one of the country's biggest populations of kiwis.

Rock islands,
Southern Lagoon, Palau

Spirit house
These long timber buildings are places in which Melanesian tribes practice rituals. They are reserved for men.

Mount Tavurvur,
New Britain Island, Papua New Guinea

Spirit house,
Sepik River, Papua New Guinea

Parliament House,
Port Moresby, Papua New Guinea

Kakadu rock art,
Australia

Cattle stations,
Barkly Tableland, Australia

Kuranda Scenic Railwa
Queensland rainforest Australia

Florence Falls
The forests of Litchfield National Park are home to this beautiful double waterfall.

Florence Falls,
Australia

Wolfe Creek
A meteorite collision 300,000 years ago left this well-preserved crater.

Bungle Bungle,
Purnululu National Park, Australia

**Karlu Karlu
(Devil's Marbles),**
Northern Territory

Diamantina National Park
Queensland

**Wolfe Creek
meteor crater,**
Western Australia

Gosses Bluff Crater,
Australia

**Burrup Peninsula
rock art,**
Western Australia

**Uluru
(Ayers Rock),**
Northern Territory

Lake Eyre,
South Australia

**Karijini
National Park,**
Western Australia

**Trans-Australian
Railway,** *Nullarbor Plain, Australia*

Swan Bells,
Perth, Western Australia

Bunda Cliffs, *Nullarbor Plain, South Australia*

Adelaide Ova
Adelaide, Austral

○ Uluru (Ayers Rock)
This huge mass of sandstone appears to change color during the day as the sun reflects on its different minerals.

Pinnacles Desert,
Western Australia

Fremantle Prison
Built for British convicts in the 1850s, this prison is now a tourist site.

Fremantle Prison,
Western Australia

ANZAC Memorial,
Western Australia

N

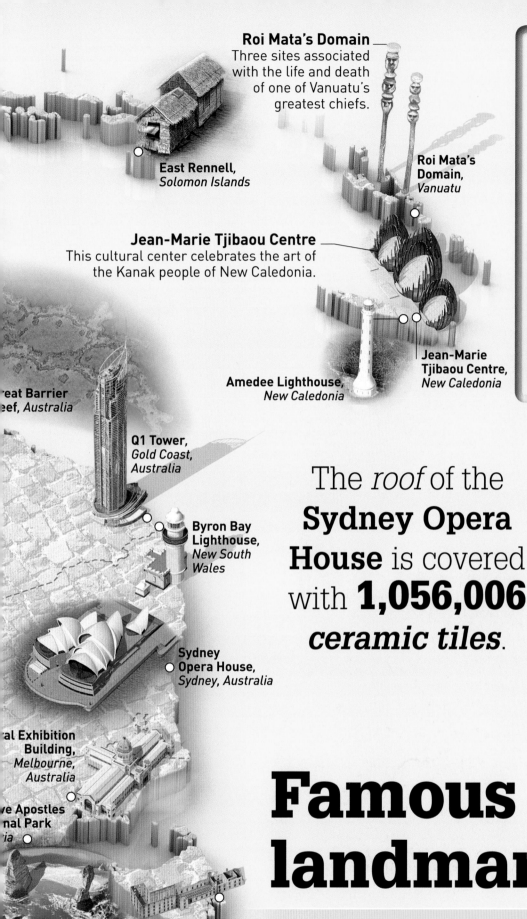

Roi Mata's Domain
Three sites associated with the life and death of one of Vanuatu's greatest chiefs.

East Rennell, *Solomon Islands*

Roi Mata's Domain, *Vanuatu*

Jean-Marie Tjibaou Centre
This cultural center celebrates the art of the Kanak people of New Caledonia.

Amedee Lighthouse, *New Caledonia*

Jean-Marie Tjibaou Centre, *New Caledonia*

reat Barrier eef, *Australia*

Q1 Tower, *Gold Coast, Australia*

Byron Bay Lighthouse, *New South Wales*

Sydney Opera House, *Sydney, Australia*

al Exhibition Building, *Melbourne, Australia*

e Apostles nal Park ia

Port Arthur Historic Site, *Tasmania*

The *roof* of the **Sydney Opera House** is covered with **1,056,006** *ceramic tiles*.

● **The Great Barrier Reef**
One of the natural wonders of the world, the Great Barrier Reef stretches for 2,600 km (1,600 miles) along the northeastern coast of Australia. The reef is made of coral, which is built by billions of tiny creatures over hundreds of years. It is home to about 1,500 species of fish, 14 species of sea snake, and more than 3,000 different types of mollusc.

Sky Tower, *Auckland, New Zealand*

Mount Ngauruhoe,
This active volcano is situated at the heart of New Zealand's oldest national park.

Mount Ngauruhoe, *Tongariro National Park, New Zealand*

Milford Sound, *Te Wahipounamu, New Zealand*

Moeraki Boulders, *Hampden, New Zealand*

Famous landmarks

The rock formations of the Australian Outback and the dramatic scenery of New Zealand's fjordland are just two of the region's many natural wonders. The region is also home to some iconic modern architecture, such as the Sydney Opera House.

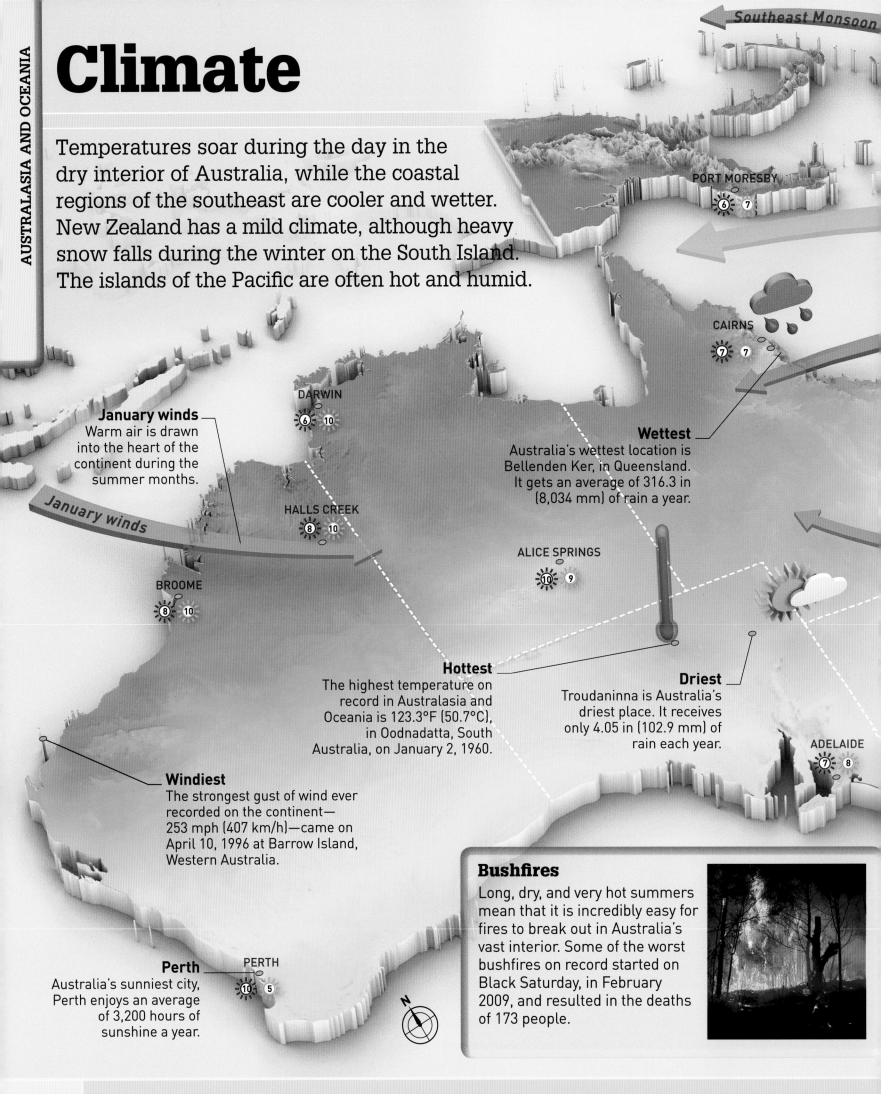

Climate

Temperatures soar during the day in the dry interior of Australia, while the coastal regions of the southeast are cooler and wetter. New Zealand has a mild climate, although heavy snow falls during the winter on the South Island. The islands of the Pacific are often hot and humid.

Southeast Monsoon

PORT MORESBY
6 7

CAIRNS
7 7

DARWIN
6 10

January winds
Warm air is drawn into the heart of the continent during the summer months.

January winds

Wettest
Australia's wettest location is Bellenden Ker, in Queensland. It gets an average of 316.3 in (8,034 mm) of rain a year.

HALLS CREEK
8 10

ALICE SPRINGS
10 9

BROOME
8 10

Hottest
The highest temperature on record in Australasia and Oceania is 123.3°F (50.7°C), in Oodnadatta, South Australia, on January 2, 1960.

Driest
Troudaninna is Australia's driest place. It receives only 4.05 in (102.9 mm) of rain each year.

ADELAIDE
7 8

Windiest
The strongest gust of wind ever recorded on the continent— 253 mph (407 km/h)—came on April 10, 1996 at Barrow Island, Western Australia.

Bushfires
Long, dry, and very hot summers mean that it is incredibly easy for fires to break out in Australia's vast interior. Some of the worst bushfires on record started on Black Saturday, in February 2009, and resulted in the deaths of 173 people.

PERTH
10 5

Perth
Australia's sunniest city, Perth enjoys an average of 3,200 hours of sunshine a year.

N

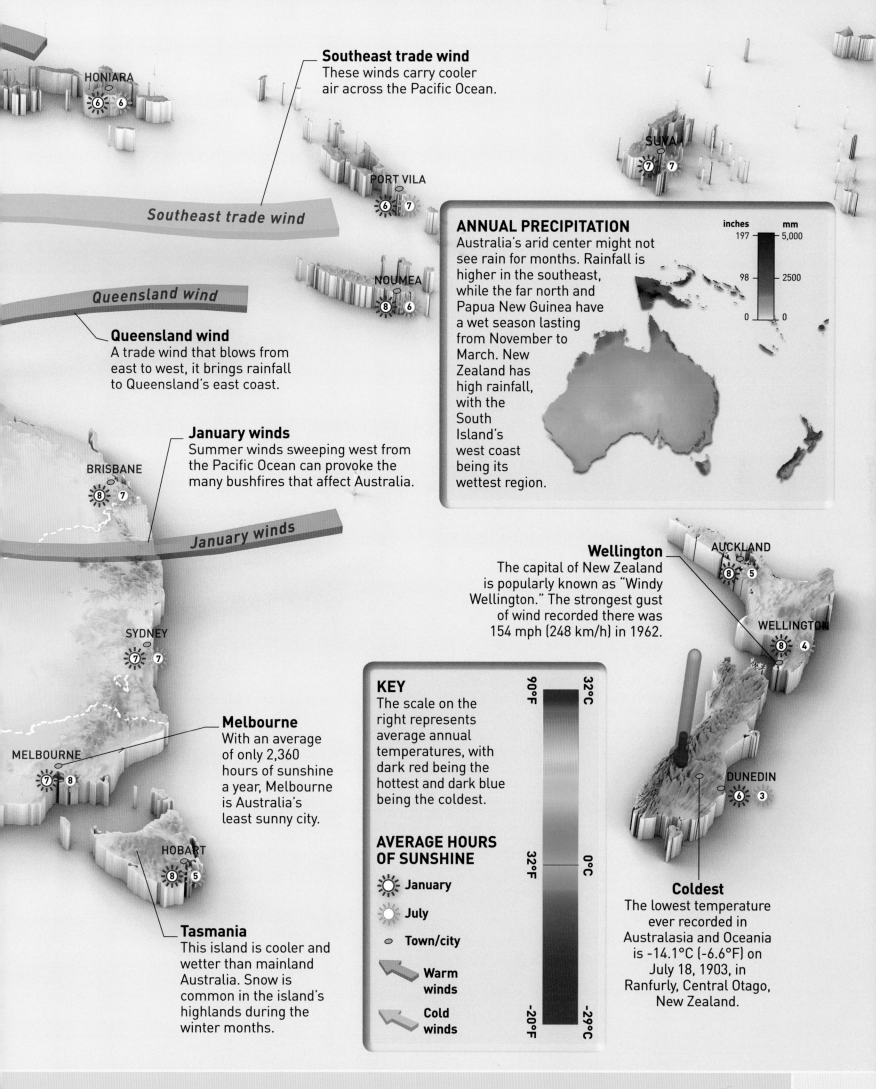

Southeast trade wind
These winds carry cooler air across the Pacific Ocean.

HONIARA
6 6

SUVA
7 7

Southeast trade wind

PORT VILA
6 7

Queensland wind

NOUMEA
8 6

Queensland wind
A trade wind that blows from east to west, it brings rainfall to Queensland's east coast.

ANNUAL PRECIPITATION
Australia's arid center might not see rain for months. Rainfall is higher in the southeast, while the far north and Papua New Guinea have a wet season lasting from November to March. New Zealand has high rainfall, with the South Island's west coast being its wettest region.

inches   mm
197 ┌─┐ 5,000
98 │ │ 2500
0   └─┘ 0

January winds
Summer winds sweeping west from the Pacific Ocean can provoke the many bushfires that affect Australia.

BRISBANE
8 7

January winds

Wellington
The capital of New Zealand is popularly known as "Windy Wellington." The strongest gust of wind recorded there was 154 mph (248 km/h) in 1962.

AUCKLAND
8 5

WELLINGTON
8 4

SYDNEY
7 7

KEY
The scale on the right represents average annual temperatures, with dark red being the hottest and dark blue being the coldest.

90°F   32°C
32°F   0°C
-20°F   -29°C

Melbourne
With an average of only 2,360 hours of sunshine a year, Melbourne is Australia's least sunny city.

MELBOURNE
7 8

AVERAGE HOURS OF SUNSHINE

☀ January

☀ July

⬭ Town/city

⬅ Warm winds

⬅ Cold winds

DUNEDIN
6 3

HOBART
8 5

Coldest
The lowest temperature ever recorded in Australasia and Oceania is -14.1°C (-6.6°F) on July 18, 1903, in Ranfurly, Central Otago, New Zealand.

Tasmania
This island is cooler and wetter than mainland Australia. Snow is common in the island's highlands during the winter months.

TO FIND THOUSANDS OF SPIDERS HAD RAINED ONTO THEIR TOWN.

BIOMES

Deserts and temperate broadleaf forest are dominant in Australia, while the mountain habitat of the Southern Alps dominates New Zealand.

- Temperate broadleaf forest
- Temperate grassland
- Mediterranean
- Tropical broadleaf forest
- Tropical dry broadleaf forest
- Tropical/subtropical grassland
- Mountain
- Desert
- Mangrove

Sir David's echidna
This spiny anteater, named for British naturalist Sir David Attenborough, is critically endangered.

Southern cassowary
Its hornlike crest helps this bird push head-first through vegetation.

Queen Alexandra birdwing butterfly
The world's largest butterfly, it has a wingspan of up to 12 in (31 cm).

Cuscus
This possum uses its strong tail to climb through trees.

Clownfish
This fish hides amo the poisonous tentacles of sea anemo

Saltwater crocodile
The largest of the reptiles, this crocodile drowns its prey by rolling it in the water.

Frilled lizard
When threatened, this lizard opens a flap of skin to warn off predators.

Black flying fox
This fruit bat's wingspan reaches up to 6.6 ft (2 m).

Dingo
Descended from prehistoric domestic dogs, dingoes are widespread throughout Australia.

Cockatoo
These noisy parrots gather in flocks that can include several hundred birds.

Walla
Like their larg cousin, the kangar wallabies carry th young in pouch

Blue-spotted stingray
Hiding patiently on the seabed, this ray ambushes passing snails and crabs.

Kangaroo
These animals are marsupials, meaning that females nurture their young in pouches.

Spiny anteater
One of the few mammals to lay eggs, the spiny anteater is protected by sharp spines.

Wombat
This marsupial lives in complex burrows that can be up to 660 ft (200 m) long.

Inland taipan
The most venomou land snake in the world, its prey includes rats and ot small mammals.

Dwarf bearded dragon
This small lizard lives off insects, invertebrates, and small mammals.

Western brown snake
This fast-moving snake preys on mice and lizards.

Redback spider
A bite from this spider can cause pain, sickness, and convulsions.

Emu
Australia's largest bird can reach up to 6.2 ft (1.9 m) in height. Its shaggy plumage resembles hair.

Tiger snake
This extremely venomous snake preys on frogs, lizards, birds, and small mammals.

Numbat
This marsupial rips open termite nests with its powerful front teeth and claws.

Poisonous snakes

Some of the world's most dangerous snakes live in Australia. The eastern brown snake causes the most deaths, followed by the western brown snake, and the tiger snake.

The eastern brown snake car be extremely aggressive.

Banded sea krait
The coral reef provides a hunting ground for this highly venomous sea snake.

Fijian monkey-faced bat
This bat can only be found on Fiji, but is endangered due to habitat loss.

Coconut crab
The largest land-living crab in the world uses its pincers to pierce coconut shells.

The *platypus* has a pair of **venomous spurs** on its hind legs.

Giant manta ray
To feed, this ray pulls in water through its mouth, collecting up to 66 lb (30 kg) of plankton each day.

Koala
Eucalyptus leaves provide the koala with its staple diet.

Green turtle
This turtle feeds on seagrasses and is found throughout the region's seas.

Kiwi
This nocturnal, flightless bird preys on earthworms and other invertebrates.

Regent bowerbird
The male's plumage is glossy black and gold, while the female's is drab olive-brown.

Dusky dolphin
Highly acrobatic, these dolphins can be found in the coastal waters around New Zealand.

Lyrebird
During courtship, the male displays an extraordinary repertoire of songs.

Kakapo
This large, flightless parrot lives off seeds and fruit.

Duck-billed platypus
With its webbed feet and paddlelike tail, the platypus is well equipped for its semi-aquatic life.

New Zealand sea lion
This highly endangered sea lion preys on crabs and penguins in the seas around New Zealand's South Island.

okaburra
own for its ghing call, kookaburra s mice and all reptiles.

Tasmanian devil
The size of a small dog, this ferocious marsupial feeds on animal carcasses.

Wildlife

Australia and New Zealand are home to some weird and wonderful animals, among them egg-laying mammals, marsupials, and flightless birds. The seas of Oceania, meanwhile, are home to turtles, dolphins, and an extraordinary range of tropical fish.

POLAR REGIONS

Extreme cold

The North and South Poles are the northernmost and southernmost points on Earth. The climate there is extremely harsh, with temperatures rarely rising above 32°F (0°C).

South Pole Station
The Amundsen-Scott research station is located at the Geographical South Pole. First opened in 1956, it can house up to 200 researchers.

Southern elephant seal
The largest of all seals, males can be over 20 ft (6 m) long and weigh up to 8,800 lb (4,000 kg).

Vinson Massif
Part of a large mountain range by the Ronne Ice Shelf, this massif contains Antarctica's highest peak, Mount Vinson, at 16,050 ft (4,892 m).

Antarctic minke whale
This small whale lives in groups of two to four.

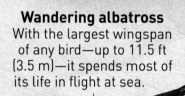

Antarctic ice fish
A type of anti-freeze in its blood enables this fish to survive in ice-cold water.

Wandering albatross
With the largest wingspan of any bird—up to 11.5 ft (3.5 m)—it spends most of its life in flight at sea.

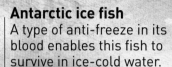

Snowy sheathbill
This bird does not swim, so it steals fish, and eggs or chicks, from penguins.

South polar skua
Up to 21 in (53 cm) tall, this large bird breeds in Antarctica before returning to a life on the oceans.

Antarctic toothfish
Growing up to 5.6 ft (1.7 m) long, this fish feeds on squid, crabs, shrimp, and smaller fish.

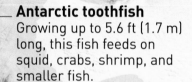

Leopard seal
This fierce, sharp-toothed predator hunts other seals, penguins, and fish.

Antarctica

Earth's southernmost continent is the coldest region in the world, with temperatures reaching as low as -135.8°F (-93.2°C). Despite the harsh conditions, the continent is home to a number of animals. However, climate change is a threat to both Antarctica's animals and landscape.

Ross Ice Shelf
This enormous layer of floating ice is over 370 miles (600 km) long. About 90 percent of its ice lies underwater.

ANTARCTICA CONTAINS ABOUT 90 PERCENT OF THE WORLD'S ICE. IF

Orca
In fact the largest of all dolphins, this is one of the world's most powerful predators.

Colossal squid
This squid is up to 46 ft (14 m) long, and has sharp hooks on its limbs.

Antarctic fur seal
Males battle for territory during the breeding season when these seals gather in vast numbers on land.

Adelie penguin
Parents take turns in feeding and keeping their eggs safe from predators.

Geographical South Pole
This is Earth's southernmost point. The Ceremonial South Pole, situated 590 ft (180 m) from the Geographical South Pole, is marked by a pole surrounded by the flags of the nations that signed the Antarctic Treaty, an agreement that set aside the continent for scientific research.

Extreme climate
The average annual temperature in Antarctica is around -58°F (-50°C). Winds often reach storm force, there is little snowfall, and the sun does not rise at all between March and September.

Emperor penguin
The largest of all penguins has an average height of 45 in (115 cm). They can survive in temperatures as low as -76° F (-60° C).

Gentoo penguin
These speedy swimmers have red beaks, white feather caps, and orange feet.

Mount Erebus
One of the world's most active volcanoes and, at 12,448 ft (3,794 m), the highest active volcano in Antarctica, Mount Erebus has a very rare, bubbling, lava lake.

Snow petrel
These birds nest on cliffs, but prefer to gather on pack ice.

KEY
Antarctica is a cold desert. Where it is not covered in ice, the barren ground is gravel or rock.

☐ Ice
☐ Tundra

IT MELTED, WORLD SEA LEVELS WOULD RISE BY ABOUT 200 FT (60 M).

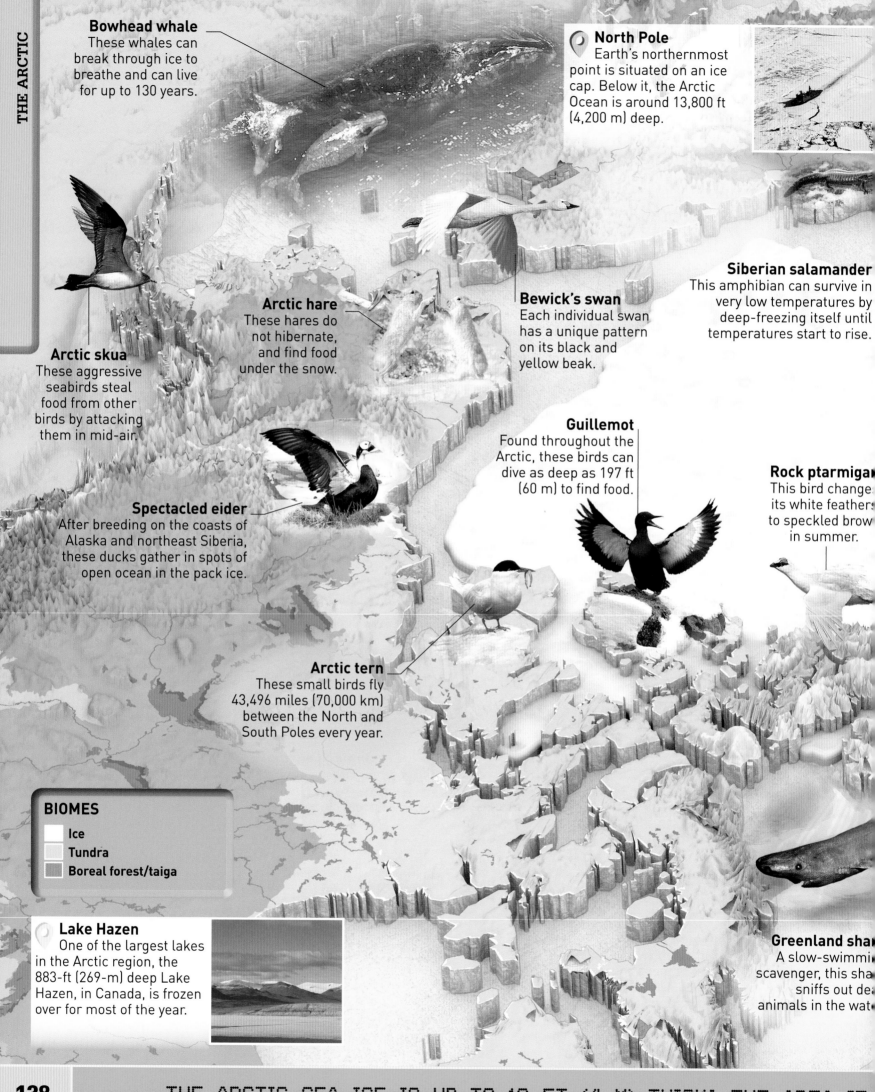

Bowhead whale
These whales can break through ice to breathe and can live for up to 130 years.

North Pole
Earth's northernmost point is situated on an ice cap. Below it, the Arctic Ocean is around 13,800 ft (4,200 m) deep.

Arctic hare
These hares do not hibernate, and find food under the snow.

Bewick's swan
Each individual swan has a unique pattern on its black and yellow beak.

Siberian salamander
This amphibian can survive in very low temperatures by deep-freezing itself until temperatures start to rise.

Arctic skua
These aggressive seabirds steal food from other birds by attacking them in mid-air.

Guillemot
Found throughout the Arctic, these birds can dive as deep as 197 ft (60 m) to find food.

Rock ptarmigan
This bird changes its white feathers to speckled brown in summer.

Spectacled eider
After breeding on the coasts of Alaska and northeast Siberia, these ducks gather in spots of open ocean in the pack ice.

Arctic tern
These small birds fly 43,496 miles (70,000 km) between the North and South Poles every year.

BIOMES
☐ Ice
☐ Tundra
☐ Boreal forest/taiga

Lake Hazen
One of the largest lakes in the Arctic region, the 883-ft (269-m) deep Lake Hazen, in Canada, is frozen over for most of the year.

Greenland shark
A slow-swimming scavenger, this shark sniffs out dead animals in the water.

THE ARCTIC SEA ICE IS UP TO 13 FT (4 M) THICK; THE AREA IT

Yenisei
The Yenisei river in Russia is the largest river to flow out into the Arctic Ocean. Its 31-mile (50-km) wide estuary is frozen for long parts of the year.

The Arctic

Unlike Antarctica, the Arctic is not a continent, but the area of frozen waters surrounding the North Pole. It includes the northernmost parts of three continents—North America, Europe, and Asia. Many different animals have made a home in this inhospitable region.

Siberian crane
This bird easily snips off roots and catches fish with its saw-edged beak.

Ermine
This mammal's coat turns from brown to white in winter for camouflage.

Beluga whale
White in color, this small whale speaks in clicks and whistles.

Porbeagle shark
This shark grows up to 8.2 ft (2.5 m) in length and feeds on squid and fish.

Spiny dogfish
This fish is one of the most numerous species of shark in the world.

Brent goose
Unlike other geese, the Brent flies in long lines instead of in a V-shape.

Narwhal
The tusks of this small whale can grow to 9.8 ft (3 m).

Lemming
Soft, warm fur helps this rodent stay active through the winter.

Polar bear
A powerful predator, this bear roams over land and pack ice to find prey.

Bluntnose sixgill shark
This fast-swimming shark has six gills instead of the five normal in most sharks.

Puffin
60 percent of the world's puffins live in Iceland.

Murmansk
Around 300,000 people live in the Russian port of Murmansk, the largest city inside the Arctic Circle.

THE OCEANS

Mighty seas
Oceans cover approximately 71 percent of Earth's surface and contain 97 percent of the water found on our planet.

Pacific Ocean

The Pacific is by far the world's largest ocean. At its widest point (stretching from Colombia to Indonesia), it extends for 12,300 miles (19,800 km) —almost halfway around the world. The deepest trenches on Earth can be found here, along with massive volcanoes that rise up from the ocean's floor.

FAST FACTS

Total area:
60,060,893 sq miles
(155,557,000 sq km)

Coastline:
84,297 miles (135,663 km)

Average depth:
13,025 ft (3,970 m)

Lowest point:
Challenger Deep, Mariana Trench—
35,840 ft (10,924 m)

Major access points:

1 **Panama Canal**

2 **Strait of Magellan**

3 **Tsugaru Strait**

4 **Tsushima**

5 **Torres Straits**

2

The Strait of Magellan, in southern Chile/Argentina, connects the Pacific and Atlantic Oceans.

The Emperor Seamounts
These underwater mountains extend northwest from Hawaii. Each mount is named after a Japanese emperor.

Mariana Trench
The lowest point on Earth, its deepest point lies almost 7 miles (11 km) beneath the ocean's surface.

New Caledonia
This island and New Zealand are all that remain of an ancient continent called Zealandia that was half the size of Australia.

The Tonga Trench
Lying north of New Zealand's North Island, this trench reaches an average depth of 34,448 ft (10,500 m).

ALL SEVEN OF THE EARTH'S CONTINENTS COULD

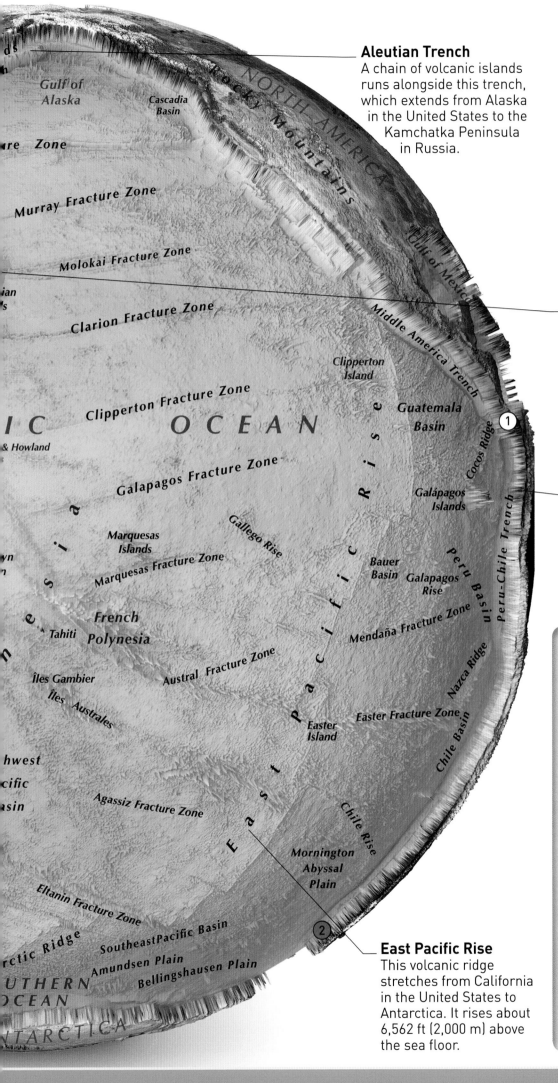

Aleutian Trench
A chain of volcanic islands runs alongside this trench, which extends from Alaska in the United States to the Kamchatka Peninsula in Russia.

Gulf of Alaska

Cascadia Basin

re Zone

NORTH AMERICA

Rocky Mountains

Murray Fracture Zone

Molokai Fracture Zone

Gulf of Mexico

Clarion Fracture Zone

Middle America Trench

Clipperton Island

Clipperton Fracture Zone

OCEAN

Guatemala Basin

Cocos Ridge

Galapagos Fracture Zone

Galápagos Islands

Peru-Chile Trench

Marquesas Islands

Gallego Rise

Bauer Basin

Galapagos Rise

Peru Basin

Marquesas Fracture Zone

French Polynesia

Mendaña Fracture Zone

Nazca Ridge

Tahiti

Îles Gambier

Austral Fracture Zone

Îles Australes

Easter Fracture Zone

Easter Island

Chile Basin

East Pacific Rise

hwest cific asin

Agassiz Fracture Zone

Chile Rise

Mornington Abyssal Plain

Eltanin Fracture Zone

ctic Ridge

SoutheastPacific Basin

Amundsen Plain

Bellingshausen Plain

SOUTHERN OCEAN

ANTARCTICA

The Pacific Ocean contains *just over half* of all the world's **seawater**.

Mauna Loa
Measuring 29,500 ft (9,000 m) in height from the ocean floor to its summit, the world's largest active volcano looms over Hawaii.

Peru-Chile Trench
This 3,660-mile (5,900-km) long trench is the longest in the Pacific Ocean. It follows the line of the Andes Mountains.

Ring of Fire
The Pacific Ocean is surrounded by a band of volcanoes called the Ring of Fire. This ring extends from New Zealand to South America and contains more than three-quarters of the world's volcanoes, including Mount Fuji, in Japan, and Mount St. Helens in the United States.

East Pacific Rise
This volcanic ridge stretches from California in the United States to Antarctica. It rises about 6,562 ft (2,000 m) above the sea floor.

Atlantic Ocean

The Atlantic is the world's second-largest ocean. It stretches from the Arctic to the Antarctic, separating Europe and Africa from the Americas. The Atlantic Ocean covers about one-fifth of the planet's surface, is home to some of the world's richest fishing waters, and contains a plentiful supply of gas and oil.

FAST FACTS

Total area:
29,637,974 sq miles (76,762,000 sq km)

Coastline:
69,510 miles (111,866 km)

Average depth:
11,962 ft (3,646 m)

Lowest point:
Milwaukee Deep, Puerto Rico Trench— 28,232 ft (8,605 m)

Major access points:

1 English Channel

2 Panama Canal

3 Straits of Florida

4 Strait of Gibraltar

5 Strait of Magellan

The Panama Canal, one of the world's busiest waterways, connects the Pacific and Atlantic Oceans.

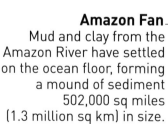

Puerto Rico Trench
This trench stretches for 497 miles (800 km) and contains the Atlantic Ocean's deepest point.

Mid-Atlantic Ridge
This underwater mountain range runs for about 10,000 miles (16,000 km) along the ocean floor.

Amazon Fan
Mud and clay from the Amazon River have settled on the ocean floor, forming a mound of sediment 502,000 sq miles (1.3 million sq km) in size.

Icebergs
The icebergs of the Antarctic are usually much larger than those found in the Arctic. They can reach lengths of up to 50 miles (80 km).

Map labels: Labrador Sea, Grand Banks of Newfoundland, Lab. B., Newfound. Basin, NORTH AMERICA, Sohm Plain, Bermuda, Bermuda Rise, Hatteras Plain, Mid Atlantic, Sargasso Sea, Kane Fracture Zone, Nares Plain, Puerto Rico Trench, Greater Antilles, Lesser Antilles, Caribbean Sea, ATL, Doldrums Fracture Zo, Demerara Plain, OC, Panama Basin, Amazon Fan, Amazon, Amazon Basin, Ceará, SOUTH AMERICA, Andes, Vi Sea, PACIFIC OCEAN, Santos Plateau, Rio Gr Rise, Argenti Basin, Falkland Escarpment, Falkland Islands, Falkland Plateau, Yaghan Basin, Cape Horn, Drake Passage, Scot, We S, G

THE FIRST PERSON TO FLY ACROSS THE ATLANTIC WAS

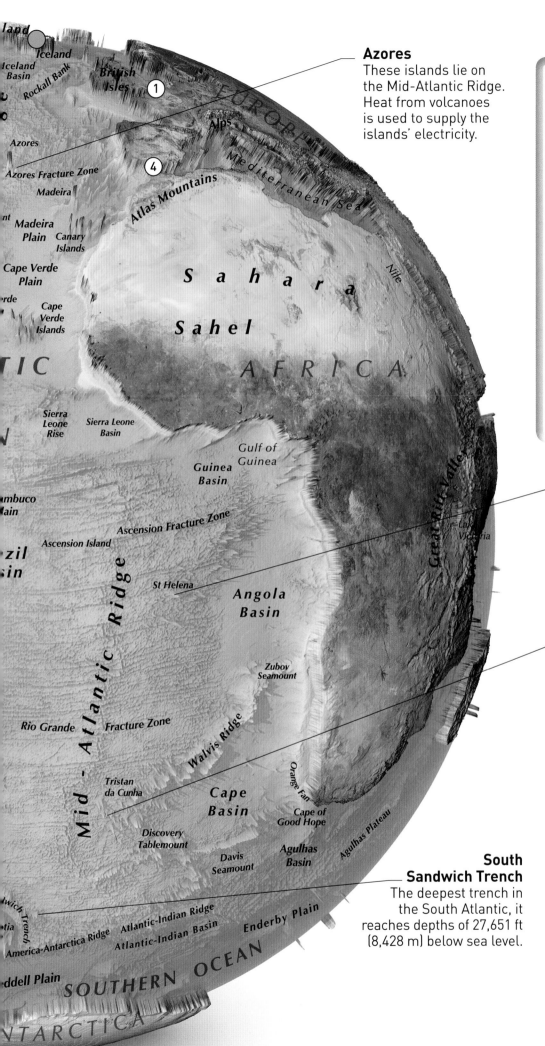

Azores
These islands lie on the Mid-Atlantic Ridge. Heat from volcanoes is used to supply the islands' electricity.

Iceland
With an area of 39,769 sq miles (103,000 sq km), Iceland is the largest of the islands that lie on the Mid-Atlantic Ridge. It is home to more than 100 volcanoes, many of which are still active, as well as to many geysers and hot springs.

Saint Helena
This tiny volcanic island has an area of just 47 sq miles (122 sq km). It has been under British control since 1676.

Tristan da Cunha
Lying 1,250 miles (2,000 km) from the nearest inhabited land (Saint Helena), this is the most isolated group of inhabited islands in the world. Just over 250 people live there.

South Sandwich Trench
The deepest trench in the South Atlantic, it reaches depths of 27,651 ft (8,428 m) below sea level.

The **Atlantic** is **widening** by up to **3.9 in** (10 cm) every year as its **continental plates** move **slowly** apart.

Map labels: land, Iceland, Iceland Basin, Rockall Bank, British Isles, Azores, Azores Fracture Zone, Madeira, Madeira Plain, Canary Islands, Cape Verde Plain, Cape Verde Islands, Sierra Leone Rise, Sierra Leone Basin, Guinea Basin, Gulf of Guinea, Ascension Fracture Zone, Ascension Island, St Helena, Angola Basin, Zubov Seamount, Rio Grande Fracture Zone, Walvis Ridge, Tristan da Cunha, Cape Basin, Orange Fan, Discovery Tablemount, Davis Seamount, Agulhas Basin, Cape of Good Hope, Agulhas Plateau, America-Antarctica Ridge, Atlantic-Indian Ridge, Atlantic-Indian Basin, Enderby Plain, Sandwich Trench, Weddell Plain, EUROPE, Alps, Mediterranean Sea, Nile, Atlas Mountains, Sahara, Sahel, AFRICA, Great Rift Valley, Lake Victoria, Mid-Atlantic Ridge, SOUTHERN OCEAN, ANTARCTICA, (1), (4)

Indian Ocean

The Indian Ocean is the smallest of the world's major oceans, but it provides important sea routes connecting the Middle East, Africa, and East Asia, with Europe and the Americas. As with the Pacific Ocean, its warm waters are dotted with coral atolls and islands. Around one-fifth of the world's population live on its shores.

FAST FACTS

Total area:
26,469,620 sq miles (68,556, 000 sq km)

Coastline:
41,337 miles (66,526 km)

Average depth:
12,274 ft (3,741 m)

Lowest point:
Diamantina Deep, Java Trench— 23,812 ft (7,258 m)

Major access points:

1 Bab El Mandeb

2 Strait of Hormuz

3 Strait of Malacca

4 Suez Canal

5 Torres Straits

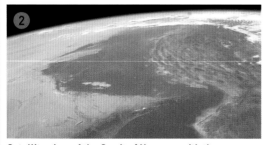

Satellite view of the Strait of Hormuz, with the United Arab Emirates on the left of the image.

Mid-Indian Ridge
Heading southeast from the Gulf of Aden, this ridge meets the Southwest Indian Ridge mid-ocean.

Seychelles
This group of 115 islands lies 1,130 miles (1,819 km) to the north of Madagascar. It forms part of the Mascarene Plateau.

Southwest Indian Ridge
This ridge connects the Mid-Indian Ridge to the Mid-Atlantic Ridge.

Prince Edward Islands
These two small islands are the peaks of volcanoes that extend 3 miles (5 km) from the sea bed.

Caspian Sea

Iran Plat

Gulf of

Arabian Peninsula

Murray Ridge

Nile

Red Sea

Socotra

Owen Fracture Zo

Ar

Gulf of Aden

Ethiopian Highlands

Horn of Africa

Chain Ridge

Carlsbe

AFRICA

Lake Victoria

Somali Basin

Mascarene

Seychelles

Mascarene Basin

Lake Nyasa

Mascarene Plain

Ma Réunio

Madagascar

Madagascar Basin

ATLANTIC OCEAN

Mozambique Channel

Mozambique Plateau

Natal Basin

Madagascar Plateau

Indomed Fracture Zone

Southwest In Rid

Cape Horn

Agulhas Plateau

Croz Plate

Agulhas Basin

Del Cano Rise

Croze Island

Prince Edward Islands

Lena Tablem

Ob' Tablemount

End Pl

Atlantic-Indian Basin

NONE OF THE MALDIVES, A GROUP OF ABOUT 1,200 ISLANDS SOUTH

ASIA
Tien Shan
Himalayas
Ganges
Brahmaputra
Irrawaddy
Ganges Fan
Bay of Bengal
Andaman Islands
Sri Lanka
Nicobar Islands
Andaman Sea
Mekong
Gulf of Thailand
South China Sea
Borneo
Sumatra
Celebes
Java Sea
Java
Christmas Island
Java Trench
North Australian Basin
Exmouth Plateau
Cuvier Plateau
Australia
Chagos-Laccadive Plateau
Ceylon Plain
Cocos Basin
Mid-Indian Basin
Ninetyeast Ridge
Investigator Ridge
Cocos Islands
INDIAN
OCEAN
Wharton Basin
East Indiaman Ridge
Perth Basin
Naturaliste Plateau
Broken Ridge
Amsterdam Fracture Zone
Diamantina Fracture Zone
Southeast Indian Ridge
Kerguelen Plateau
Banzare Seamounts
South Indian Basin
SOUTHERN OCEAN
ANTARCTICA
PACIFIC OCEAN

The Ganges Fan
Two of the world's great rivers—the Ganges and the Brahmaputra—flow into the Indian Ocean here. Sediment from the rivers collects in a huge fan shape in the Bay of Bengal.

Indian Ocean tsunami
On December 26, 2004, an earthquake (the third largest ever recorded) off the coast of Sumatra, Indonesia, triggered a tsunami (a huge wave that destroys everything in its path). It had catastrophic consequences for many countries bordering the Indian Ocean, when waves of up to 100 ft (30 m) high left as many as 230,000 people dead.

Java Trench
The Indian Ocean's only major trench runs for 1,600 miles (2,570 km) south of the Indonesian islands of Java and Sumatra.

Ninety East Ridge
This ridge is named for the line of longitude it follows. At 3,100 miles (5,000 km), it is the world's longest sea ridge, and also its straightest.

Kerguelen Plateau
Only a few uninhabited islands remain of what was once a small continent.

Southern Ocean
The Indian, Pacific, and Atlantic Oceans come together in the seas around Antarctica.

The **Indian Ocean** is the world's **warmest**. *Water temperatures reach 82.4°F (28°C)* in its **eastern** parts.

REFERENCE

Night and day
While Asia, the Middle East, and East Africa are bathed in sunlight, in Europe and West Africa, the lights continue to shine in the dark hours before dawn.

Countries of the world

This section includes 195 of the world's countries. With the exception of Taiwan and the Vatican City, all of them are member states of the United Nations.

* denotes official language

NORTH AND CENTRAL AMERICA

CANADA
North America
Capital: Ottawa
Population: 35.1 million / 9 people per sq mile (4 people per sq km)
Total area: 3,855,103 sq miles (9,984,670 sq km)
Languages: English*, French*, Punjabi, Italian, German, Cantonese, Inuktitut
Currency: Canadian dollar = 100 cents

UNITED STATES OF AMERICA
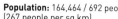
North America
Capital: Washington, DC
Population: 324 million / 85 people per sq mile (33 people per sq km)
Total area: 3,796,742 sq miles (9,833,517 sq km)
Languages: English, Spanish
Currency: US dollar = 100 cents

MEXICO
North America
Capital: Mexico City
Population: 123.2 million / 162 people per sq mile (63 people per sq km)
Total area: 758,449 sq miles (1,964,375 sq km)
Languages: Spanish*, Nahuatl, Mayan
Currency: Mexican peso = 100 centavos

BELIZE
Central America
Capital: Belmopan
Population: 347,370 / 39 people per sq mile (15 people per sq km)
Total area: 8,867 sq miles (22,966 sq km)
Languages: English*, English Creole, Spanish, Mayan, Garifuna (Carib)
Currency: Belizean dollar = 100 cents

COSTA RICA
Central America
Capital: San José
Population: 4.8 million / 243 people per sq mile (94 people per sq km)
Total area: 19,730 sq miles (51,100 sq km)
Languages: Spanish*, English
Currency: Costa Rican colón = 100 céntimos

EL SALVADOR
Central America
Capital: San Salvador
Population: 6.1 million / 750 people per sq mile (290 people per sq km)
Total area: 8,124 sq miles (21,041 sq km)
Languages: Spanish*, Nawat
Currency: US dollar = 100 cents

GUATEMALA
Central America
Capital: Guatemala City
Population: 15.2 million / 362 people per sq mile (140 people per sq km)
Total area: 42,042 sq miles (108,889 sq km)
Languages: Spanish*, indigenous languages
Currency: Quetzal = 100 centavos

HONDURAS
Central America
Capital: Tegucigalpa
Population: 8.9 million / 206 people per sq mile (79 people per sq km)
Total area: 43,278 sq miles (112,090 sq km)
Languages: Spanish*, Indigenous languages
Currency: Lempira = 100 centavos

NICARAGUA
Central America
Capital: Managua
Population: 6 million / 119 people per sq mile (46 people per sq km)
Total area: 50,336 sq miles (130,370 sq km)
Languages: Spanish*, Miskito
Currency: Córdoba = 100 centavos

PANAMA
Central America
Capital: Panama City
Population: 3.7 million / 127 people per sq mile (49 people per sq km)
Total area: 29,120 sq miles (75,420 sq km)
Languages: Spanish*, English Creole, Indigenous languages including Ngabere
Currency: Balboa = 100 centesimos

ANTIGUA AND BARBUDA
West Indies
Capital: St. John's
Population: 92,436 / 540 people per sq mile (209 people per sq km)
Total area: 171 sq miles (443 sq km)
Languages: English*, Antiguan Creole
Currency: Eastern Caribbean dollar = 100 cents

THE BAHAMAS
West Indies
Capital: Nassau
Population: 324,600 / 61 people per sq mile (23 people per sq km)
Total area: 5,359 sq miles (13,880 sq km)
Languages: English*, English Creole, French Creole
Currency: Bahamian dollar = 100 cents

BARBADOS
West Indies

Capital: Bridgetown
Population: 290,600 / 1,750 people per sq mile (676 people per sq mile)
Total area: 166 sq miles (430 sq km)
Languages: English*, Bajan (Barbadian English)
Currency: Barbados dollar = 100 cents

CUBA
West Indies
Capital: Havana
Population: 11 million / 256 people per sq mile (99 people per sq km)
Total area: 42,803 sq miles (110,860 sq km)
Languages: Spanish*
Currency: Cuban peso = 100 centavos

DOMINICA
West Indies
Capital: Roseau
Population: 73,607 / 254 people per sq mile (98 people per sq km)
Total area: 290 sq miles (751 sq km)
Languages: English*, French Creole
Currency: East Caribbean dollar = 100 cents

DOMINICAN REPUBLIC
West Indies
Capital: Santo Domingo
Population: 10.5 million / 559 people per sq mile (216 people per sq km)
Total area: 18,792 sq miles (48,670 sq km)
Languages: Spanish*
Currency: Dominican Republic peso = 100 centavos

GRENADA
West Indies
Capital: St. George's
Population: 111,000 / 836 people per sq mile (323 people per sq km)
Total area: 133 sq miles (344 sq km)
Languages: English*, French Patois
Currency: East Caribbean dollar = 100 cents

HAITI
West Indies
Capital: Port-au-Prince
Population: 10.5 million / 979 people per sq mile (378 people per sq km)
Total area: 10,714 sq miles (27,750 sq km)
Languages: French*, French Creole*
Currency: Gourde = 100 centimes

JAMAICA
West Indies
Capital: Kingston
Population: 3 million / 613 people per sq mile (237 people per sq km)
Total area: 4,243 sq miles (10,991 sq km)
Languages: English*, English Creole
Currency: Jamaican dollar = 100 cents

SAINT KITTS AND NEVIS
West Indies
Capital: Basseterre
Population: 52,329 / 519 people per sq mile (201 people per sq km)
Total area: 101 sq miles (261 sq km)
Language: English*
Currency: Eastern Caribbean dollar = 100 cents

SAINT LUCIA
West Indies

Capital: Castries
Population: 164,464 / 692 people per sq mile (267 people per sq km)
Total area: 238 sq miles (616 sq km)
Languages: English*, French Creole
Currency: Eastern Caribbean dollar = 100 cents

SAINT VINCENT AND THE GRENADINES
West Indies
Capital: Kingstown
Population: 102,350 / 682 people per sq mile (263 people per sq km)
Total area: 150 sq miles (389 sq km)
Languages: English*, English Creole
Currency: Eastern Caribbean dollar = 100 cents

TRINIDAD AND TOBAGO
West Indies
Capital: Port-of-Spain
Population: 1.2 million / 606 people per sq mile (234 people per sq km)
Total area: 1,980 sq miles (5,128 sq km)
Languages: English*, Caribbean Hindustani, French, Spanish
Currency: Trinidad and Tobago dollar = 100 cents

SOUTH AMERICA

COLOMBIA
South America
Capital: Bogotá
Population: 46.7 million / 106 people per sq mile (41 people per sq km)
Total area: 439,736 sq miles (1,138,910 sq km)
Languages: Spanish*, Amerindian languages, English Creole
Currency: Colombian peso = 100 centavos

GUYANA
South America
Capital: Georgetown
Population: 735,900 / 9 people per sq mile (3 people per sq km)
Total area: 83,000 sq miles (214,969 sq km)
Languages: English*, English Creole, Indigenous languages, Indian languages
Currency: Guyana dollar = 100 cents

SURINAME
South America
Capital: Paramaribo
Population: 585,800 / 9 people per sq mile (4 people per sq km)
Total area: 63,251 sq miles (163,820 sq km)
Languages: Dutch*, English, Sranan Tongo
Currency: Suriname dollar = 100 cents

VENEZUELA
South America
Capital: Caracas
Population: 30.9 million / 88 people per sq mile (34 people per sq km)
Total area: 352,143 sq miles (912,050 sq km)
Languages: Spanish*, numerous indigenous languages
Currency: Bolivar fuerte = 100 centimos

SOUTH SUDAN IS THE WORLD'S NEWEST COUNTRY. IT BECAME A

OLIVIA
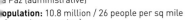
outh America
apital: Sucre (judicial);
a Paz (administrative)
opulation: 10.8 million / 26 people per sq mile
0 people per sq km)
otal area: 424,165 sq miles (1,098,581 sq km)
anguages: Spanish*, Quechua*, Aymara*
urrency: Boliviano = 100 centavos

CUADOR
outh America
apital: Quito
opulation: 15.9 million / 145 people per sq mile
6 people per sq km)
otal area: 109,484 sq miles (283,561 sq km)
anguages: Spanish*, Quechua*, other
idigenous languages
urrency: US dollar = 100 cents

ERU
outh America
apital: Lima
opulation: 30.7 million / 62 people per sq mile
24 people per sq km)
otal area: 496,225 sq miles (1,285,216 sq km)
anguages: Spanish*, Quechua*, Aymará*, other
idigenous languages
urrency: New sol = 100 centimos

RAZIL
outh America
apital: Brasília
opulation: 204.3 million / 62 people per sq mile
24 people per sq km)
otal area: 3,287,957 sq miles (8,515,770 sq km)
anguages: Portuguese*, German, Italian,
panish, Polish, Japanese
urrency: Real = 100 centavos

ARGENTINA
outh America
apital: Buenos Aires
opulation: 43.4 million / 40 people per sq mile
6 people per sq km)
otal area: 1,073,518 sq miles (2,780,400 sq km)
anguages: Spanish*, Italian, English, German,
rench, Indigenous languages
urrency: Argentine Peso = 100 centavos

URUGUAY
outh America
apital: Montevideo
opulation: 3.4 million / 70 people per sq mile
27 people per sq km)
otal area: 68,036 sq miles (176,215 sq km)
anguages: Spanish*, Portuñol
urrency: Uruguayan peso = 100 centesimos

CHILE
outh America
apital: Santiago
opulation: 17.5 million / 60 people per sq mile
23 people per sq km)
otal area: 291,932 sq miles (756,102 sq km)
anguages: Spanish*, Indigenous languages
urrency: Chilean peso = 100 centavos

PARAGUAY
outh America
apital: Asunción
opulation: 6.9 million / 44 people per sq mile
17 people per sq km)
otal area: 157,048 sq miles (406,752 sq km)
anguages: Spanish*, Guaraní*
urrency: Guaraní = 100 centimos

AFRICA

ALGERIA
North Africa
Capital: Algiers

Population: 39.5 million / 43 people per sq mile
(17 people per sq km)
Total area: 919,595 sq miles (2,381,740 sq km)
Languages: Arabic*, Tamazight*, French
Currency: Algerian dinar = 100 santeems

LIBYA
North Africa
Capital: Tripoli
Population: 6.5 million / 10 people per sq mile
(4 people per sq km)
Total area: 679,362 sq miles (1,759,540 sq km)
Languages: Arabic*, Berber languages
Currency: Libyan dinar = 1,000 dirhams

MOROCCO
North Africa
Capital: Rabat

Population: 33.7 million / 196 people per sq mile
(76 people per sq km)
Total area: 172,414 sq miles (446,550 sq km)
Languages: Arabic*, Tamazight*, French
Currency: Moroccan dirham = 100 santim

TUNISIA
North Africa
Capital: Tunis
Population: 11.1 million / 176 people per sq mile
(68 people per sq km)
Total area: 63,170 sq miles (163,610 sq km)
Languages: Arabic*, French, Berber
Currency: Tunisian dinar = 1,000 millimes

BURUNDI
Central Africa
Capital: Bujumbura
Population: 10.7 million / 996 people per sq mile
(384 people per sq km)
Total area: 10,745 sq miles (27,830 sq km)
Languages: Kirundi*, French*, Kiswahili
Currency: Burundi franc = 100 centimes

DJIBOUTI
East Africa
Capital: Djibouti

Population: 828,324 / 92 people per sq mile
(36 people per sq km)
Total area: 8,958 sq miles (23,200 sq km)
Languages: French*, Arabic*, Somali, Afar
Currency: Djibouti franc = 100 centimes

EGYPT
North Africa
Capital: Cairo
Population: 88.5 million / 229 people per sq mile
(88 people per sq km)
Total area: 386,660 sq miles (1,001,450 sq km)
Languages: Arabic*, French, English
Currency: Egyptian pound = 100 piastres

ERITREA
East Africa
Capital: Asmara
Population: 5.9 million / 130 people per sq mile
(50 people per sq km)
Total area: 45,406 sq miles (117,600 sq km)
Languages: Tigrinya*, Arabic*, English*, Tigre,
Afar, Bilen, Kunama, Nara
Currency: Nafka = 100 cents

ETHIOPIA
East Africa
Capital: Addis Ababa

Population: 102.3 million / 235 people per sq mile
(91 people per sq km)
Total area: 426,373 sq miles (1,104,300 sq km)
Languages: Amharic*, Oromo, Tigrinya
Currency: Ethiopian birr = 100 santim

KENYA
East Africa
Capital: Nairobi
Population: 45.5 million / 208 people per sq mile
(80 people per sq km)
Total area: 224,081 sq miles (580,367 sq km)
Languages: Kiswahili*, English*
Currency: Kenya shilling = 100 cents

RWANDA
Central Africa
Capital: Kigali
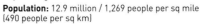
Population: 12.9 million / 1,269 people per sq mile
(490 people per sq km)
Total area: 10,169 sq miles (26,338 sq km)
Languages: French*, Kinyarwanda*, English
Currency: Rwandan franc = 100 centimes

SOMALIA
East Africa
Capital: Mogadishu
Population: 10.8 million / 44 people per sq mile
(17 people per sq km)
Total area: 246,199 sq miles (637,657 sq km)
Languages: Somali*, Arabic*, English, Italian
Currency: Somali shilling = 100 cents

SOUTH SUDAN
East Africa
Capital: Juba

Population: 12.5 million / 50 people per sq mile
(19 people per sq km)
Total area: 248,777 sq miles (644,329 sq km)
Languages: English*, Arabic, Dinka, Nuer
Currency: South Sudanese pound = 100 piasters

SUDAN
East Africa
Capital: Khartoum

Population: 36.7 million / 51 people per sq mile
(20 people per sq km)
Total area: 718,723 sq miles (1,861,484 sq km)
Languages: Arabic*, English*, Nubian, Fur
Currency: Sudanese pound = 100 plastres

TANZANIA
East Africa
Capital: Dodoma

Population: 52.5 million / 144 people per sq mile
(55 people per sq km)
Total area: 365,755 sq miles (947,300 sq km)
Languages: English*, Swahili*, Sukuma, Chagga,
Nyamwezi, Hehe, Makonde
Currency: Tanzanian shilling = 100 cents

UGANDA
East Africa
Capital: Kampala
Population: 38.3 million / 412 people per sq mile
(159 people per sq km)
Total area: 93,065 sq miles (241,038 sq km)
Languages: English*, Luganda
Currency: Uganda shilling = 100 cents

BENIN
West Africa
Capital: Porto-Novo
Population: 10.4 million / 239 people per sq mile
(92 people per sq km)
Total area: 43,483 sq miles (112,622 sq km)
Languages: French*, Fon, Bariba, Yoruba, Adja,
Houeda, Somba
Currency: West African CFA franc = 100 centimes

BURKINA FASO
West Africa
Capital: Ouagadougou
Population: 18.9 million / 179 people per sq mile
(69 people per sq km)
Total area: 105,869 sq miles (274,200 sq km)
Languages: French*, various languages belonging
to the Sudanic family
Currency: West African CFA franc = 100 centimes

CAPE VERDE
Atlantic Ocean
Capital: Praia
Population: 545,993 / 351 people per sq mile
(135 people per sq km)
Total area: 1,557 sq miles (4,033 sq km)
Languages: Portuguese*, Portuguese Creole
Currency: Cape Verde escudo = 100 centavos

IVORY COAST
West Africa
Capital: Yamoussoukro
Population: 23.7 million / 190 people per sq mile
(74 people per sq km)
Total area: 124,504 sq miles (322,463 sq km)
Languages: French*, Dioula
Currency: West African CFA franc = 100 centimes

GAMBIA
West Africa
Capital: Banjul
Population: 2 million / 458 people per sq mile
(177 people per sq km)
Total area: 4,363 sq miles (11,300 sq km)
Languages: English*, Mandinka, Fula, Wolof
Currency: Dalasi = 100 butut

GHANA
West Africa
Capital: Accra
Population: 26.9 million / 292 people per sq mile
(113 people per sq km)
Total area: 92,098 sq miles (238,533 sq km)
Languages: English*, Asante, Ewe, Fante, Boron
Currency: Cedi = 100 pesewas

GUINEA
West Africa
Capital: Conakry
Population: 12.1 million / 128 people per sq mile
(49 people per sq km)
Total area: 94,925 sq miles (245,857 sq km)
Languages: French*, Fulani, Malinke, Soussou
Currency: Guinea franc = 100 centimes

GUINEA BISSAU
West Africa
Capital: Bissau
Population: 1.8 million / 124 people per sq mile
(49 people per sq km)
Total area: 13,948 sq miles (36,125 sq km)
Languages: Portuguese*, West African Crioulo
Currency: West African CFA franc = 100 centimes

LIBERIA
West Africa
Capital: Monrovia
Population: 4.3 million / 101 people per sq mile
(39 people per sq km)
Total area: 43,000 sq miles (111,370 sq km)
Languages: English*
Currency: Liberian dollar = 100 cents

MALI
West Africa
Capital: Bamako
Population: 17.5 million / 37 people per sq mile
(14 people per sq km)
Total area: 478,764 sq miles (1,240,000 sq km)
Languages: French*, Bambara, Peul, Dogon
Currency: West African CFA franc = 100 centimes

MAURITANIA
West Africa
Capital: Nouakchott

Population: 3.7 million / 9 people per sq mile (4 people per sq km)
Total area: 397,953 sq miles (1,030,700 sq km)
Languages: Arabic*, Hassaniyah Arabic, Pulaar, Soninke
Currency: Ouguiya = 5 khoums

NIGER
West Africa
Capital: Niamey
Population: 18.6 million / 38 people per sq mile (15 people per sq km)
Total area: 489,189 sq miles (1,267,000 sq km)
Languages: French*, Hausa, Djerma
Currency: West African CFA franc = 100 centimes

NIGERIA
West Africa
Capital: Abuja
Population: 186 million / 522 people per mile km (201 people per sq km)
Total area: 356,667 sq miles (923,768 sq km)
Languages: English*, Hausa, Yoruba, Ibo
Currency: Naira = 100 kobo

SENEGAL
West Africa
Capital: Dakar
Population: 14.3 million / 188 people per sq mile (73 people per sq km)
Total area: 75,955 sq miles (196,722 sq km)
Languages: French*, Wolof, Pulaar
Currency: West African CFA franc = 100 centimes

SIERRA LEONE
West Africa
Capital: Freetown
Population: 6 million / 217 people per sq mile (84 people per sq km)
Total area: 27,669 sq miles (71,740 sq km)
Languages: English*, Mende, Temne, Krio
Currency: Leone = 100 cents

TOGO
Western Africa
Capital: Lomé
Population: 7.8 million / 356 people per sq mile (137 people per sq km)
Total area: 21,925 sq miles (56,785 sq km)
Languages: French*, Ewe, Mina, Kabye
Currency: West African CFA franc = 100 centimes

CAMEROON
Central Africa
Capital: Yaoundé
Population: 23.7 million / 130 people per sq mile (50 people per sq km)
Total area: 183,567 sq miles (475,440 sq km)
Languages: English*, French*, Bamileke, Fang, Fulani
Currency: Central African CFA franc = 100 centimes

CENTRAL AFRICAN REPUBLIC

Central Africa
Capital: Bangui
Population: 5.4 million / 23 people per sq mile (9 people per sq km)
Total area: 240,535 sq miles (622,984 sq km)
Languages: French*, Sangho, Banda, Gbaya
Currency: CFA franc =100 centimes

CHAD
Central Africa
Capital: N'Djaména
Population: 13 million / 27 people per sq mile (10 people per sq km)
Total area: 495,752 sq miles (1,284,000 sq km)
Languages: French*, Arabic*, Sara, Maba
Currency: Central African CFA franc = 100 centimes

CONGO
Central Africa
Capital: Brazzaville
Population: 4.8 million / 36 people per sq mile (14 people per sq km)
Total area: 132,046 sq miles (342,000 sq km)
Languages: French*, Monokutuba, Mikongo, Lingala
Currency: Central African CFA franc = 100 centimes

CONGO, DEM. REP.
Central Africa
Capital: Kinshasa
Population: 79.4 million / 88 people per sq mile (34 people per sq km)
Total area: 905,355 sq miles (2,344,858 sq km)
Languages: French*, Tshiluba, Kikongo, Lingala, Kingwana
Currency: Congolese Franc = 100 centimes

EQUATORIAL GUINEA

Central Africa
Capital: Malabo
Population: 759,451 / 70 people per sq mile (27 people per sq km)
Total area: 10,830 sq miles (28,051 sq km)
Languages: Spanish*, Fang, Bubi
Currency: Central African CFA franc = 100 centimes

GABON
Central Africa
Capital: Libreville
Population: 1.7 million / 16 people per sq mile (6 people per sq km)
Total area: 103,346 sq miles (267,667 sq km)
Languages: French*, Fang, Myene, Bapounou, Nzebi
Currency: Central African CFA franc = 100 centimes

SÃO TOMÉ AND PRINCIPE
West Africa
Capital: São Tomé
Population: 197,541 / 531 people per sq mile (204 people per sq km)
Total area: 372 sq miles (964 sq km)
Languages: Portuguese*, Forro
Currency: Dobra = 100 centimos

ANGOLA
Southern Africa
Capital: Luanda
Population: 25.7 million / 54 people per sq mile (21 people per sq km)
Total area: 481,351 sq miles (1,246,700 sq km)
Languages: Portuguese*, Umbundu, Kimbundu, Kikongo
Currency: Kwanza = 100 centimos

BOTSWANA
Southern Africa
Capital: Gaborone
Population: 2.2 million / 10 people per sq mile (4 people per sq km)
Total area: 224,607 sq miles (581,730 sq km)
Languages: English*, Setswana, Shona, San, Khoikhoi, Ndebele
Currency: Pula = 100 thebe

COMOROS
Indian Ocean
Capital: Moroni
Population: 780,972 / 905 people per sq mile (349 people per sq km)
Total area: 863 sq miles (2,235 sq km)
Languages: Arabic*, French*, Comoran*
Currency: Comoros franc = 100 centimes

LESOTHO
Southern Africa
Capital: Maseru
Population: 2 million / 171 people per sq mile (66 people per sq km)
Total area: 11,720 sq miles (30,355 sq km)
Languages: Sesotho*, English*, Zulu
Currency: Loti = 100 lisente

MADAGASCAR
Indian Ocean
Capital: Antananarivo
Population: 24.4 million / 108 people per sq mile (42 people per sq km)
Total area: 226,658 sq miles (587,041 sq km)
Languages: French*, Malagasy*
Currency: Malagasy ariary = 5 iraimbilanja

MALAWI
Southern Africa
Capital: Lilongwe
Population: 18.6 million / 407 people per sq mile (157 people per sq km)
Total area: 45,747 sq miles (118,484 sq km)
Languages: English*, Chichewa*, Chinyanja, Chiyao
Currency: Malawi kwacha = 100 tambala

MAURITIUS
Indian Ocean
Capital: Port Louis
Population: 1.4 million / 1,778 people per sq mile (686 people per sq km)
Total area: 788 sq miles (2,040 sq km)
Languages: English, French, French Creole
Currency: Mauritian rupee = 100 cents

MOZAMBIQUE
Southern Africa
Capital: Maputo
Population: 26 million / 84 people per sq mile (32 people per sq km)
Total area: 308,642 sq miles (799,380 sq km)
Languages: Portuguese*, Emakhuwa, Xichangana
Currency: Metical = 100 centavos

NAMIBIA
Southern Africa
Capital: Windhoek
Population: 2.4 million / 8 people per sq mile (3 people per sq km)
Total area: 318,261 sq miles (824,292 sq km)
Languages: English*, Oshiwambo languages, Nama, Afrikaans
Currency: Namibian dollar = 100 cents

SEYCHELLES
Indian Ocean
Capital: Victoria
Population: 93,200 / 531 people per sq mile (205 people per sq km)
Total area: 176 sq miles (455 sq km)
Languages: Seychellois Creole*, English*, French*
Currency: Seychelles rupee = 100 cents

SOUTH AFRICA
Southern Africa
Capital: Pretoria (administrative)
Population: 54.3 million / 115 people per sq mile (45 people per sq km)
Total area: 470,693 sq miles (1,219,090 sq km)
Languages: IsiZulu*, IsiXhosa*, Afrikaans*, English*
Currency: Rand = 100 cents

SWAZILAND
Southern Africa
Capital: Mbabane
Population: 1.5 million / 224 people per sq mile (86 people per sq km)
Total area: 6,704 sq miles (17,364 sq km)
Languages: Siswati*, English*
Currency: Lilangeni = 100 cents

ZAMBIA
Southern Africa
Capital: Lusaka
Population: 15.5 million / 53 people per sq mile (21 people per sq km)
Total area: 290,587 sq miles (752,618 sq km)
Languages: English*, Bemba, Nyanja, Tonga
Currency: Zambian kwacha = 100 ngwee

ZIMBABWE
Southern Africa
Capital: Harare
Population: 14.5 million / 96 people per sq mile (37 people per sq km)
Total area: 150,872 sq miles (390,757 sq km)
Languages: Shona*, Ndebele*, English
Currency: US dollar = 100 cents

EUROPE

ICELAND
Northwest Europe
Capital: Reykjavík
Population: 335,900 / 8 people per sq mile (3 people per sq km)
Total area: 39,768 sq miles (103,000 sq km)
Languages: Icelandic*, English
Currency: Icelandic króna = 100 aurar

DENMARK
Northern Europe
Capital: Copenhagen
Population: 5.4 million / 325 people per sq mile (125 people per sq km)
Total area: 16,639 sq miles (43,094 sq km)
Languages: Danish*, Faroese, Inuit
Currency: Danish krone = 100 øre

FINLAND
Northern Europe
Capital: Helsinki
Population: 5.5 million / 42 people per sq mile (16 people per sq km)
Total area: 130,559 sq miles (338,145 sq km)
Languages: Finnish*, Swedish, Sami
Currency: Euro = 100 cents

NORWAY
Northern Europe
Capital: Oslo
Population: 5.3 million / 42 people per sq mile (16 people per sq km)
Total area: 125,021 sq miles (323,802 sq km)
Languages: Norwegian* (Bokmål and Nynorsk), Sami, Finnish
Currency: Norwegian krone = 100 øre

SWEDEN
Northern Europe
Capital: Stockholm
Population: 9.9 million / 57 people per sq mile (22 people per sq km)
Total area: 173,860 sq miles (450,295 sq km)
Languages: Swedish*, Finnish, Sami
Currency: Swedish krona = 100 öre

BELGIUM
Northwest Europe
Capital: Brussels
Population: 11.3 million / 874 people per sq mile (338 people per sq km)
Total area: 11,787 sq miles (30,528 km)
Languages: Dutch*, French*, German*, Flemish
Currency: Euro = 100 cents

LUXEMBOURG
Northwest Europe
Capital: Luxembourg
Population: 582,300 / 583 people per sq mile (225 people per sq km)
Total area: 998 sq miles (2,586 km)
Languages: French*, German*, Luxembourgish*, Portuguese
Currency: Euro = 100 cents

NETHERLANDS
Northwest Europe
Capital: Amsterdam/The Hague
Population: 17 million / 1,060 people per sq mile (409 people per sq km)
Total area: 16,040 sq miles (41,543 km)
Languages: Dutch*, Frisian
Currency: Euro = 100 cents

IRELAND
Northwest Europe
Capital: Dublin
Population: 4.9 million / 181 people per sq mile (70 people per sq km)
Total area: 27,133 sq miles (70,273 km)
Languages: English*, Irish*
Currency: Euro = 100 cents

UNITED KINGDOM

Northwest Europe
Capital: London
Population: 64.4 million / 685 people per sq mile (264 people per sq km)
Total area: 94,058 sq miles (243,610 km)
Languages: English*, Welsh
Currency: Pound sterling = 100 pence

FRANCE
Western Europe
Capital: Paris
Population: 62.8 million / 295 people per sq mile (114 people per sq km)
Total area: 212,935 sq miles (551,500 km)
Languages: French*, Provencal, Breton, Catalan, Basque, Corsican
Currency: Euro = 100 cents

MONACO
Southern Europe
Capital: Monaco
Population: 30,581 / 39,602 people per sq mile (15,291 people per sq km)
Total area: 0.77 sq miles (2 km)
Languages: French*, Italian, Monégasque, English
Currency: Euro = 100 cents

ANDORRA
Southwest Europe
Capital: Andorra la Vella
Population: 85,580 / 474 people per sq mile (183 people per sq km)
Total area: 181 sq miles (468 km)
Languages: Catalan*, Spanish, French, Portuguese
Currency: Euro = 100 cents

PORTUGAL
Southwest Europe

Capital: Lisbon
Population: 10.8 million / 281 people per sq mile (109 people per sq km)
Total area: 35,556 sq miles (92,090 km)
Languages: Portuguese*, Mirandese
Currency: Euro = 100 cents

SPAIN
Southwest Europe

Capital: Madrid
Population: 48.6 million / 249 people per sq mile (96 people per sq km)
Total area: 195,125 sq miles (505,370 km)
Languages: Castilian Spanish*, Catalan*, Galician*, Basque*
Currency: Euro = 100 cents

AUSTRIA
Central Europe
Capital: Vienna
Population: 8.7 million / 269 people per sq mile (104 people per sq km)
Total area: 32,383 sq miles (83,871 km)
Languages: German*, Turkish, Serbian, Croatian, Slovene, Hungarian (Magyar)
Currency: Euro = 100 cents

GERMANY
Northern Europe
Capital: Berlin
Population: 81 million / 588 people per sq mile (227 people per sq km)
Total area: 137,847 sq miles (357,022 km)
Languages: German*
Currency: Euro = 100 cents

LIECHTENSTEIN
Central Europe
Capital: Vaduz
Population: 37,937 / 614 people per sq mile (237 people per sq km)
Total area: 62 sq miles (160 km)
Languages: German*, Alemannish dialect, Italian
Currency: Swiss franc = 100 centimes

SLOVENIA
Central Europe

Capital: Ljubljana
Population: 2 million / 256 people per sq mile (99 people per sq km)
Total area: 7,827 sq miles (20,273 km)
Languages: Slovene*, Serbo-Croat
Currency: Euro = 100 cents

SWITZERLAND
Central Europe
Capital: Bern
Population: 8.2 million / 515 people per sq mile (199 people per sq km)
Total area: 15,937 sq miles (41,277 km)
Languages: German*, French*, Italian*, Romansch*
Currency: Swiss franc = 100 centimes

ITALY
Southern Europe
Capital: Rome
Population: 62 million / 533 people per sq mile (206 people per sq km)
Total area: 116,348 sq miles (301,340 km)
Languages: Italian*, German, French, Slovene
Currency: Euro = 100 cents

MALTA
Southern Europe
Capital: Valletta
Population: 415,196 / 3,403 people per sq mile (1,314 people per sq km)
Total area: 122 sq miles (316 km)
Languages: Maltese*, English
Currency: Euro = 100 cents

SAN MARINO
Southern Europe
Capital: San Marino
Population: 33,285 / 1,413 people per sq mile (546 people per sq km)
Total area: 24 sq miles (61 km)
Language: Italian*
Currency: Euro = 100 cents

VATICAN CITY
Southern Europe
Capital: Vatican City
Population: 1000 / 5,886 people per sq mile (2,273 people per sq km)
Total area: 0.17 sq miles (0.44 km)
Languages: Italian*, Latin*
Currency: Euro = 100 cents

CZECH REPUBLIC
Central Europe
Capital: Prague
Population: 10.6 million / 348 people per sq mile (134 people per sq km)
Total area: 30,450 sq miles (78,867 km)
Languages: Czech*, Slovak,
Currency: Czech koruna = 100 halers

HUNGARY
Central Europe

Capital: Budapest
Population: 9.9 million / 276 people per sq mile (106 people per sq km)
Total area: 35,918 sq miles (93,028 km)
Languages: Hungarian*
Currency: Forint = 100 fillér

POLAND
Northern Europe

Capital: Warsaw
Population: 38.5 million / 319 people per sq mile (123 people per sq km)
Total area: 120,728 sq miles (312,685 km)
Languages: Polish*, Silesian
Currency: Zloty = 100 groszy

SLOVAKIA
Central Europe

Capital: Bratislava
Population: 5.5 million / 291 people per sq mile (112 people per sq km)
Total area: 18,933 sq miles (49,035 km)
Languages: Slovak*, Hungarian (Magyar), Romany
Currency: Euro = 100 cents

ALBANIA
Southeast Europe
Capital: Tirana
Population: 3 million / 270 people per sq mile (104 people per sq km)
Total area: 11,100 sq miles (28,748 km)
Languages: Albanian*, Greek, Macedonian
Currency: Lek = 100 qindarkas

BOSNIA AND HERZEGOVINA
Southeast Europe

Capital: Sarajevo
Population: 3.9 million / 197 people per sq mile (76 people per sq km)
Total area: 19,767 sq miles (51,197 km)
Languages: Bosnian*, Croatian*, Serbian*
Currency: Marka = 100 pfenigs

CROATIA
Southeast Europe

Capital: Zagreb
Population: 4.5 million / 206 people per sq mile (80 people per sq km)
Total area: 21,851 sq miles (56,594 km)
Languages: Croatian*, Serbian, Hungarian
Currency: Kuna = 100 lipa

MACEDONIA
Southeast Europe

Capital: Skopje
Population: 2.1 million / 212 people per sq mile (82 people per sq km)
Total area: 9,928 sq miles (25,713 km)
Languages: Macedonian*, Albanian, Turkish
Currency: Macedonian denar = 100 deni

MONTENEGRO
Southern Europe
Capital: Podgorica
Population: 644,578 / 121 people per sq mile (47 people per sq km)
Total area: 5,322 sq miles (13,812 km)
Languages: Montenegrin*, Serbian, Bosnian, Albanian
Currency: Euro = 100 cents

SERBIA
Southern Europe
Capital: Belgrade
Population: 7.1 million / 238 people per sq mile (92 people per sq km)
Total area: 29,913 sq miles (77,474 km)
Languages: Serbian*, Hungarian
Currency: Serbian dinar = 100 para

CYPRUS
Southeast Europe
Capital: Nicosia
Population: 1.2 million / 336 people per sq mile (130 people per sq km)
Total area: 3,751 sq miles (9,250 km)
Languages: Greek*, Turkish*, English
Currency: Euro = 100 cents

BULGARIA
Southeast Europe

Capital: Sofia
Population: 7.2 million / 168 people per sq mile (65 people per sq km)
Total area: 42,811 sq miles (110,879 km)
Languages: Bulgarian*, Turkish, Roma
Currency: Lev = 100 stotinki

GREECE
Southeast Europe
Capital: Athens
Population: 10.7 million / 210 people per sq mile (81 people per sq km)
Total area: 50,949 sq miles (131,957 km)
Languages: Greek*
Currency: Euro = 100 cents

BELARUS
Eastern Europe
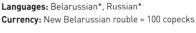
Capital: Minsk
Population: 9.6 million / 120 people per sq mile (46 people per sq km)
Total area: 80,154 sq miles (207,600 km)
Languages: Belarussian*, Russian*
Currency: New Belarussian rouble = 100 copecks

ESTONIA
Northeast Europe

Capital: Tallinn
Population: 1.3 million / 74 people per sq mile (29 people per sq km)
Total area: 17,463 sq miles (45,228 km)
Languages: Estonian*, Russian
Currency: Euro = 100 cents

LATVIA
Northeast Europe
Capital: Riga
Population: 2 million / 80 people per sq mile (31 people per sq km)
Total area: 24,938 sq miles (64,589 km)
Languages: Latvian*, Russian
Currency: Euro = 100 cents

LITHUANIA
Northeast Europe
Capital: Vilnius
Population: 2.8 million / 111 people per sq mile (43 people per sq km)
Total area: 25,213 sq miles (65,300 sq km)
Languages: Lithuanian*, Russian
Currency: Euro = 100 cents

MOLDOVA
Southeast Europe
Capital: Chisinau
Population: 3.5 million / 268 people per sq mile (103 people per sq km)
Total area: 13,070 sq miles (33,851 sq km)
Languages: Moldovan*, Romanian, Russian
Currency: Moldovan leu = 100 bani

ROMANIA
Southeast Europe
Capital: Bucharest
Population: 21.6 million / 235 people per sq mile (91 people per sq km)
Total area: 91,699 sq miles (237,500 sq km)
Languages: Romanian*, Hungarian, Romany
Currency: Romanian leu = 100 bani

UKRAINE
Eastern Europe
Capital: Kiev
Population: 44.2 million / 190 people per sq mile (73 people per sq km)
Total area: 233,031 sq miles (603,550 sq km)
Languages: Ukrainian*, Russian
Currency: Hryvnia = 100 kopiykas

RUSSIAN FEDERATION
Europe/Asia
Capital: Moscow
Population: 142.4 million 22 people per sq mile / (8 people per sq km)
Total area: 6,601,668 sq miles (17,098,242 sq km)
Languages: Russian*, Tatar
Currency: Russian Rouble = 100 kopeks

ASIA

KAZAKHSTAN
Central Asia
Capital: Astana
Population: 18.4 million / 15 people per sq mile (6 people per sq km)
Total area: 1,052,090 sq miles (2,724,900 sq km)
Languages: Kazakh*, Russian
Currency: Tenge = 100 tiin

ARMENIA
Southwest Asia
Capital: Yerevan
Population: 3.1 million / 270 people per sq mile (104 people per sq km)
Total area: 11,484 sq miles (29,743 sq km)
Languages: Armenian*, Russian, Kurdish
Currency: Dram = 100 luma

AZERBAIJAN
Southwest Asia
Capital: Baku
Population: 9.8 million / 293 people per sq mile (113 people per sq km)
Total area: 33,436 sq miles (86,600 sq km)
Languages: Azeri*, Russian
Currency: Manat = 100 qopiks

GEORGIA
Southwest Asia
Capital: Tbilisi
Population: 4.9 million / 182 people per sq mile (70 people per sq km)
Total area: 26,911 sq miles (69,700 sq km)
Languages: Georgian*, Russian
Currency: Lari = 100 tetri

TURKEY
Asia/Europe
Capital: Ankara
Population: 80.3 million / 265 people per sq mile (103 people per sq km)
Total area: 302,535 sq miles (783,562 sq km)
Languages: Turkish*, Kurdish
Currency: Turkish lira = 100 kurus

ISRAEL
Southwest Asia
Capital: Jerusalem (disputed)
Population: 8.2 million / 1,023 people per sq mile (395 people per sq km)
Total area: 8,019 sq miles (20,770 sq km)
Languages: Hebrew*, Arabic, English
Currency: Shekel = 100 agorot

JORDAN
Southwest Asia
Capital: Amman
Population: 8.2 million / 143 people per sq mile (55 people per sq km)
Total area: 34,495 sq miles (89,342 sq km)
Languages: Arabic*
Currency: Jordanian dinar = 1,000 fils

LEBANON
Southwest Asia
Capital: Beirut
Population: 6.2 million / 1,544 people per sq mile (596 people per sq km)
Total area: 4,015 sq miles (10,400 sq km)
Languages: Arabic*, French, Armenian, Assyrian
Currency: Lebanese pound = 100 piastres

SYRIA
Southwest Asia
Capital: Damascus
Population: 17.2 million / 241 people per sq mile (93 people per sq km)
Total area: 71,498 sq miles (185,180 sq km)
Languages: Arabic*, Kurdish, Armenian, Circassian, Aramaic
Currency: Syrian pound = 100 piastres

BAHRAIN
Southwest Asia
Capital: Manama
Population: 1.3 million / 4,590 people per sq mile (1,772 people per sq km)
Total area: 293 sq miles (720 sq km)
Languages: Arabic*, English, Urdu, Farsi
Currency: Bahraini dinar = 1,000 fils

IRAN
Southwest Asia
Capital: Tehran
Population: 82.8 million / 130 people per sq mile (50 people per sq km)
Total area: 636,372 sq miles (1,648,195 sq km)
Languages: Farsi (Persian)*, Azeri, Gilaki, Balochi, Mazandarani, Kurdish, Arabic
Currency: Iranian rial = 10 tomans

IRAQ
Southwest Asia
Capital: Baghdad
Population: 38.2 million / 226 people per sq mile (87 people per sq km)
Total area: 169,235 sq miles (438,317 sq km)
Languages: Arabic*, Kurdish*, Armenian, Assyrian, Turkic languages
Currency: Iraqi dinar = 100 fils

KUWAIT
Southwest Asia
Capital: Kuwait City
Population: 2.8 million / 407 people per sq mile (157 people per sq km)
Total area: 6,880 sq miles (17,820 sq km)
Languages: Arabic*, English
Currency: Kuwaiti dinar = 1,000 fils

OMAN
Southwest Asia
Capital: Muscat
Population: 3.4 million / 28 people per sq mile (11 people per sq km)
Total area: 119,499 sq miles (309,500 sq km)
Languages: Arabic*, Baluchi
Currency: Omani rial = 1000 baizas

QATAR
Southwest Asia
Capital: Doha
Population: 2.3 million / 514 people per sq mile (198 people per sq km)
Total area: 4,473 sq miles (11,586 sq km)
Languages: Arabic*
Currency: Qatar riyal = 100 dirhams

SAUDI ARABIA
Southwest Asia
Capital: Riyadh
Population: 28.1 million / 34 people per sq mile (13 people per sq km)
Total area: 830,000 sq miles (2,149,690 sq km)
Languages: Arabic*
Currency: Saudi riyal = 100 halalas

UNITED ARAB EMIRATES
Southwest Asia
Capital: Abu Dhabi
Population: 5.9 million / 183 people per sq mile (71 people per sq km)
Total area: 32,278 sq miles (82,600 sq km)
Languages: Arabic*, Farsi, English, Indian and Pakistani languages
Currency: UAE dirham = 100 fils

YEMEN
Southwest Asia
Capital: Sana
Population: 27.4 million / 134 people per sq mile (52 people per sq km)
Total area: 203,850 sq miles (527,968 sq km)
Languages: Arabic*
Currency: Yemeni rial = 100 fils

AFGHANISTAN
Central Asia
Capital: Kabul
Population: 32 million / 129 people per sq mile (50 people per sq km)
Total area: 251,827 sq miles (652,230 sq km)
Languages: Persian*, Pashto*, Uzbek, Turkmen
Currency: Afghani = 100 puls

KYRGYZSTAN
Central Asia
Capital: Bishkek
Population: 5.7 million / 74 people per sq mile (29 people per sq km)
Total area: 77,202 sq miles (199,951 sq km)
Languages: Krygyz*, Russian*, Uzbek
Currency: Som = 100 tyiyn

TAJIKISTAN
Central Asia
Capital: Dushanbe
Population: 8.3 million / 149 people per sq mile (58 people per sq km)
Total area: 55,637 sq miles (144,100 sq km)
Languages: Tajik*, Russian
Currency: Somoni = 100 diram

TURKMENISTAN
Central Asia
Capital: Ashgabat
Population: 5.3 million / 28 people per sq mile (11 people per sq km)
Total area: 188,455 sq miles (488,100 sq km)
Languages: Turkmen*, Russian, Uzbek
Currency: Manat = 100 tenge

UZBEKISTAN
Central Asia
Capital: Tashkent
Population: 29.5 million / 171 people per sq mile (66 people per sq km)
Total area: 172,741 sq miles (447,400 sq km)
Languages: Uzbek*, Russian
Currency: Som = 100 tiyin

CHINA
East Asia
Capital: Beijing
Population: 1.37 billion / 370 people per sq mile (143 people per sq km)
Total area: 3,705,960 sq miles (9,596,960 sq km)
Languages: Mandarin*, Wu, Cantonese, Xiang, Min, Hakka, Gan
Currency: Yuan (Renminbi) = 100 fen

MONGOLIA
East Asia
Capital: Ulan Bator
Population: 3 million / 4 people per sq mile (2 people per sq km)
Total area: 603,909 sq miles (1,566,116 sq km)
Languages: Khalkha Mongolian*, Kazakh, Chinese, Russian
Currency: Tögrög = 100 möngös

NORTH KOREA
East Asia
Capital: Pyongyang
Population: 25.1 million / 539 people per sq mile (208 people per sq km)
Total area: 46,540 sq miles (120,538 sq km)
Languages: Korean*
Currency: North Korean won = 100 chon

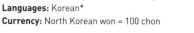

SOUTH KOREA
East Asia
Capital: Seoul
Population: 50.9 million / 1,322 people per sq mile (510 people per sq km)
Total area: 38,502 sq miles (99,720 sq km)
Languages: Korean*
Currency: South Korean won = 100 jeon

TAIWAN
East Asia
Capital: Taipei
Population: 22.5 million / 1,620 people per sq mile (625 people per sq km)
Total area: 13,892 sq miles (35,980 sq km)
Languages: Mandarin Chinese*, Taiwanese (Min), Hakka Chinese
Currency: Taiwan dollar = 100 cents

JAPAN
East Asia
Capital: Tokyo
Population: 127.7 million / 868 people per sq mile (335 people per sq km)
Total area: 145,914 sq miles (377,915 sq km)
Languages: Japanese
Currency: Yen = 100 sen

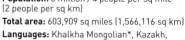

INDIA
South Asia
Capital: New Delhi
Population: 1.27 billion / 1,001 people per sq mile (386 people per sq km)
Total area: 1,269,219 sq miles (3,287,263 sq km)
Languages: Hindi*, English*, Urdu, Bengali, Marathi, Telugu, Tamil, Kannada, other
Currency: Indian rupee = 100 paise

SRI LANKA
South Asia
Capital: Colombo
Population: 22.2 million / 876 people per sq mile (338 people per sq km)
Total area: 25,332 sq miles (65,610 sq km)
Languages: Sinhalese*, Tamil, English
Currency: Sri Lanka rupee = 100 cents

MALDIVES
Indian Ocean
Capital: Malé
Population: 393,000 / 3,415 people per sq mile (1,319 people per sq km)
Total area: 115 sq miles (298 sq km)
Languages: Dhivehi*, English
Currency: Rufiyaa = 100 laari

PAKISTAN
South Asia
Capital: Islamabad
Population: 202 million / 657 people per sq mile (254 people per sq km)
Total area: 307,374 sq miles (796,095 sq km)
Languages: Urdu*, Punjabi, Sindhi, Pashtu, Balochi
Currency: Pakistani rupee = 100 paise

BANGLADESH
South Asia
Capital: Dhaka
Population: 169 million / 2,948 people per sq mile (1,138 people per sq km)
Total area: 57,321 sq miles (148,460 sq km)
Languages: Bengali*, Urdu, Chakma
Currency: Taka = 100 poisha

BHUTAN
South Asia
Capital: Thimphu
Population: 741,919 / 50 people per sq mile (19 people per sq km)
Total area: 14,824 sq miles (38,394 sq km)
Languages: Dzongkha*, Sharchhopka, Lhotshamkha
Currency: Ngultrum = 100 chetrum

NEPAL
South Asia
Capital: Kathmandu
Population: 29 million / 510 people per sq mile (197 people per sq km)
Total area: 56,827 sq miles (147,181 sq km)
Languages: Nepali*, Maithili, Bhojpuri
Currency: Nepalese rupee = 100 paise

CAMBODIA
Southeast Asia
Capital: Phnom Penh
Population: 15.7 million / 225 people per sq mile 87 people per sq mile
Total area: 69,898 sq miles (181,035 sq km)
Languages: Khmer*, French, Chinese, Vietnamese, Cham
Currency: Riel = 100 sen

LAOS
Southeast Asia
Capital: Vientiane
Population: 7 million / 77 people per sq mile 30 people per sq mile
Total area: 91,428 sq miles (236,800 sq km)
Languages: Lao*, various local dialects, French
Currency: New kip = 100 att

MYANMAR (BURMA)
Southeast Asia
Capital: Nay Pyi Taw
Population: 56.9 million / 218 people per sq mile (84 people per sq km)
Total area: 261,228 sq miles (676,578 sq km)
Languages: Burmese*
Currency: Kyat = 100 pyas

THAILAND
Southeastern Asia
Capital: Bangkok
Population: 68.2 million / 344 people per sq mile (133 people per sq km)
Total area: 198,117 sq miles (513,120 sq km)
Languages: Thai*, Burmese
Currency: Baht = 100 satangs

VIETNAM
Southeast Asia
Capital: Hanoi
Population: 95.3 million / 745 people per sq mile (288 people per sq km)
Languages: Vietnamese*, Chinese, Khmer
Currency: Dông = 10 hao = 100 xu

BRUNEI
Southeast Asia
Capital: Bandar Seri Begawan
Population: 429,646 / 193 people per sq mile (75 people per sq km)
Total area: 2,226 sq miles (5,765 sq km)
Languages: Malay*, English, Chinese
Currency: Brunei dollar = 100 cents

EAST TIMOR
Southeast Asia
Capital: Dili
Population: 1.2 million / 210 people per sq mile (81 people per sq km)
Total area: 3,756 sq miles (14,874 sq km)
Languages: Tetum*, Indonesian, Portuguese*
Currency: US dollar = 100 cents

INDONESIA
Southeast Asia
Capital: Jakarta
Population: 258 million / 351 people per sq mile (135 people per sq km)
Total area: 735,358 sq miles (1,904,569 sq km)
Languages: Bahasa Indonesia*, more than 700 other languages are used
Currency: Rupiah = 100 sen

MALAYSIA
Southeast Asia
Capital: Kuala Lumpur
Population: 31 million / 243 people per sq mile (94 people per sq km)
Total area: 127,355 sq miles (329,847 sq km)
Languages: Bahasa Malaysia*, Chinese*, English, Tamil
Currency: Ringgit = 100 sen

PHILIPPINES
Southeast Asia
Capital: Manila
Population: 102.6 million / 886 people per sq mile (342 people per sq km)
Total area: 115,830 sq miles (300,000 sq km)
Languages: Filipino*, English*, Cebuano
Currency: Philippine Peso = 100 centavos

SINGAPORE
Southeast Asia
Capital: Singapore
Population: 5.8 million / 21,552 people per sq mile (8,321 people per sq km)
Total area: 269 sq miles (697 sq km)
Languages: Malay*, Mandarin*, English*, Tamil*
Currency: Singapore dollar = 100 cents

AUSTRALASIA AND OCEANIA

FIJI
Australasia and Oceania

Capital: Suva
Population: 915,303 / 130 people per sq mile (50 people per sq km)
Total area: 7,055 sq miles (18,274 sq km)
Languages: Fijian*, English*, Hindi, Urdu, Tamil, Telegu
Currency: Fijian dollar = 100 cents

KIRIBATI
Australasia and Oceania
Capital: Tarawa Atoll
Population: 106,925 / 342 people per sq mile (132 people per sq km)
Total area: 313 sq miles (811 sq km)
Languages: English*, Kiribati
Currency: Australian dollar = 100 cents

MARSHALL ISLANDS
Australasia and Oceania
Capital: Majuro
Population: 73,376 / 1,050 people per sq mile (405 people per sq km)
Total area: 70 sq miles (181 sq km)
Languages: Marshallese*, English*
Currency: US dollar = 100 cents

MICRONESIA
Australasia and Oceania
Capital: Palikir
Population: 104,700 / 490 people per sq mile (189 people per sq km)
Total area: 271 sq miles (702 sq km)
Languages: English, Trukese, Pohnpeian, Mortlockese, Kosrean
Currency: US dollar = 100 cents

NAURU
Australasia and Oceania
Capital: No official capital
Population: 9,591 / 1,183 people per sq mile (457 people per sq km)
Total area: 8 sq miles (21 sq km)
Languages: Nauruan*, English, Kiribati, Chinese
Currency: Australian dollar = 100 cents

PALAU
Australasia and Oceania
Capital: Melekeok
Population: 21,347 / 121 people per sq mile (47 people per sq km)
Total area: 177 sq miles (459 sq km)
Languages: Palauan, English*, Sonsorolese*
Currency: US dollar = 100 cents

PAPUA NEW GUINEA
Australasia and Oceania
Capital: Port Moresby
Population: 6.8 million / 38 people per sq mile (15 people per sq km)
Total area: 178,703 sq miles (462,840 sq km)
Languages: Tok Pisin*, English*, Hiri Motu*, over 800 native languages
Currency: Kina = 100 toea

SAMOA
Australasia and Oceania
Capital: Apia
Population: 198,930 / 182 people per sq mile (70 people per sq km)
Total area: 1,093 sq miles (2,831 sq km)
Languages: Samoan*, English
Currency: Tala = 100 sene

SOLOMON ISLANDS
Australasia and Oceania
Capital: Honiara
Population: 635,000 / 57 people per sq mile (22 people per sq km)
Total area: 11,157 sq miles (28,896 sq km)
Languages: English*, Melanesian Pidgin, 120 indigenous languages
Currency: Solomon Islands dollar = 100 cents

TONGA
Australasia and Oceania
Capital: Nuku'alofa
Population: 106,500 / 366 people per sq mile (141 people per sq km)
Total area: 288 sq miles (747 sq km)
Languages: Tongan*, English
Currency: Pa'anga = 100 seniti

TUVALU
Australasia and Oceania
Capital: Funafuti Atoll
Population: 10,900 / 1,086 people per sq mile (419 people per sq km)
Total area: 10 sq miles (26 sq km)
Languages: Tuvaluan*, English*, Kiribati
Currency: Australian/Tuvaluan dollar = 100 cents

VANUATU
Australasia and Oceania
Capital: Port Vila
Population: 277,600 / 59 people per sq mile (23 people per sq km)
Total area: 4,706 sq miles (12,189 sq km)
Languages: Bislama*, English*, French*
Currency: Vatu

AUSTRALIA
Australasia and Oceania
Capital: Canberra
Population: 22.8 million / 8 people per sq mile (3 people per sq km)
Total area: 2,988,902 sq miles (7,741,220 sq km)
Languages: English*, Mandarin, Greek, Arabic, Italian, Aboriginal languages
Currency: Australian dollar = 100 cents

NEW ZEALAND
Australasia and Oceania
Capital: Wellington
Population: 4.5 million / 43 people per sq mile (17 people per sq km)
Total area: 103,799 sq miles (268,838 sq km)
Languages: English*, Maori*
Currency: New Zealand dollar = 100 cents

THAT IS NOT SQUARE OR RECTANGULAR IN SHAPE.

Glossary

Alkaline
Describes something that contains high levels of salts, such as a lake.

Amerindian
The peoples native to America, who lived there long before the arrival of European explorers and settlers.

Amphibious
Term used to describe a cold-blooded animal that is able to live both on land and in water, such as frogs, toads, and salamanders.

Aquatic
Animal or plant that lives in water.

Arachnid
Type of animal, such as a spider or a scorpion, that has a two-part body and four pairs of legs.

Archipelago
A group, or chain, of islands.

Arthropod
An animal without a backbone but with a hard outer shell, and with legs that can bend in many places, such as crabs, spiders, and centipedes.

Asteroid
A small body of rock or metal that circles the Sun, mainly between the orbits of Mars and Jupiter.

Atmosphere
The layer of gases, including oxygen and nitrogen, that surrounds Earth and protects us from radiation and debris coming in from space.

Atoll
A circular, or horseshoe-shaped, coral reef enclosing a shallow area of water (lagoon).

Biome
A large area that has a particular climate, type of vegetation, and species of animals living in it.

Birth rate
The number of children born in an area, usually measured in the number of live births per 1,000 individuals within a population, or the average number of children per woman in that area.

Boreal forest
A type of coniferous forest— *see* taiga.

Broadleaf forest
A type of forest that can be temperate (with trees such as oak) or tropical (with various types of palm trees).

Caldera
A huge crater in a volcano, often formed by the collapse of the volcano's cone during an eruption.

Canyon
A steep valley that has been carved through rock by a river.

Civil war
A war between people living in the same country, because of political, religious, or racial differences.

Climate
What the weather is usually like, over a long time, in a specific area.

Climate change
When the climate is changing, due to Earth's atmosphere getting hotter because of human activity, such as pollution. Higher temperatures will affect weather systems, which in turn will affect the people, animals, and plants living in an area.

Coniferous
A type of tree or shrub, such as pine or fir, that has needles instead of leaves. They are found in both temperate and boreal forests.

Continent
One of the seven large landmasses on Earth: North America, South America, Europe, Africa, Asia, Australasia and Oceania, and Antarctica.

Crust
The hard, thin, outer shell of Earth.

Deciduous forest
A type of broadleaf forest found in temperate regions.

Deforestation
The cutting down of trees for timber or to clear the land for farming or for roads. It can lead to soil erosion.

Delta
A low-lying, fan-shaped area at a river mouth, usually where it flows into the sea. It is formed by layers of sediment brought along by the river.

Democracy
A system of ruling a country in which the people have a say, usually in the form of voting for who will be the country's leader (such as a president or prime minister).

Desert
A very arid (dry) region that has little or no precipitation. Some are cold deserts, such as the barren areas of rock and ice in the Arctic and Antarctic.

Dictatorship
The rule of a country by a person who often came to, or held on to, power without the vote of their people; the opposite of democracy.

Disputed territory
An area, or country, that wants to be independent from another, but that has not been officially recognized by the original nation, or the United Nations (UN).

Diversity
The variety of plants and animals in an ecosystem; or of different people living in an area.

Dormant
Describes a volcano which is not extinct, but that has not erupted for a long time, although is likely to do so in the future.

Ecosystem
How all living things in an area interact with each other, the climate, and the various habitats there.

Elevation
The height of land above sea level.

Endemic
An animal or plant that is native and particular to one specific area.

Equator
The 0° line of latitude. It divides Earth into the northern and southern hemispheres.

Erosion
The wearing down of the land surface by running water, waves, ice, wind, and weather.

Evolution
How animals and plants change and develop over a long time, in order to adapt and survive.

Extinct
Refers to an animal that no longer exists, due to overhunting or loss of habitat.

Fjord
A long, narrow, and deep inlet of sea situated between steep, coastal mountain sides.

Geyser
A fountain of hot water that erupts regularly as underground streams come into contact with hot rocks.

Glaciation
When ice sheets and glaciers grow and how that changes the landscape.

Glacier
A mass of ice made up of compacted and frozen snow, which moves slowly down a mountain, eroding and depositing rocks as it flows.

Gravity
The pulling force that attracts objects to each other—it keeps us on Earth, and planets in their orbits.

Habitat
The environment or place in which an animal or plant normally lives.

Hemisphere
The northern hemisphere is the half of Earth that sits above the Equator; the southern hemisphere is the half of the globe that falls below it.

Hominin
Humans, including the very first type of human ancestor, that first appeared in Africa about 7 million years ago.

Hurricane
A violent, tropical storm, also known as a cyclone in the Indian Ocean, and as a typhoon in the Pacific Ocean.

Iceberg
A large, floating mass of ice that has broken off from a glacier, or ice shelf, with most of its body underwater.

Ice sheet
A permanent layer of ice that covers large areas of land, such as in Antarctica or Greenland.

Ice shelf
A permanent layer of ice that floats on water, but which is partly attached to land.

Inca empire
A powerful ancient empire located in the Andes mountains of South America, which was conquered by the Spanish in the 16th century.

Indigenous
A plant, animal, or people native to a geographical area.

Infrastructure
A term used to describe the things that make a country or region function, such as roads, transportation, communications, schools, and industry.

Interstellar
Means "between stars."

Invertebrate
Animals that do not have a backbone, such as insects, crabs, and worms.

Isthmus
A narrow strip of land with water on either side that connects two larger landmasses.

Lagoon
A shallow stretch of coastal salt-water that is partly sheltered behind a barrier, such as a sandbank or coral reef; see atoll.

Latitude
A series of imaginary lines that run parallel to the Equator, measured in degrees north or south of it. The Equator is 0°, the North Pole 90°N, and the South Pole 90°S.

Longitude
As latitude, but giving the distance for how far east or west something is from 0° longitude in Greenwich, London, in the United Kingdom.

Mammal
Warm-blooded animals that give birth to babies that feed on milk.

Mangrove
Trees and shrubs that grow along muddy shores and riverbanks, often in salty water, and with many of their roots exposed.

Marsupial
A type of mammal, such as a kangaroo, that keeps its young in a pouch on its stomach until they can take care of themselves.

Mayan empire
An ancient civilization in South America that existed from around 2,000 BCE to the 16th century, when they were conquered by the Spanish.

Metropolitan area
The built-up, often densely populated area surrounding a city, including suburbs and nearby urban areas.

Migration
The movement of animals or people from one place to another, often to find food or to breed.

Molten
Rock or metal that has been heated to liquid form; lava is molten rock.

Monsoon
A seasonal wind in South and East Asia that brings heavy rains.

Montane
The type of biome (climate, plants, and wildlife) found in mountains.

Nomad
People who move around a region to find fresh pasture for their herds.

Oasis
A fertile, green area in a desert that usually gets its water from underground sources.

Peninsula
A thin strip of land that sticks out from the mainland into the ocean.

Plain
A flat, low-lying region of land.

Plateau
A flat area of land on a highland.

Population density
Describes how crowded or sparsely populated an area is, based on how many people live per square mile or square kilometer—it is worked out by dividing a country's (or city's) population by its area.

Precipitation
The moisture that falls from the atmosphere onto Earth, in the form of rain, snow, hail, or sleet.

Prevailing winds
Commonly occurring winds that blow in the same direction, and which influence the climate of a particular region.

Rain forest
Dense forests growing in tropical zones, with high rainfall, temperature, and humidity.

Rift valley
A long depression in Earth's crust, formed by the sinking of rocks between two faults or plates.

River basin
The land into which water (usually in the form of rivers) gathers.

Rural
Relating to unbuilt areas, usually countryside; the opposite of urban.

Sea ice
The ice that forms when ocean water in the polar regions freezes.

Steppe
Large areas of dry grassland in the northern hemisphere—especially in southeast Europe and central Asia.

Subcontinent
A large landmass that is part of a continent, such as India (subcontinent) in Asia (continent).

Subtropical
An area or climate that is nearly tropical, located to the north or south of the tropics.

Taiga
The Russian word for a coniferous forest.

Tectonic plates
Huge interlocking plates that make up Earth's surface. A plate boundary is the point at which plates meet, and where earthquakes often occur.

Temperate
The mild, variable climate found in areas between the tropics and cold polar regions.

Tetrapod
Any vertebrate (animal that has a spine) with four limbs (arms or legs).

Time zone
The world is split into 39 different time zones. Most are set whole hours ahead or behind Coordinated Universal Time (UTC)—the time at the Greenwich Meridian in London, UK. Some, however, are whole hours plus 30 or 45 minutes ahead or behind UTC.

Trade wind
A prevailing wind that blows toward the Equator, either from northeast or southeast.

Trench
A deep valley in the ocean floor, formed when tectonic plates collide.

Tributary
A stream or small river that feeds into a larger one.

Tropical
Referring to the climate or biomes in the areas just north and south of the Equator. These areas are characterized by heavy rainfall, high temperatures, and no clearly defined seasons.

Tundra
A biome in the very cold, northern parts of Europe, North America, and Asia, in which the ground never thaws beneath the surface (called permafrost).

United Nations (UN)
An organization of 193 states that work together to keep peace in the world, and make it better for all people who live here.

UNESCO
Part of the UN, UNESCO works for peace by helping people understand each other through their cultures. They have made a list of heritage sites that should be protected, ranging from natural landscapes to historic buildings.

Urban
Built up; relating to living in a town or a city.

Urbanization
A term that refers to both the growth of towns and cities, and to the number of people that move from rural to urban areas.

Index

Acknowledgments

The publisher would like to thank the following for their kind permission to reproduce their photographs:

(Key: a-above; b-below/bottom; c-center; f-far; l-left; r-right; t-top)

4-5 Science Photo Library: Mark Garlick. 6 Science Photo Library: Richard Bizley (bl). 7 Science Photo Library: Mark Garlick (br). 8 123RF.com: Tolga Tezcan / tolgatezcan (bc); Oleg Znamenskiy / znm (bl). 9 Dr. Brian Choo: (tl). Dorling Kindersley: Natural History Museum, London (br, bl); Royal Museum of Scotland, Edinburgh (bc). 11 Dorling Kindersley: Natural History Museum, London (br); Jon Hughes (tr); Swedish Museum of Natural History (bl). Science Photo Library: Christian Darkin (tl). 12 Dorling Kindersley: Jon Hughes (bl). 13 Dorling Kindersley: Natural History Museum, London (bc). Dreamstime.com: Mr1805 (tl). 14 Alamy Stock Photo: Kostyantyn Ivanyshen / Stocktrek Images, Inc. (bl). Dorling Kindersley: Natural History Museum, London (tc). Dreamstime.com: Roberto Caucino / Rcaucino (bc); Digitalstormcinema (br). 15 Getty Images: Robert Postma / First Light (bl). 21 PunchStock: Peter Adams (cra). 22 Dreamstime.com: Bryan Busovicki (cr); Paul Lemke (tl). 23 123RF.com: bennymarty (cr). Dreamstime.com: Harryfn (tl). 24 Dreamstime.com: Rafael Ben-ari (tc). 25 123RF.com: Kan Khampanya (cra). Alamy Stock Photo: Kike Calvo / Vwpics (tc). 26 Getty Images: Carol Polich Photo Workshops (bc). 27 Alamy Stock Photo: Danita Delimont (tc); Henk Meijer (tr); Colleen Miniuk-Sperry (cr). Getty Images: Bloomberg (bc). 28 Alamy Stock Photo: IE204 (tc). 29 123RF.com: ishtygashev (cr). 30 Alamy Stock Photo: Iuliia Bycheva (tc). 33 123RF.com: Menno Schaefer (cr). 34 Getty Images: Chris Moore - Exploring Light Photography (tc). 35 Alamy Stock Photo: Reynold Mainse / Perspectives (cra); Martin Shields (ca). Dreamstime.com: Altinosmanaj (cr). Getty Images: Walter Bibikow (c). 38 Alamy Stock Photo: Mary Evans Picture Library (br). 39 Alamy Stock Photo: Yadid Levy (cr). 41 Dreamstime.com: Paweł Opaska (cr). 42 Alamy Stock Photo: Barbagallo Franco / hemis.fr (tl); Francisco Negroni (tr). Dreamstime.com: Olegmj (br). 43 Dreamstime.com: Achilles Moreaux / Almor67 (c). 44 Dreamstime.com: King Ho Yim (br). 45 Alamy Stock Photo: David Davis Photoproductions (crb). 46 123RF.com: Matyas Rehak (bc). Alamy Stock Photo: HUGHES Herve / hemis.fr (br). Dreamstime.com: André Costa (tl); Rosendo Francisco Estevez Rodriguez (cl). Getty Images: Alex Robinson (tc). 47 Alamy Stock Photo: Roger Bacon (cra); Lee Dalton (tc). 48 Dreamstime.com: Renato Machado / Froogz (br). 49 Dreamstime.com: Paura (cr). 51 123RF.com: steba (bc). 53 Dreamstime.com: Igor Terekhov / Terex (cra). 55 Dreamstime.com: piccaya (cra). 59 Alamy Stock Photo: F. Schneider / Arco Images GmbH (br). Dreamstime.com: Demerzel21 (cra). 61 Alamy Stock Photo: frans lemmens (cra). Getty Images: Peter Adams (br). 62 Dreamstime.com: Evgeniy Fesenko (cr); Marcin Okupniak (bl). Getty Images: Danita Delimont (crb). 63 Dreamstime.com: Mwitacha (tl). Getty Images: Richard Roscoe / Stocktrek Images (cb); Westend61 (tr). 64 Getty Images: Alex Saberi / National Geographic (crb). 65 Alamy Stock Photo: Hutchison / Hutchison Archive / Eye Ubiquitous (cr). 66 Alamy Stock Photo: Nigel Pavitt (tl); Jan Wlodarczyk (tc). Dreamstime.com: Dmitry Kuznetsov (bc). 67 Alamy Stock Photo: david tipling (cr). Getty Images: Harri Jarvelainen Photography (ca). 68 Getty Images: Peter Adams (br). 69 Getty Images: Westend61 (cra). 71 Alamy Stock Photo: Richard Roscoe / Stocktrek Images (crb). 73 Alamy Stock Photo: Eyal Bartov (cra). 74 Getty Images: George Steinmetz (crb). 75 Alamy Stock Photo: Konrad Wothe (cra). 80 Dreamstime.com: Danil Nikonov (bl). 81 Alamy Stock Photo: Zoonar / Julialine (crb). 82 Alamy Stock Photo: Martin Plöb (bl). Dreamstime.com: Rostislav Glinsky (cb). 83 123RF.com: Alexander Baron (tl). Dreamstime.com: Ebastard129 (crb). 84 123RF.com: Luciano Mortula (bl). 85 123RF.com: Stefan Holm (br). 86 123RF.com: jakezc (bl); myrtilleshop (tl). Dreamstime.com: Claudio Giovanni Colombo (tc); Reinhardt (tr). 87 123RF.com: Santi Rodriguez Fontoba (tr); Janos Gaspar (cr). 88 123RF.com: Aitor Munoz Munoz (bl); Alexey Stiop (clb). 89 123RF.com: Roman Babakin (crb); dr. Le Thanh Hung (br). 93 Alamy Stock Photo: David & Micha Sheldon (tr). 94 Dreamstime.com: Palaine (cl). 95 Getty Images: simonbyrne (crb). 98 Alamy Stock Photo: Foto 28 (cb). 100 Dreamstime.com: Noracarol (cb). 102 Dreamstime.com: Michal Knitl (br); Yinan Zhang (cra). 103 Alamy Stock Photo: EPA (tc). Getty Images: Edward L. Zhao (br). 104 Dreamstime.com: Simone Matteo Giuseppe Manzoni (cb). 105 123RF.com: Jiang Yifan / bassphoto (crb). 106 Dreamstime.com: Bayon (tr); Daniel Boiteau (clb). Getty Images: Holly Wilmeth (bc). 107 Alamy Stock Photo: Stefan Auth (bc); Jian Liu (cra). 108 123RF.com: sophiejames (c). 109 Dreamstime.com: Sean Pavone (crb). 113 Getty Images: Barry Kusuma (crb). 114 Dreamstime.com: Nohead Lam (c). 115 Alamy Stock Photo: Matthew Williams-Ellis (br). 119 Getty Images: UniversalImagesGroup (tr). 120 Alamy Stock Photo: Ingo Oeland (tc). 121 Alamy Stock Photo: Excitations (tr). 122 Alamy Stock Photo: Fullframe Photographics / redbrickstock.com (bl). 123 Alamy Stock Photo: Simon Browitt (tl). Dreamstime.com: Gábor Kovács / Kovgabor79 (tr). Getty Images: Raimund Linke / Photodisc (br). 125 Dreamstime.com: Chu-wen Lin (cra). 126 Alamy Stock Photo: Bhaskar Krishnamurthy (br). Dreamstime.com: Rawpixelimages (bc). 127 Alamy Stock Photo: Tui De Roy (bc); John Rendle NZ (crb). Dreamstime.com: Dmitry Pichugin (tr). 129 Alamy Stock Photo: Norbert Probst (cra). 130 Alamy Stock Photo: Horizon (br). 132 Dreamstime.com: Kristian Bell (br). 134-135 Alamy Stock Photo: Adam Burton. 136 Alamy Stock Photo: John Higdon (br). Getty Images: Galen Rowell (tc); Gordon Wiltsie (tl). 137 Alamy Stock Photo: Dan Leeth (bl). Dreamstime.com: Staphy (c). 138 Alamy Stock Photo: JTB Photo (bc). Getty Images: Per Breiehagen (tr). 139 123RF.com: Irina Borsuchenko / vodolej (br); Aleksei Ruzhin (tl). 140-141 Alamy Stock Photo: H. Mark Weidman Photography. 142 Alamy Stock Photo: Mark Hannaford / John Warburton-Lee Photography (bl). 143 Alamy Stock Photo: Kevin Schafer (crb). 144 Dreamstime.com: Richardpross (bl). 145 Dreamstime.com: Naten (tr). 146 Getty Images: Stocktrek Images (bl). 147 Getty Images: Jim Holmes / Perspectives (tr)

Climate data
Hijmans, R. J., S. E. Cameron, J. L. Parra, P. G. Jones and A. Jarvis, 2005. Very high resolution interpolated climate surfaces for global land areas.

Population data
Center for International Earth Science Information Network—CIESIN—Columbia University. 2016. Gridded Population of the World, Version 4 (GPWv4): Population Density. Palisades, NY: NASA Socioeconomic Data and Applications Center (SEDAC).

Paleogeography globes
Derived from original maps produced by Colorado Plateau Geosystems Inc.

Landsat satellite data for feature spread 3D models
These data are distributed by the Land Processes Distributed Active Archive Center (LP DAAC), located at USGS/EROS, Sioux Falls, SD. http://lpdaac.usgs.gov

Nighttime
Data courtesy Marc Imhoff of NASA GSFC and Christopher Elvidge of NOAA NGDC. Image by Craig Mayhew and Robert Simmon, NASA GSFC.

Wildlife biomes data
WWF Terrestrial Ecoregions of the World (TEOW). Olson, D. M., Dinerstein, E., Wikramanayake, E. D., Burgess, N. D., Powell, G. V. N., Underwood, E. C., D'Amico, J. A., Itoua, I., Strand, H. E., Morrison, J. C. Loucks, C. J., Allnutt, T. F., Ricketts, T. H., Kura, Y., Lamoreux, J. F., Wettengel, W. W., Hedao, P., Kassem, K. R. 2001. Terrestrial ecoregions of the world: a new map of life on Earth. Bioscience 51(11):933-938.

All other images © Dorling Kindersley
For further information see:
www.dkimages.com

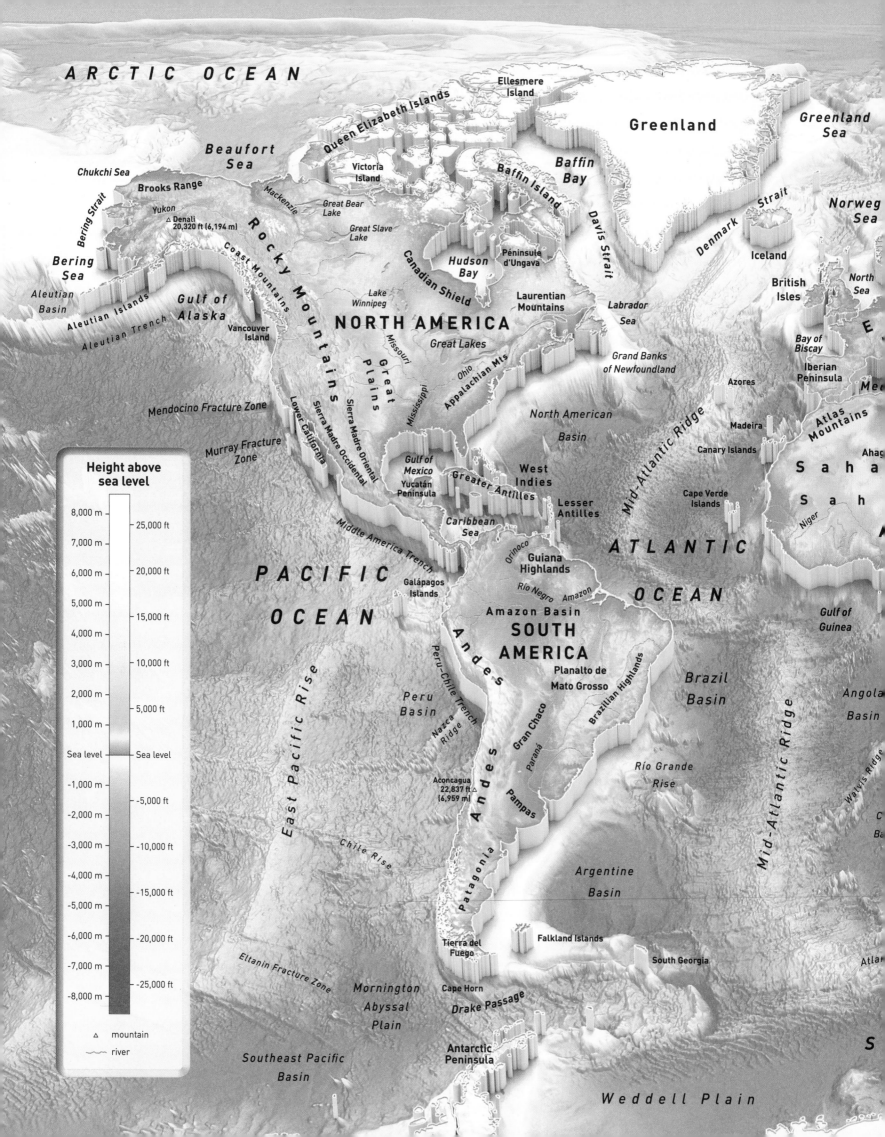

ARCTIC OCEAN

Chukchi Sea

Beaufort Sea

Queen Elizabeth Islands

Ellesmere Island

Greenland

Greenland Sea

Victoria Island

Baffin Island

Baffin Bay

Bering Strait

Brooks Range

Yukon

Mackenzie

Great Bear Lake

△ Denali 20,320 ft (6,194 m)

Rocky Mountains

Great Slave Lake

Canadian Shield

Hudson Bay

Péninsule d'Ungava

Davis Strait

Denmark Strait

Norweg Sea

Iceland

Bering Sea

Aleutian Basin

Aleutian Islands

Aleutian Trench

Gulf of Alaska

Coast Mountains

Vancouver Island

NORTH AMERICA

Lake Winnipeg

Great Lakes

Laurentian Mountains

Labrador Sea

British Isles

North Sea

Bay of Biscay

Iberian Peninsula

Mendocino Fracture Zone

Missouri

Great Plains

Ohio

Appalachian Mts

Mississippi

Grand Banks of Newfoundland

Azores

Madeira

Atlas Mountains

Med

Murray Fracture Zone

Lower California

Sierra Madre Occidental

Sierra Madre Oriental

Gulf of Mexico

Yucatán Peninsula

Greater Antilles

West Indies

North American Basin

Mid-Atlantic Ridge

Canary Islands

Saha

Sah

Ahag

Middle America Trench

Caribbean Sea

Lesser Antilles

Cape Verde Islands

Niger

PACIFIC OCEAN

Galápagos Islands

Orinoco

Guiana Highlands

ATLANTIC OCEAN

Río Negro

Amazon

Gulf of Guinea

Amazon Basin

SOUTH AMERICA

Peru-Chile Trench

Andes

Planalto de Mato Grosso

Brazilian Highlands

Brazil Basin

Angola Basin

Peru Basin

Nazca Ridge

Gran Chaco

Paraná

Río Grande Rise

Aconcagua 22,837 ft △ (6,959 m)

Pampas

Mid-Atlantic Ridge

Chile Rise

Andes

Patagonia

Argentine Basin

Watvis Ridge

C Ba

Eltanin Fracture Zone

Mornington Abyssal Plain

Cape Horn

Drake Passage

Tierra del Fuego

Falkland Islands

South Georgia

Atlan

S

Southeast Pacific Basin

Antarctic Peninsula

Weddell Plain

Height above sea level

8,000 m	25,000 ft
7,000 m	
6,000 m	20,000 ft
5,000 m	15,000 ft
4,000 m	
3,000 m	10,000 ft
2,000 m	
1,000 m	5,000 ft
Sea level	Sea level
-1,000 m	-5,000 ft
-2,000 m	-10,000 ft
-3,000 m	
-4,000 m	-15,000 ft
-5,000 m	
-6,000 m	-20,000 ft
-7,000 m	
-8,000 m	-25,000 ft

△ mountain

river